CHILDLESS BY CHOICE

J. E. Veevers
The University of Western Ontario

BUTTERWORTHS
Toronto

Printed and bound in Canada

CANADA: BUTTERWORTH & CO. (CANADA) LTD.
TORONTO: 2265 Midland Avenue, Scarborough, M1P 4S1
VANCOUVER: 856–409 Granville Street, Vancouver, V6C 1T8

UNITED KINGDOM: BUTTERWORTH & CO. (PUBLISHERS) LTD.
LONDON: 88 Kingsway, WC2B 6AB

AUSTRALIA: BUTTERWORTH PTY. LTD.
SYDNEY: 586 Pacific Highway, Chatswood, NSW 2067
MELBOURNE: 343 Little Collins Street, 3000
BRISBANE: 240 Queen Street, 4000

NEW ZEALAND: BUTTERWORTHS OF NEW ZEALAND LTD.
WELLINGTON: 77–85 Custom House Quay, 1

SOUTH AFRICA: BUTTERWORTH & CO. (SOUTH AFRICA) (PTY.) LTD.
DURBAN: 152/154 Gale Street

Canadian Cataloguing in Publication Data

Veevers, Jean E.
Childless by choice

Bibliography: p.
ISBN 0-409-87474-4

1. Childlessness. I. Title.

HQ755.8.V44 306.8 C80-094004-0

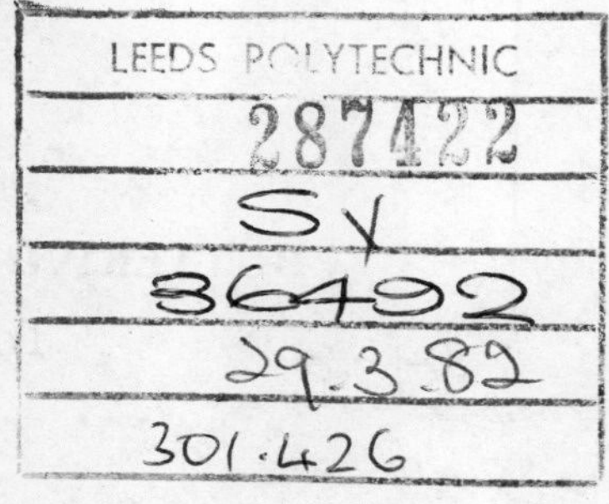

This book is dedicated to
CHARLES AND VICKIE FIGLEY
a childfree couple par excellence

Foreword

This book has been anxiously awaited by those of us who are dedicated to the scientific study of marriage and the family. Prior to the recent upsurge in academic interest in the "childfree" lifestyle, Dr. Veevers had published more on the topic than all other scholars combined. For the past eight years Professor Veevers has interviewed the childless by choice, meticulously analyzed their lives, consulted other researchers and theorists, collated and summarized her own published works and the works of hundreds of others, and organized it all into a highly readable form in the present volume.

Childless by Choice is destined to become the seminal work in this area primarily because of Professor Veevers' success in blending scholarship with a crisp, even writing style spiced with excerpts from hundreds of hours of interviews. Unlike most scholarly reports which satisfy only scientific standards, this book transcends the artificial barriers of academic theorizing and pedantic style and communicates directly to everyone about the alleged mysteries of the childless by choice. Veevers succeeds in her attempt to convey both the substance and the form of the childfree life style with fairness and without proselytization.

This book will certainly be welcomed as an important addition to the sociology of the family. In this single volume Professor Veevers has effectively woven together almost everything that has been written on the subject. In addition, she presents elegant interpretations of a wide variety of scholarly perspectives, masterfully blending them into her own unique theoretical constructs and models, liberally illustrated with candid disclosures by the true experts here—the childless themselves.

Another sign of a truly seminal work, beyond its impact on its field, is its impact on the public. With sufficient exposure, this book may well usher in a much needed re-examination of the social script of parenthood: the social press on us all to become parents. Past attempts to discuss options to parenthood objectively most often raised tempers and turned off all but the true believers. Though frequently provocative in substance, the tone of the book is balanced and non-threatening, and it should serve as interesting reading to a broad cross-section of western and westernized cultures. A good illustration of this is Professor Veevers' success in delicately maneuvering the reader through the emotion-laden discussions of pronatalism and anti-natalism while embracing neither.

Many readers unfamiliar with the voluntarily childless will expect to find child-haters, but discover instead mostly aficionados of the adult-centered lifestyle. Indeed, it is remarkable how similar the childless by choice are to everyone else. Most of us, with or without children, have marital problems, career pressures, and varying bouts with self-doubt and self-indulgence. We try to enjoy life's peaks and muddle through the valleys as best we can. In the later years of life we are all eventually childless and experience a welcomed independent and adult-oriented life.

But comprising the most important audience for this book are those who must soon decide one of life's most important questions: to parent or not. Professor Veevers' masterpiece will most certainly destroy the myths about the childless by choice, and even some of the mysteries.

Charles R. Figley, Ph.D.
Director, Family Research Institute
Purdue University

Acknowledgements

Writing *Childless by Choice* has required nearly a decade of intermittent reflection and research, during which time I have incurred a number of intellectual and personal debts. My initial inspiration to work on this topic came from my confederate and confidant, Dr. Douglas F. Cousineau, now of Simon Fraser University. From the inception of the project, our endless conversations about childlessness were a source of inspiration, and he will certainly recognize many of his insights masquerading as my own. He took part in the initial interviewing, reacted to preliminary drafts of the manuscript, and in other ways provided crucial support to getting the research under way.

Research on childlessness is not possible without the wholehearted cooperation of the childless themselves. I deeply appreciate the men and women who volunteered to participate, and who persevered through the time-consuming and sometimes painful process of in-depth interviewing. I also appreciate suggestions made by two family sociologists: Dr. Norman W. Bell of The University of Toronto and Dr. Kenneth Kiser of Oklahoma State University.

The penultimate draft of the manuscript benefitted from suggestions of Dr. Robert N. Whitehurst of the University of Windsor. My mother, Mrs. Edith L. Gratz of Victoria, has read and reacted to virtually every word I have ever written. I was pleased that she also read and approved of this manuscript.

I have a special debt of gratitude to Dr. Charles R. Figley of the University of Purdue. In collaborating with me in the final stages of the project, he shared freely of his expertise and enthusiasm. While acting as both a colleague and a coach, he worked diligently in organizing, rewriting, and editing the final manuscript. Without his timely intervention, *Childless by Choice* would never have been actualized.

Finally, I am indebted to my close friend, Dr. James M. Wanklin of The University of Western Ontario, who over the years has perused all my manuscripts in all their stages. Although imbued with quite a different perspective, James manfully suppresses his skepticism as often as possible, and maintains my sense of humor at the tribulations associated with unorthodox, unfunded research. For these and many other reasons, I value his comradeship and support.

Prologue

The irrepressible Tom Lehrer, amusing the sixties generation with his satire, observed: "From the Bible to the popular song,/There's one theme that we find right along;/Of all ideals they hail as good,/The most sublime is *motherhood*!" As every politician knows, one attacks motherhood at one's peril. *Childless by Choice* is emphatically not an attack on motherhood. Neither is it an apologist's view of the childfree lifestyle. It will be readily apparent to the reader that I am not pronatalist in my views, in the sense of endorsing an inappropriate exaltation of parenthood, but it would be incorrect to conclude that I am therefore an antinatalist. Treading my way between these extreme views, I anticipate some displeasure from both sides. Persons with a familistic ideology may be disturbed by the questioning of generally unquestionable assumptions concerning the parenthood mystique; persons ideologically committed to nonparenthood may chafe at the use of child*less* rather than child*free*. Advocating a condition in which most couples should be encouraged to remain childless seems as patently absurd as endorsing the commonly held view that *all* married couples should have children. To the extent that I dare dabble in the politics of natalism, I am advocating the not-very-radical contention that it is in everyone's best interest to make having children the result of a deliberate choice, rather than of sexual happenstance. To achieve this goal, a necessary first step entails some preliminary consciousness-raising, in which the option of remaining childless is at least brought to the level of awareness.

Voluntary childlessness remains a sensitive issue. Although becoming more visible, persons who deliberately avoid parenthood still place themselves beyond the moral pale of conventional society. As social deviants who are stigmatized and stereotyped, they are understandably reluctant to expose themselves to additional censure by expounding their views. *Childless by Choice* is based on in-depth interviews with one hundred and fifty-six childless persons who, under the cloak of anonymity, volunteered to discuss in detail all aspects of their variant lifestyle. Our approach is admittedly unorthodox. It is also the only approach deemed feasible for an intensive, exploratory work. Our intention is to describe and to analyze the nature and meaning of childlessness, as seen from the perspective of the childless themselves. While it seems likely that the respondents interviewed share a great deal in common with other voluntarily childless couples, there is no way of knowing the extent to which they are actually representative of this larger group. In referring to our data, we must explicitly and implicitly qualify our remarks with the admonition that our data indicate such and such *about the childless persons interviewed*, who are a purposive, not a random, sample. Definitive descriptions of childless couples, and definitive comparisons of them with parental couples, must await more extensive and more structured research.

Exploratory research has the advantage of being relatively inexpensive, a fortunate circumstance since the present work was financed entirely out-of-pocket. While this permits one considerable freedom, it also drastically limits one's scope. I would hope that future researchers would not be so independent, and that if nothing else, *Childless by Choice* helps to establish childlessness as a legitimate area for funded research.

Table of Contents

Chapter One: THE PARENTHOOD PRESCRIPTION

In the Western world, there is one expectation about which almost everyone agrees: married couples should have children. Moreover, it is not enough that couples have children; they are also expected to want to have them. Parenthood is almost universally lauded as an intrinsically desirable social role. Many factors combine to create a milieu wherein having children is defined as both inevitable and desirable. However, in spite of a pervasive cultural press towards parenthood, since earliest times there have always been some individuals who have questioned and, ultimately, rejected the dominant norms of having and wanting children.[1] Some individuals who do want to get married do not also want to become parents. *Childless by Choice* is concerned with the lives of those unusual couples who decide never to have children.

In the past, unless couples were willing to place their legitimate offspring in foundling homes, the choice of remaining childless generally necessitated the corollary of remaining unmarried. Except for abortion or the more drastic alternative of infanticide, deliberate lifelong childlessness required either absolute celibacy or at least very infrequent intercourse. Although presumably there have always been some married couples who achieved voluntary childlessness, the social

---

[1] For example, historians have noted the manifest tolerance of voluntary childlessness during the later days of the Roman empire (Kenkel, 1966: 77-87). In New England during the later nineteenth century, deliberate childlessness occasioned considerable comment (Calhoun, 1919) and the increase in the number of childless wives was viewed as an indicator of the "appalling decadence" of native American stock (Crum, 1914).

unacceptability of their behavior has meant that most of the time they have been prudently inconspicuous.

Voluntary childlessness has been feasible since the development and dissemination of reliable birth control techniques. Until the past decade, however, voluntarily childless couples were largely an invisible minority, and were virtually ignored by social scientists. Since the start of the seventies, voluntary childlessness has begun to emerge as an alternative to conventional marriage, and there has been a burgeoning of public and professional interest in it. At the present time in Canada and the United States, deliberate childlessness is estimated to characterize at least five to seven per cent of all couples. Current fertility trends suggest that among women who are now in their childbearing years, twice that number may ultimately decide not to become mothers (Westoff, 1978: 55). In the near future, it would not be suprising if one couple in ten were to reject parenthood and to decide to remain childless.

The purpose of the present book is to report on some of the causes and consequences of being childless by choice. Between 1972 and 1978, I undertook an intensive exploratory study of voluntary childlessness. In-depth interviews were conducted with 156 married men and women who had deliberately avoided having children, and who were almost certainly to remain childless permanently. The goals of the research were to explore the neglected area of voluntary childlessness, and to offer plausible hypotheses relevant to understanding how some persons come to remain childless, why they choose to do so, and what becomes of them as a result. Toward this end, I present my own results in juxtaposition with the results of other research which is, directly or indirectly, germane to the study of childlessness. Hopefully, the ensuing discussions will contribute to the description of the social meanings of childlessness, and to the explanation of the dynamics of entering and defending the childless lifestyle.[2]

---

[2] Characterizing a segment of the population in terms of an attribute which they do *not* have is, at best, linquistically awkward. Synonyms for childlessness lend themselves readily to the nuances of rhetoric. The word *unmothered* (Albert, 1966) is ambiguous, in that it can imply either a person who does not have a child or a person who does not have a mother. Demographers discuss the phenomenon in terms of *zero parity* (Mommsen and Lund, 1977), while physicians are concerned with *nullipara* (Kaij and Malmquist, 1971). Contrasting the childless with the *childed* (Poston, 1976) is somewhat unwieldy, but not as cumbersome as comparing the progenied with the *non-progenied* (Cameron *et al.*, 1976). The straightforward term child*less* is considered by some to be pejorative, in that it seems to imply a negative statement of a lack or a flaw. Persons with this opinion prefer the term child*free* which is considered to have more positive connotations (Cooper *et al.*, 1978: 72). Following the same logic, some persons prefer to refer to childfree *families* rather than couples, thereby asserting the position that a husband and wife are in and of themselves sufficient to warrent definition as a family unit (Whelan, 1975: 125).

The Social Meanings of Parenthood

Family institutions in Canada and the United States are basically pronatalistic, in the sense that they place an inordinate emphasis upon the many advantages attendant upon having children.[3] The very high value placed on having children is reflected in two major fertility norms: first, the norm that *all* married couples should have children, and second, that *all* married couples should want to have them. Acceptance of these norms is widespread internationally,[4] and appears to transcend the usual divisions by sex, age, race, religion, ethnicity, and social class which are associated with divergent opinions on other issues.

> On the matter of the desirability of having children, traditionalists, middle-of-the-roaders, and radicals are in essential agreement. The traditionalists are inclined to think of the bearing of children as a duty to God, church and country. Liberals, affected by the child-centered orientation of our culture, think of children as the natural outcome of a happy marriage. Those in the middle range of orientation may have mixed reasons for desiring children, but . . . they do tend to favor them (Stroup, 1966: 349).

The desire for children is assumed to be universal. Consequently, expectations regarding normal and socially acceptable adult roles implicitly incorporate expectations regarding procreation and child-care. The motherhood mystique[5]—or more accurately the parenthood mystique—asserts that having children is not only compatible with self-

---

[3] Pronatalism is a neologism coined to refer to attitudes which encourage fertility. Its basic meaning is quite straightforward: "natal" referring to "birth," with the prefix "pro" meaning "to be in favor." Originally, pronatalism was used by demographers to refer to official governmental policies which are intended to encourage fertility (Blake, 1973). An obvious example of such a policy is the Canadian program of family allowance payments, in which each mother receives a monthly "baby bonus" of cash for each child in her care. With the diffusion of the concept into general social science, pronatalism came to refer indiscriminantly to all actions, official or otherwise, which are intended to encourage fertility. Finally, pronatalism has come to incorporate all actions which might have the effect of encouraging fertility, whether or not they are manifestly intended to do so. Thus, Peck and Senderowitz (1974: 1) use the term loosely to mean: "any attitude or policy that is 'pro-birth,' that encourages reproduction, that exalts the role of parenthood."

[4] For example, Van Keep (1971) conducted an extensive survey of ideal family size in Belgium, Great Britain, France, West Germany, and Italy. He found that among wives aged sixteen to forty-five, only one or two per cent felt that being childless was ideal; among husbands, the rate was higher, but was still less than five per cent. In another study in Britain, Peel and Carr (1975) found only four per cent of couples did not want children.

[5] Friedan's classic analysis *The Feminine Mystique* (1963) documented the discontent and malaise of many suburban housewives, and argued that being a housewife-mother was

Table 1. The Social Meaning of Parenthood and Childlessness

Dimension	Parenthood	Childlessness
Morality	Desire for parenthood is a *religious obligation*; being a parent is being *moral*	Desire for childlessness is a *flouting of religious authority;* not being a parent is being *immoral.*
Responsibility	Desire for parenthood is a *civic obligation;* being a parent is being *responsible.*	Desire for childlessness is *avoidance of responsibility;* not being a parent is being *irresponsible.*
Marriage	Desire for parenthood is *the the meaning of marriage;* being a parent *improves marital adjustment* and *prevents divorce*	Desire for childlessness *destroys the meaning of marriage;* not being a parent *hinders marital adjustment* and *increases divorce proneness.*
Sexuality	Desire for parenthood *is acceptance of gender* role; for a woman, being a mother is *proof of femininity*; for a man, being a father is *proof of masculinity.*	Desire for childlessness is *rejection of gender* role; for a woman, not being a mother indicates *lack of femininity;* for a man, not being a father indicates *lack of masculinity.*
Normalcy	Desire for parenthood is a sign of *normal mental health*; being a parent contributes to *social maturity and stability of personality.*	Desire of childlessness is a sign of *abnormal mental health;* not being a parent is associated with *social immaturity and emotional maladjustment.*

actualization but is, indeed, necessary for it. Advocates of the mystique no longer argue that parenthood *per se* is sufficient for fulfillment, but they do continue to assert that it is a necessary factor. The social meanings of childlessness are essentially the obverse of the social meanings of parenthood, and childlessness is therefore defined almost

---

not a sufficient *raison d'être* for fulfillment. It is significant that Friedan's proposed solution to the "problem that had no name" was that women became involved in intrinsically interesting careers, or absorbed in meaningful forms of self-expression, *in addition to* being mothers. Although acutely aware of the existence of the feminine mystique and very critical of its implications, she was apparently completely unaware of a pervasive motherhood mystique as a separate part of it. The alternative of maximizing personal fulfillment by avoiding motherhood apparently did not occur to her, and the topic of childlessness does not even appear in the index.

exclusively in negative terms. As shown in Table 1, these operate at three levels: the sociocultural, involving morality and responsibility; the interpersonal, involving marriage and sexuality; and the individual, involving maturity and normalcy.

Virtually all societies are, of necessity, pronatalistic to some extent, in that parenthood is normative in all societies (Pohlman, 1969), and is generally defined as a moral imperative for married persons (Rosenblatt *et al.*, 1973).[6] Given the complete vulnerability of the human infant, if a society is to be maintained, each generation must recruit a large number of persons who will devote a major proportion of their lives to having and raising children. Although these tasks are to some extent intrinsically gratifying, the sacrifices required are considerable, and it is necessary to provide some extrinsic incentives to induce adults to undertake parenthood roles and to remain committed to them. Pronatalist philosophies contribute to this end, in that they stress the advantages of having children while ignoring or minimizing the attendant disadvantages. The recruitment of willing parents for their essential but difficult tasks requires considerable social support. "The crucial link in the interdependence of biology and socialization is that the child is taught not only to want to rear children but also to rear his children *in turn* so that they want to care for *their* children" (Goode, 1964: 19).

The norms that married persons should have children and should rejoice at the prospect of becoming parents are tantamount to a parenthood "prescription." In the dictionary sense, the verb *to prescribe* has two meanings: "to lay down as a course to be followed" and "to order as a remedy or treatment" (Stein and Urdang, 1971: 1138). In the first meaning of the term, parenthood tends to be prescribed as a moral imperative for socially acceptable persons, especially those who are also religious. In the second usage, parenthood is also prescribed, in the sense that it is frequently recommended, if not as a panacea, then at least as a partial "solution" to a number of problems of personal

---

[6] Although almost all societies are pronatalistic, some antinatalistic exceptions have been recorded. For example, among the Mundugumor, a pre-literate people in New Guinea, women detest bearing and rearing children (Mead, 1949: 48) and men detest their wives for being pregnant (Mead, 1949: 82). Pregnancy and nursing are hated and are avoided as much as possible. Although sexual intercourse and sexual attraction are very significant themes in the society for both men and women, children are viewed as an undesirable consequence whose coming, if it cannot be prevented, is unfortunate and disruptive. A similar disinclination to parenthood is reported to have occurred in the later days of the Roman empire when there was a basic devaluation in the worth of a child and "childlessness became an enviable state and abortion, infanticide, and the abandonment of infants were resorted to when unwanted children were conceived" (Kenkel, 1966: 77).

growth and adjustment. Parenthood is believed to provide experiences which are crucial to the development of full emotional and sexual maturity. In a real sense, having a child affirms one's adult status in the community, making a boy into a man and a girl into a woman (LeMasters, 1957b: 522). Children are thought to give life purpose and meaning and, especially for women, to be necessary if not sufficient for fullfillment. Parenthood is often considered a mandatory adjunct of husband-wife roles, providing a cohesive focal point which helps to cement the marriage. On a wider scale, having children is believed to increase one's sense of civic and social responsibility.

Stigmas and stereotypes

In light of the parenthood "prescription," not having, nor wanting to have, children becomes a noteworthy kind of social deviance, in clear violation of the dominant fertility norms. Once a particular group of people have been identified as deviant for whatever reason, how do others react to them? Goffman includes in his list of social deviants: ". . . the metropolitan unmarried and merely married who disavail themselves of the opportunity to raise a family" (Goffman, 1963: 154). The voluntarily childless are defined as deviant, and, hence, like other deviants, are also stigmatized.[7] Goffman distinguishes among three kinds of stigma: ". . . abominations of the body . . . blemishes of individual character . . . and tribal stigma through race, nation, and religion" (Goffman, 1963: 4). The sterile or subfecund are stigmatized in terms of their bodily abnormalities which do not allow them to reproduce and thus render them as less-than-whole persons.[8] The

[7] A subtle aspect of the stigmatizing process is that the specific terms used to refer to the stigma become part of our daily discourse and a source of metaphor and imagery. Although we do not give much thought to the original meanings when we call people bastards, cripples or morons, the continued use of such terms as pejorative reinforces their negative connotations (Goffman, 1963: 5). In everyday speech, something which is "fruitful" is "productive of good results, profitable," and to be "fecund" is to be "very productive or creative intellectually" (Stein and Urdang, 1971: 572, 520). By contrast, in addition to the meaning of not producing offspring, or not being capable of producing offspring, the word "barren" means: "unproductive, without capacity to interest or attract, mentally unproductive, dull, stupid, not producing results, destitute and bereft" (Stein and Urdang, 1971: 122). "Sterile" can be used to mean both "incapable of producing offspring" and "not productive of results and ideas, fruitless" (Stein and Urdang, 1971: 1394). Such pejorative connotations associated with words "barren" and "sterile" serve to perpetuate the stigmatic connotations of childlessness.

[8] Goffman does not deal directly with childlessness as stigma. However, he does make reference to a long quote which points out that: "I began to realize that the words of the crippled girl . . . (words of bitterness) could have just as well been spoken by young women who had never needed crutches, women who felt inferior and different because of ugliness, or *inability to bear children* . . . or many other reasons" (Goffman, 1963: 12; emphasis ours).

childless by choice are stigmatized in terms of their blemished characters. The subfecund may be considered unfortunate and hence deserving of sympathy, but the voluntarily childless are considered immoral and hence deserving of censure.

The stigmatization of the childless as social deviants leads to a second component of the negative image of childlessness, namely the attribution of a negative stereotype. People who violate important social norms, either in their behavior or in their motivation, tend to be perceived as deviant not only in terms of these specific transgressions but also in terms of their total personalities. Once individuals have been stigmatized, for whatever reason, "we tend to impute [to them] a wide range of imperfections on the basis of the original one" (Goffman, 1963: 5). Both lay explanations of deviance, and to some extent "scientific" theories as well, lend great credibility to the idea that only special kinds of people could or would perform deviant acts. "By definition . . . we believe that the person with a stigma is not quite human. On this assumption . . . we construct stigma theory, an ideology to explain his inferiority and account for the danger he represents, sometimes rationalizing an animosity based on other differences" (Goffman, 1963: 5).

The process of stereotyping serves to explain the behavior of the childless, and to justify a wide range of negative reactions to them. Both laymen and social scientists tend to stereotype the childless in terms of a plethora of social pathologies, characterizing them *inter alios* as psychologically maladjusted, emotionally immature, immoral, selfish, lonely, unhappy, unfulfilled, sexually inadequate, unhappily married, and prone to divorce (Pohlman, 1970; Blake, 1973; Thompson, 1974).

Although parenthood is prescribed for all married adults, it is clear that it is judged to be more important for women than for men. Part of this discrepancy may be a legacy of the double standard, in which any immoral or quasi-immoral behavior among women is traditionally judged more harshly than the same behavior among men. More significant, however, is the fact that motherhood is much more salient to the female role than fatherhood is to the male. Whereas masculinity can be affirmed by occupational success or sexual prowess, femininity has traditionally been closely linked with bearing and caring for children, with other roles remaining relatively peripheral. Although the paternal role is also important, it does not have the same centrality that makes motherhood almost a woman's *raison d'être*. Fatherhood is preferred to non-fatherhood, but there is no male equivalent to the "motherhood mandate" (Russo, 1976: 14). As a consequence, childlessness is more cogent and salient in the lives of wives than of their husbands

(Lichtman, 1976). In spite of sex role changes, motherhood is still viewed as an integral part of the female gender role—more than fatherhood is of the male role—and having or not having children still remains primarily a "woman's issue" (Cooper *et al.*, 1978).

Usually the use of the term "stereotype" implies a set of beliefs which are by definition false. In common usage, the idea of a "valid" stereotype seems to be a contradiction in terms. However, from our perspective, the social import of the stereotype of childlessness lies not so much in its validity or invalidity, but in the extent to which it is *believed* to be true, and thus to influence social behavior. Early discussions of pronatalism as expressed in stereotypes of childlessness relied on very impressionistic and essentially anecdotal data, but recent research has confirmed the acceptance of such stereotypes among the general public (Centers and Blumberg, 1954; Rainwater, 1960; Griffith, 1973; Polit, 1978; Blake, 1978). The extent to which the stereotype of voluntarily childless persons is valid or invalid is not yet established and is an important question for further research.[9]

Models of childlessness: causes and consequences

Consensus regarding the social meanings of childlessness and the stereotype of deliberately childless persons does not necessarily imply a comparable consensus regarding the underlying epidemiological conundrum: do atypical persons tend to remain childless, or does remaining childless tend to make persons atypical? The negative meanings imputed to voluntary childlessness derive from at least three models concerning the causes and/or consequences of such behavior. Although these models are interrelated—and are often only stated implicitly—for the purposes of discussion it is convenient to designate them as the diagnostic model, the deprivation model, and the labelling model.

The **diagnostic model** is based on the premise that not wanting children constitutes *de facto* evidence of psychological maladjustment. It is not so much that childlessness is considered problematic *per se* as that it is defined as a symptom of abnormality that can therefore be expected to be associated with other symptoms of precarious mental health. Within this perspective, whatever correlations might be

---

9 In many cases, the validity of a stereotype is not only unknown but unknowable because the descriptive terms used do not refer to objective conditions (for example, rich, poor, intelligent, stupid), but to evaluations (persistent, stubborn, clannish, loyal) or to relative states (happy, unhappy, adjusted, maladjusted). The word "stereotype" as used here refers to a set of adjectives which people *believe* to constitute an accurate description of childless persons.

observed between voluntary childlessness and other aberrant behavior would be interpreted as resulting from the factors operating to select out a group of childless persons intrinsically different in some way from others. Such correlations would then be regarded as spurious, rather than accorded causal importance.

When a particular kind of behavior is ubiquitous in a society, there is a tendency for social scientists as well as laymen to attribute the cause of that behavior not to social learning, but to human nature itself. Until a few decades ago, reproduction could not be efficiently controlled and almost all individuals who married became parents. The "explanation" most frequently offered to account for this behavior was that there existed a reproductive drive, a maternal or even paternal instinct, and that people therefore had children because it was "natural" for them to do so. Given the additional fact that most parents make more or less adequate provisions for the care and feeding of their offspring, it required only a short logical leap to assert that this aspect of familial behavior could also be "explained" in terms of intrinsic attributes of human nature, which naturally made adults interested in and devoted to their children.[10] Persons who are chary of the term "instinct" but who wish to refer to essentially the same kind of phenomenon may consider instead "biological proclivities" or, more generally, "hormonal factors." Recent explorations of the biology of parenthood, especially motherhood, have lent renewed credence to the possibility of an important physiological component in parenthood aspirations and experiences.[11]

---

[10] For example, Fletcher (1968) proposes a contemporary theory of instincts, which explains parental activity as an instinct due to primary impulses, with the physiological source to be found in the sexual organs and sexual hormones. He considers the instinct to be triggered by the sight of a dependent human baby (especially, but not only, one's own) and to be associated with related behaviors such as "holding, nursing, fondling, and playing with a child." Fletcher even goes so far as to postulate the existence of a "home-making" instinctive tendency which involves "desiring permanent presence of the sexual mate or love object and the desire to protect and care for children" and includes "seeking or constructing a dwelling place and providing manifold domestic requirements." Eickhoff (1966: 173) postulates a "drive for procreation" which he equates with a "drive for immortality through one's own children" and argues that "most psychologists" would agree. The psychoanalytic perspective has been most adamant in its contention that parenthood is related to basic innate drives. Benedek (1970: 137-138), a psychoanalyst, discusses parenthood and its pathology in terms of an instinctive organizing of motherliness in the female personality as well as an instinctive drive for fatherhood and an instinctually rooted character trend which enables men to act toward children with fatherliness, and immediate empathetic responsiveness.

[11] Bardwick (1974: 59-60), in discussing evolution and parenting, concludes that:

> Parenthood has been the most accessable means available to the majority of humanity to express their existential needs for creativity and generativity . . . [thus] one could surmise that

Among persons adhering to the diagnostic model, the presumed association between childlessness and unsatisfactory mental health is accounted for primarily by reference to the supposed existence of a parenthood instinct. If wanting children is "natural," then by inference not wanting them is "unnatural," and the absence of a basic instinct is therefore considered indicative of serious pathology.[12] One of the disconcerting characteristics of theories of instinct is that, like theories of the subconscious or the unconscious, there is no way to disprove them. The fact that some adults do not appear to have any biological proclivities towards parenthood does not prove that such proclivities do not exist in other adults. Hypothetically, deviant cases in which instinctive desires for childbearing are not apparent may be accounted for by explanations that, owing to special circumstances, the drives have been repressed, attenuated, or even extinguished altogether. In social sciences, explanations of human behavior in terms of instincts have generally been discredited (Berelson and Steiner, 1964: 38-51). However, we cannot simply conclude, as does Veenhoven (1974: 496) that: "The instinct theory of human procreation is wrong." While we cannot disprove the existence of a maternal instinct, it does not seem a heuristic model for the study of procreation. We begin with the premise, with which most social scientists would now agree, that the desire to have or not to have a child is rooted in socialization and experiences which lead to definitions of motherhood and fatherhood as rewarding or unrewarding social roles.[13] In more general terms, the

---

> our evoluntionary heritage includes not only the *ability* to parent but the *need* to parent—especially for women (emphasis in original).

Rossi (1977: 24), in discussing the biosocial perspective on parenthood, suggests that it seriously questions the cultural determinism of contemporary social science. She notes the significant influences of physiological factors on women as a consequence of hormonal cyclicity, pregnancy, and birth, and concludes that:

> . . . there may be a biologically based potential for heightening maternal investment in the child, at least through the first months of life, that exceeds the potential for investment by men in fatherhood.

12 For example, Bardwick (1974: 58-59) is very explicit in her interpretation of childlessness as pathological.

> As Harlow's disturbed monkeys could neither reproduce nor effectively nurture, that seems true for people too. It is as though to some extent one of nature's fail-safe mechanisms is infertility in those who are not psychologically healthy enough to nurture. . . . Thus the potential or pre-disposition to reproduce and to parent seems a normative human development but, responsive to stress, it may not be part of the behavioral repertoire of disturbed individuals, groups, or cultures. . . .

13 For example, after a comprehensive *Comparative Study of Human Reproduction* based on the Human Relations Area Files, Ford (1945: 96) concludes that:

ubiquity of the desire for parenthood seems to be primarily a product of the general cultural expectations included under the rubric of "pronatalism."

The **deprivation model** is based on the premise that remaining childless has a detrimental effect, in that persons who do not have the experience of parenthood are perceived to be at a disadvantage compared with those who do. Childbearing, or more particularly, childrearing, is considered a crucial developmental task which is essential for good mental health (Parsons and Bales, 1955: 21; Simpson, 1966: 427; Benedek, 1970; Greenbaum, 1973: 1262). For example, Erikson (1951: 267) stresses the importance of generativity—the interest in establishing and guiding the next generation—in the development and stabilization of mature personalities. This view is expressed concisely in the aphorism: "The value of marriage is not that adults produce children but that children produce adults" (*Reader's Digest*, 1975: 108). In this perspective, the cause of childlessness is less important than the fact of deprivation from the protective benefits believed to accrue from interaction with young children. The sterile are expected to suffer as much as the voluntarily childless; conversely, adoptive parents are expected to derive the advantages attendant in participation in parenthood roles.

The **labelling model** is based on the premise that voluntary childlessness is labelled as immoral and unacceptable behavior, and that individuals who do not want children are therefore stigmatized and in other ways sanctioned for their deviance. This primary deviance is believed to lead to secondary deviance, in the sense that once persons are labelled as undesirable and treated accordingly, their response to such sanctions does in fact lead to undesirable characteristics (Lemert, 1951). Regardless of the mental health of persons when they decide to remain childless, after a number of years they may come to be maladjusted, not because they are deprived of the benefits of children, but because of the adverse effects of living with social disapproval and of being subjected to various kinds of punishments and pressures (Mead, 1949: 178). Within this perspective, persons who are expected to remain childless, such as the unmarried or those in

---

> Human reproduction is effected by biological processes assisted by learned behavior. . . . The wish for offspring is not an innate component of human nature; it is not a basic drive. On the contrary, it is an acquired motive which is constantly being reinforced by social rewards and punishments. Promises and security, approval and prestige support the desire for children; threats of insecurity, punishment and ridicule block incipient wishes to escape the pains and cares of childbirth and parenthood. . . . Conflicting with the desire for parenthood are other motives. . . . If people are to reproduce, social life must offer enough rewards for bearing children to more than outweigh the punishments involved in reproduction.

religious orders, would not be expected to suffer ill-effects from not having had children, since they would be applauded rather than criticized for that decision.

Neglect of the Study of Childlessness

Given the existence of a negative stereotype of the voluntarily childless, and given three implicit models that purport to explain it, the next logical question in the study of childlessness is the extent to which the attributed traits do or do not actually characterize deliberately childless persons. Unfortunately, in spite of the extensive theoretical and empirical concern devoted to the study of the family, relatively little attention has been paid to voluntary childlessness, and we still cannot say with any certainty which of the proposed models, if any, is a valid interpretation of comparisons of childless persons and those with children.

The initial discussions of deliberate childlessness did not come from social scientists, but rather from journalists who reported, usually in a satiric vein, on their own experiences.[14] In examining the parent-child relationship, social scientists have been so preoccupied with the impact that parents have upon the lives of their children that they have virtually precluded consideration of the reciprocal impact that children may have upon the lives of their parents.[15] Although demographers have taken note of zero parity as the logical extreme in the study of differential fertility, other social scientists have generally failed to make direct comparisons between parents and nonparents. Consequently, although there is a well-developed ideology concerning the supposed benefits of parenthood, only limited data are available concerning the actual relationship between remaining childless or

---

14 The first article of this ilk was Greene's (1963) "A Vote Against Motherhood," followed by Balchin's (1965) opinion that "Children Are A Waste of Time." Rollin's (1971) query, "Motherhood: Who Needs It?" has been widely reprinted. Nonparents later become more articulate and vociferous in presenting their views. Proselytizing interpretations of childfree philosophies were offered simultaneously by Peck (1971) in her description of *The Baby Trap* and by the Silvermans (1971) who purported to make *The Case Against Having Children.* Two years later, Radl (1973) made the more polemic statement, proclaiming that *Mother's Day Is Over.*

15 For example it is not incidental that when Terhune and Pilie (1974) offer *A Review of the Actual and Expected Consequences of Family Size,* nine out of ten chapters are devoted to the consequences for children, leaving only one out of ten concerned with consequences for parents.

becoming a parent, and subsequent individual satisfaction and social adjustment.

Ideally, the sociological study of the family should be equally concerned with all aspects of the institution. In reality, however, sociologists have focused on some aspects to the virtual exclusion of related aspects. Because the discipline is relatively young, and because the resources and facilities for research are limited, it is inevitable that some topics will not yet have been fully explored, and some relevant data will not yet have been collected. Although some omissions may be due simply to random oversight and error, others involve ". . . selective inattention" in that ". . . persistent avoidance by a group of scholars of *pertinent* topics is not purely or chiefly accidental" (Dexter, 1958: 176). The subjects selected for study in the field of marriage and the family reflect to a large extent the value preferences and biases of the participating social scientists. Instead of researching with equal enthusiasm all questions which are theoretically interesting, they choose to research only those which are personally interesting and which are supportive of their own value preferences. Such processes of selective inattention lead to a neglect of the phenomenon of voluntary childlessness as a research area.

The lack of attention paid to childlessness has been unfortunate from several perspectives. In addition to being a relevant and significant topic in its own right, the study of childlessness is also of central importance for those persons concerned with the study of the famliy, in that procreation of necessity remains a major function of the family. Having and/or wanting children are still major components of expectations for male-female roles in general and husband-wife roles in particular. Rational fertility decision-making is predicated upon being able to make accurate predictions concerning the consequences of parenthood. While assessing such consequences remains difficult, theoretically it would be facilitated greatly if reference could be made to a comparison group of childless persons who have deliberately avoided the experience of parenthood. "Often you get the best insights by considering extremes—by thinking of the opposite of that with which you are directly concerned" (Mills, 1959: 214). In studying the impact of one element of family life on other elements, it is important to be able to hold other factors constant, and to manipulate only one aspect at a time. Sociological studies of the causes and effects of parenthood have generally failed to consider adequate control groups. An intensive study of voluntarily childless couples is one potential source of hypotheses about the reasons people become parents and the effects their parental roles have on their life adjustments.

During the 1970s, social scientists became increasingly aware of the implicit bias associated with pronatalist philosophies. Published accounts conerning childlessness reflected not so much an increase in its incidence as an increase in its visibility. Speculation concerning childlessness as a variant lifestyle led to some research with persons known to be deliberately childless. When the present research was begun in 1972, the only other study was by Gustavus and Henley (1971) who interviewed seventy-two childless couples seeking sterilization. Since that time, a number of researchers have been concerned with the topic.[16] Our description and analysis of voluntary childlessness is based on in-depth interviews with 120 childless wives and 36 childless husbands. A description of the ways in which respondents were found and interviewed is given in the Appendix.

---

16 Since 1975, more than twenty empirical studies have been directly concerned with one or another aspect of voluntary childlessness. These studies will be cited one at a time when their data is relevant to our own concerns. Details concerning the kinds of designs used and the samples studied, together with summaries of the major findings, are presented in a recent overview in *Marriage and Family Review* (Veevers, 1979).

Chapter Two: DECIDING TO BE CHILDLESS: THE PSYCHOLOGY OF COMMITMENT

Among the voluntarily childless, there are many persons who are above average in education, and who are consequently highly verbal and articulate, with a good command of language and an extensive vocabulary. However, when such persons are confronted with the basic question: "Why don't you want to have children?" their usual verbal fluency appears to desert them and they experience great difficulty in formulating coherent and comprehensive replies. Parents have comparable difficulties in trying to give simple and cogent explanations as to why they did have children. Reasons for wanting or not wanting children are difficult to verbalize and, even when they are articulated, often include ambivalent sentiments expressed in contradictory attitudes (Flapan, 1969). "The private covert reasons for or against having children cannot well be asked even though we know what some of them might be. In any case, they are not easily articulated though they may not always be unconscious" (Wyatt, 1967: 34). This presents minimal difficulty for parents, who are seldom called upon to explain themselves. It is, however, problematic for childless persons, who are continually pressed to account for their nonconformity, and who indeed frequently question themselves and each other.

The struggle for insight can be a long and painful process. For example, one woman of twenty-three reported that, although she had known for eight years that she never wanted to have children, she still did not know exactly why. She lamented:

> I've looked and looked, trying to figure out the exact source of my utter disregard for convention. I know that I don't want to get married, then save up for a down-payment for a house, go into hock for furniture and have two kids—and that's all there is, right? I tried to sort out why I did not want all that, but who knows why? I'm just damn sure that I don't. I sort of know when I made up my mind, back then, but it was lots of things, I guess. I do know, whatever else, I'm not cut out to be a mother.

In the same vein, another wife commented:

> I've given up an hour of talk and I haven't really told you anything about why I don't want to have children, have I? It's a thing that isn't simple, it's extremely complicated, and it's deeply rooted—in my case in my intellectual and emotional discoveries about women and families, and in my ambitions for myself.

The themes involved in voluntary childlessness are so integrated and interrelated that several may be expressed in a single sentence. Rather than describing factors in a clear and orderly sequence, our subjects presented a conglomeration of factors which could then be separated and analyzed. For example, asked why she did not want children, one wife replied at length:

> I don't know if I want kids or not. Well, I'd have to quit work and then where would we be with the bills and all? But I've had all that as a kid anyway, and Jon wants to go to Europe next year. Besides, like my mother, I'd rather not get too tied down. Maybe later, but I would not be good at all that. I don't like doing it, so I wouldn't do a good job, would I? What right do I have to take a child and spoil its whole life, because that's what parents do. Being free is so important. Well, it is all there is and once you give up freedom, well, that's it, right? I mean, the damn puppy is bad enough. But the real thing is, we don't need the motherhood thing anymore. We have enough kids getting born, right?

In unstructured interviews, as in everyday speech, the flow of conversation is erratic and, if every word were to be taken literally, would appear to be merely free association. Close attention to direct quotations, however, reveals a number of recurrent themes. For example, this woman appears to disavow her commitment, in spite of the fact that, after eleven years of deliberately avoiding children, there can be little doubt that she will never have a child. Her response to the question ("I don't know if I want kids or not") is not expressing ambivalence about what she intends to do, but ambivalence about how she evaluates being childless. Persons move quickly from short-term consequences ("Where would we be with the bills") to long-range implications ("Once you give up freedom, well, that's it, right"). Questions concerning one's competence ("I wouldn't do a good job, would I") are in conjuncture with the issue of not wanting to perform the task in any case ("I've had all that as a kid anyway"). Parenthood, which is usually defined as an obligation, is redefined as a privilege ("What right do I have") and one which has at best a dubious outcome ("and spoil its whole life"). Finally, reasons for not wanting children are placed next to justifications for that decision ("We have enough kids getting born"). This quotation is representative of the verbalizations of childless couples, in that a plurality of themes are offered in random juxtaposition rather than separate points made independently. It does not make sense to ask which of the many related reasons is *the* reason, or even the *most important* reason. The factors related to self-image, to personality, and to lifestyle are multifarious and complex. After exhaustive (and exhausting) conversations with many voluntarily childless persons, recurrent themes become apparent. The precise analysis of exactly how important individual themes are for particular kinds of childless persons awaits a different and much more structured kind of data collection and analysis.

The Childlessness Clause in the Marriage "Contract"

How do some couples come to be voluntarily childless? Although the men and women interviewed could not list precisely the reasons and motives which led them to reject parenthood, they could place in time the "state of affairs which afterward came to be labelled as the decision" (Bell, 1971). The ability to estimate that point in time provides a useful starting point for the consideration of the processes whereby couples come to define themselves as voluntarily childless. Two characteristic career paths are apparent. The couple, before they are even married, may formulate a definite and explicitly-stated intention never to become involved in parental roles. A second and more common route is less obvious, in which childbearing is postponed until such time as it is no longer considered desirable at all.

Of the childless couples interviewed, more than a third entered into their marriages with a childlessness clause clearly stated in their marriage "contract." Although none of the couples had a formal written contract in the legal sense of the word, the husband and wife explicitly agreed upon childlessness as a firm condition of marriage. The couples deliberately sought a future mate who, regardless of his or her own desirable qualities, would agree to this one condition. Generally, these couples made their negative decisions regarding the value of children during their early adolescence, before the possibility of marriage had ever been considered. Such persons are "early articulators" (Houseknecht, 1978) of an antinatalist position, in that they not only reach their decision at a very young age, but they are able to verbalize their opinions as well. For example, one nurse reported:

> When I was in residence just before we all graduated, everyone was getting married. It was the thing to do, you got your diploma, you got married, you got your first real job, all in a month or two. You know the scene, you run a picture of yourself in your cap to announce your engagement. So I got married too. But I was looking for someone who would not want children for at least ten years. Even then, I would only have them if I could have a governess like the English do. I do not think parents and children can spend twenty-four hours a day with each other and still be happy. Anyway, I did not have much luck at first. I went out with med students and interns who are really very conservative and middle-class, and they were all shocked that I would talk this way. I never tried to hide it, I was serious. And then Ron came along, and he did not like kids at all and that was great with me. I met him just before I was to graduate, and we got married five months later.

One respondent with exceptionally negative feelings on the subject of children provides a good illustration of the potential relevance of childlessness in mate selection. She reports that:

> My first decision never to have children was formed when I was fifteen and all us girls sat around talking about sex and marriage and husbands. Everyone else would always talk about the kids they were going to have, like it was just taken for granted. I couldn't sit and talk about it with the same enthusiasm as the others did. It finally came to me that I just didn't want to have children. It was a shock because all my life, you know, you're sort of groomed for it. I was groomed for it. My parents had very strict views on education for women, you know, they said you finish high school, after that you work in an office and then you get married and have children and you'll be fine. And when I said I didn't want to do that, they got very upset.

The respondent's insistence on childlessness as a necessary condition of marriage soon led her to question the possibility of marriage at all, in that the likelihood of finding a man who felt as she did about children seemed remote.

> About the time I was first wondering if I wanted kids, it also occurred to me I just couldn't see myself marrying. After I decided for sure I really did not want them, there seemed even less of a chance that I would ever marry. I didn't think any man would want a wife who refused to give him children.

This woman's rejection of motherhood led to the disruption of an otherwise satisfactory relationship. She first fell in love at the age of eighteen, and for a year and a half was enthusiastically involved in a rewarding love affair, which culminated in an informal understanding that they would be married. As marriage plans became more concrete, she even bought a wedding dress. However, as the wedding date approached, her lover became more overt in his anticipation of children, looking forward to at least two. With great distress, she finally broke her engagement, saying to him: "If I had a child, within two months of having it, I'd be gone and then where would you be?" Within several months, she moved in with "the first man I'd ever met who didn't want children." Voluntary childlessness was the first thing they found they had in common and the first basis of their attraction to each other.

In some instances, the cultural association between marriage and parenthood is so deeply ingrained that the rejection of parenthood is perceived as possible only if marriage is also rejected. The two phenomena are considered to be different aspects of the same thing, and it is not until ones mid-twenties that the option of childless marriage occurs as an alternative. For example, one respondent reported:

> As young as nine or ten years of age, I felt that if what my parents had was marriage, it was not for me. In my early teens, I concluded that the women who accomplished things did not get married and have children, and that I wouldn't either. It was not until my late teens that I realized that not all married women had children, and that a career and marriage could sometimes be combined. I still felt, however, that it wasn't for me and I was determined not to get married.

Her future husband dated her for five years and proposed three times before she was finally persuaded to become a wife.

Although a few husbands among the respondents decided as boys never to become fathers, most of the husbands who agreed before marriage never to have children associated that decision with the decision to marry a particular woman. Before considering getting married, they did not feel strongly about having or not having children. This is consistent with findings from a variety of studies regarding fertility decision-making among males: they don't think about it. As one husband explained:

> The decision about children was an irrelevant question before I actually started settling down, getting married. I just thought that kids would probably come someday; I didn't really think about it. I mean, of all the things I had on my mind, that just wasn't it. Then, when we were engaged, she started talking up the advantages, how good it would be if we did not have any kids and would that be OK, and I thought about it and, man, that was fine with me. We've done a lot better just on our own.

In most instances when childlessness is an inflexible condition of marriage, the couple recognize early in their courtship that they agree on the issue of children and readily accept permanent childlessness as part of the informal marriage "contract." In some instances, however, it is possible for the man or woman who is unsuccessful in finding a like-minded person to find someone who has no firm commitment to having children, and to convert them to the childless worldview. Two of the wives interviewed first decided to avoid motherhood and then negotiated compliance with their husbands-to-be; conversely, one wife was persuaded by her husband's strong antinatalist views.

Permanent Postponement: Childlessness as a Waiting Game

More than two-thirds of the couples interviewed remained childless as a result of a series of decisions to postpone having children until some future time, a time which never came. Rather than explicitly rejecting parenthood prior to marriage, they repeatedly deferred procreation until a more convenient time. These temporary postponements provided time during which the evaluations of parenthood were reassessed relative to other goals and possibilities. At the time of their marriages, most couples who became postponers had devoted little serious thought to the question of having children, and had no strong feelings either for or against parenthood. Typically, they simply made the conventional assumption that, like everybody else, they would probably have one or two children eventually.

The transition from wanting to not wanting children typically evolves through four separate stages, which will be described in some detail. Although it is convenient to discuss each stage separately, it must be realized that in reality the stages are not discrete and discontinuous categories, but represent overlapping foci of the marriage at various times. Movement from one stage to the next is facilitated, or in some instances retarded, by various career contingencies which will be outlined and illustrated.

Postponement for a definite time

The first stage in the postponement route to childlessness involves deferring childbearing for a definite period of time. At this stage, the voluntarily childless are difficult to distinguish from the conventional and conforming couples who will eventually become parents. In most groups, it is not necessarily desirable for the bride to conceive during her honeymoon. It is considered understandable that, before starting a family, a couple might want to achieve certain goals, such as graduating from school, travelling, buying a house, saving a nest egg, or simply getting adjusted to one another. The reasons for waiting vary, but there remains a clear commitment to have children as soon as conditions are right. For example, one wife had formulated very definite fertility plans very early in her marriage. It was her intention to work until her husband completed graduate school. His graduation was scheduled for a specific date, to be followed, if all went well, by a satisfactory job offer. When these two conditions had been met, her intentions were to conceive as soon as possible, to quit her job sometime in the middle of her pregnancy, and thereafter to devote hereself full time to raising children.

During Stage One, childless couples practice birth control conscientiously and continuously. If the couple manage to postpone pregnancy deliberately for even a few months, they have established a necessary but not a sufficient condition to voluntary childlessness, namely the habit of effective birth control within marriage. Once this has occurred, habit and inertia tend to make them continue in the same behavior. The couple must now decide whether or not they wish to stop using birth control so as to have a child. Although for the first few months of marriage the postponement of pregnancy is widely accepted, even at this stage the permanently childless are somewhat different from their pre-parental counterparts. Many conventional couples, even those who approve of birth control and have access to it, do not seriously try to control their own fertility until they have had at least one child.

Postponement for an indefinite time

The second stage of the postponement route involves a shift from postponement for a definite period of time to an indefinite one. The couple often cannot recall exactly when they shifted into this second stage. They continue to remain committed to being parents, but become increasingly vague about when the blessed event is going to take place. It may be when they can "afford it" or when "things are going better" or when they "feel more ready." For example, one immigrant couple had recently experienced a rapid series of changes in country of residence, in cities within Canada, and in occupations, some of which were terminated involuntarily and some of which were terminated because they were unsatisfactory. They had very limited savings and felt that, without any family in Canada, there was no one on whom they could rely in an emergency. After nearly five years of marriage, they still wanted to remain childless until they felt financially and occupationally secure.

A more conventional couple postponed parenthood until they were "ready" and had "had some fun" in their adult, married lifestyle. The husband summed up their situation during this stage as follows:

> We were very happy and satisfied the way things were—our jobs, friends, new house, vacation trips—and we didn't want to change it just then. Our ambivalence about kids began to grow during this time, but we still assumed that someday we'd be parents just like everybody else.

Some couples postpone parenthood until they feel that they can give children all the things they think children should have. Under these circumstances, Stage Two of the postponement process closely parallels the reticence felt by many parents who do not want children too soon. A common concern is not having children until one is living in a "large enough" space, which might be defined as a two-bedroom apartment or as a three-bedroom house. Often, couples are concerned with being able to spend enough time with their children, a condition which may depend upon the woman's readiness to quit work, and/or the couple's readiness to manage on one salary. These kinds of reasons are generally relatively acceptable, in that they are attempts to maximize the advantages available to children, rather than to minimize the disadvantages that accrue to parents. A common consequence of such reasoning, however, is that the standards to be achieved before one is truly "ready" to have a child can escalate indefinitely, resulting in a series of successive "temporary" postponements.

Deliberating the pros and cons of parenthood

Stage Three involves a qualitative change in the thinking of childless couples, in that for the first time there is an open acknowledgement of the possibility that, in the end, the couple may remain permanently childless. In this phase of the career, the only definite decision is to postpone deciding until some vague and unspecified time in the future. For example, a twenty-nine-year-old student expressed considerable indecisiveness:

> We haven't decided to have children right away, and we haven't decided never to have them either. We just keep postponing the whole thing. We might, or we might not. We can worry about it later. We have talked about not having children and that prospect is not unpleasant. [Would you think of being sterilized?] No, no. We are not that sure and it is nice to be able to change your mind. But I suppose we could adopt too. It all depends on what things are like later. Certainly not for three or four years. Or maybe five.

Another wife, when asked how certain she was that she would or would not have children, replied:

> Well, no. Well, I may. I don't know. I think eventually that we probably might, but I can't see that I will in the forseeable future. If I say I'm going to have them in the next five years—there's no way I can, and then by that time I'm thirty. I'll decide then and then I'll think, "Gee whiz, I don't know what I'm going to do." If I got too old physically to have a child, or if my doctor thinks I oughtn't get pregnant, we would adopt. It's not fair to have kids when there are all these kids without advantages. But I don't know if an adopted kid would feel completely your own. I mean, it ought to, but would it? Having a kid commits you. I don't want to be committed to anything at all right now. I want to sit on the fence for a few more years. Maybe it'll take five or ten years for me to make up my mind, then I'll just see how I—how we—feel about things.

A nurse reported a typical progression from Stage One to Stage Three:

> When we were first married, we had long discussions about children. He wanted four and I only wanted two at the most, but it was no problem because it was still at the intellectual level because we were still discussing whether we wanted children and if we did, how many we would have. But we didn't want them then, we wanted to enjoy each other. Later on, we were trying to save to buy a house, the down-payment anyway, and we did, not this one but another we have sold since. Then my husband decided to go back to school, and he talked me into going back too. So that meant no kids for several years. We had been married I guess about three years when we really started to think that maybe we wouldn't have kids at all. We still

> haven't definitely decided never-never; it is a very hard decision to make, really. But a pregnancy now would just disrupt our whole way of life. Maybe later. He is thinking of a vasectomy, has been for a year or so. Maybe later; or maybe we might adopt or—I just don't know yet.

Consistent with earlier observations, husbands are often less articulate about their rationale for avoiding parenthood because they have tended to think about it considerably less than have their wives. Since wives most often raise the issue of the advantages of a childfree lifestyle, the husband often ends up in the role of the devil's advocate, articulating the advantages of children in order to encourage his mate to consider both sides of the issue. One husband reported:

> It really became silly for a while there. She would give the routine that kids would tie us down, that they would be a big pain in the ass, etc. Then I chime in with all the "howevers" and "buts," supporting the notion of being parents and the joys of watching our own kid grow. I wasn't all that hip about the idea, but wanted to be sure she was seeing both sides of the issue.

The third stage of the postponement route to voluntary childlessness is a critical one, in that the very fact of openly considering the pros and cons of having children is deviant and probably increases the likelihood of deciding against it. As one wife pointed out:

> It's a lot more difficult to consciously decide to have children after thinking hard about it for some time than to just go ahead and have them because you're married.

When considered carefully and rationally in terms of probable consequences, the decision to become a parent is perhaps more difficult than the decision to become a husband or wife. When considering marriage, the roles to be performed can be rehearsed. A number of forms of trial marriage, or "playing house" are available for the couple who are attracted toward marriage but who are hesitant about a final commitment. For parenthood, there are no comparable forms of trial reproduction, of "playing parent." The strategy of "borrowing" children, which will be discussed later, does not provide an adequate test of parental aptitude. The only situation which even begins to approximate a trial period is the waiting time legally required before adoptions can be finalized.

To pursue the analogy, it might be noted that, in deciding to get married, there is some opportunity to assess the characteristics of the prospective mate and to evaluate his or her desirability. In deciding to become a parent, there is no opportunity to assess the characteristics of the prospective child, with the possible exception of privately arranged adoptions. The parent must be reconciled to whatever kind of child fate sends. Moreover, the decision to get married is not an irrevocable one. Divorce, although perhaps not to be preferred, is always an alternative for all but the very devout. However, with parenthood, the decision, once made, is essentially irreversible. One may be an ex-mate, but never an ex-parent.

Most couples who follow the normal moral career of parenthood cope with these questions in part by keeping them below the level of awareness. They do not have to decide to become parents because they have never questioned the inevitability of parenthood, or if they have questioned it, they have remained committed to the idealized and romanticized notions of what it will be like. A significant step in the moral career of childlessness is simply questioning the inevitability of parenthood and considering negative as well as postive aspects.

Acceptance of permanent childlessness

The fourth stage involves the definite conclusion that childlessness is a permanent rather than a transitory state. For most couples, there is never a direct decision made to avoid having children. Rather, after a number of years of postponing pregnancy until some future date, they become aware that an implicit decision has been made to forego parenthood. One wife reported a typical sequence:

> Our decision not to have children was a very gradual thing. When we first got married, we decided we were going to do a little bit of travelling before we had a family. We went to England first of all for a holiday. We decided we definitely wanted to do that before we settled down. And then when we came back from England, we decided we couldn't stand not having a car any longer; we wanted to be able to go out for drives and so on, so we figured we could wait another year and buy a car instead. And it kept getting postponed and the more we postponed, the less I really wanted to have children. Actually, I don't know that I ever really did want to have children; it was sort of a matter of this is what you do. I was never really wild about the idea. It was always going to be two at the most, and then it went down to one. We decided we would have one and if it was a girl, we would adopt a boy, and if it was a boy, we would adopt a girl. And then after that it went down to none and maybe adopt one. Or maybe just adopt one and we went to see the agency, like I told you. And then we just dropped it altogether.

The process is one of recognizing an event which has already occured, rather than of posing a question and then searching or negotiating for an answer. At first, it was "obvious" that "of course" the couple would eventually have children; later it became equally "obvious" that "of course" they would not.

> Every couple of years we'd discuss whether to have a child or not, not because we really wanted children, but because the time seemed to be right. And then we'd look at the bank balance and put it off for another two years. After five years, we sort of stopped discussing it. We just decided let's let it ride, we're really not that keen on it anymore. If he really wanted to have a family, I'd go along with it wholeheartedly. Of the two of us, I'm the wishy-washy one. I would do it just because it wouldn't destroy any preconceived ideas I had about being married: you know, you get married and have children—that was already set. This is more of an unfamiliar terrain at this point, to say you are not going to. He was the one who made the decision. I never really disputed the preconceived notion that married people have children. I never even thought about it much one way or the other.

Two years later, at the age of thirty-six, the husband decided to get a vasectomy and the wife agreed it was a good decision.

Couples who reach the fourth stage usually at least consider sterilization as an option to guarantee their childless status. Among the couples studied, about one-quarter had opted for sterilization, and another quarter were seriously considering it. In most instances, the man chose to have a vasectomy. When human sterilization first became accepted as a birth control technique, husbands were more likely to have a vasectomy than wives were to have a tubal ligation. Recently, there has been a new trend towards more-or-less equal numbers of men and women seeking surgical birth control. This trend reflects not so much a change in attitudes towards women as an improvement in the medical technology available, making it possible for women to be sterilized with relatively safe, short operations involving miniminal complications.[1]

Several factors combined to precipitate the decision to be sterilized. One obvious one is a recognition of a permanent commitment of childlessness. By itself, however, this does not suggest sterilization, as other forms of birth control provide more-or-less satisfactory alternatives. The sterilization decision is most likely to follow some dissatisfaction with previously acceptable forms of birth control. Contraceptive pills,

---

[1] Laparoscopic sterilization requires two small abdominal incisions: one in the lower abdomen, and one just below the navel for the insertion of a laparoscope, a thin steel tube with an intense light at the end to allow the surgeon to see the internal reproductive organs. An alternative technique, culdoscopy, makes use of a vaginal approach and therefore avoids the necessity of an abdominal incision. For a description and evaluation of alternative methods of sterilization, see Wortman and Piotrow (1973a, 1973b, 1973c).

which were acceptable early in marriage, may be perceived as less acceptable after the wife has been taking them for some time. Recent research suggests that they may be especially hazardous for women who are over thirty-five and who are smokers (Rosenfield, 1978). Other forms of birth control do offer protection, but never the absolute protection offered by the pill. In some instances, the sterilization decision relates directly to the acceptability of abortion. If abortion is readily available and psychologically acceptable, women may be content with less-than-perfect contraception, assuming that if they did conceive, they could simply abort. However, if legal abortions are difficult to obtain, or if abortion is felt to be immoral or unesthetic, dissatisfaction with conventional contraception may be a direct impetus to seek sterilization. Given the growing availability, acceptability, and ease of sterilization, increasing numbers of parents as well as nonparents will opt for the operation. Future research is needed to investigate the process by which couples decide if sterilization is required, and if so, whether husband, wife, or both will be sterilized.

Achieving Consensus

Many topics of disagreement in a marriage can be worked out with varying kinds of compromise. The issue of having or not having children, however, is not one of them. As one old saw has it, you can't be a little bit pregnant. Nor can you have a child one year and give it up the next. Moreover, the issue of having or not having children is of very high emotional salience, and makes a significant difference in one's life. It seems unlikely that one could be happy if "forced" against one's will to have a child; similarly, it may be equally difficult to be happy if one, wanting a child, and able to have one, is not "allowed" to do so by one's husband or wife. Among our respondents, all couples had achieved consensus on the desirability of not having children. However, it must be remembered that our respondents had all been married for at least five years. Presumably, some couples who could not achieve consensus may have agreed to disagree, and gone their separate ways after less than five years of marriage.

About half the couples who achieved consensus on not wanting children were "mutuals" (Cooper *et al.*, 1978) in that they did so spontaneously, with the gradual recognition of an emergent joint decision. Of the remaining cases, there was no apparent pattern of the will of the husband or the will of the wife's being most likely to prevail. About a quarter of our respondents reported that the final consensus had been initiated by the husband; in the remaining quarter, it was the wife who first rejected children.[2] Two brief examples may serve to illustrate the dynamics.

The youngest of our respondents to have been sterilized was a twenty-three-year-old teacher who reported she was converted to voluntary childlessness by her husband. She enjoyed her work with retarded children and was apparently quite proficient at it. She had always liked children, and before she met her husband, she assumed that eventually she would have one or two. Her husband, however, had exceedingly strong views on the subject. Initially he had been repelled and disgusted by the ways in which his mother coped with his younger siblings, especially by such things as her changing a baby's diaper at the dinner table. He decided at the age of ten that he would never have children, and although he gets along well with adolescents and preadolescents, infants in the diaper stage still make him physically ill. Prior to their marriage, they discussed their differences and reached a compromise. The wife agreed not to have a baby and the husband agreed to the possiblity of someday adopting an older child. After a year or two of marriage, the wife became convinced of the advantages of remaining childless. After three years of marriage, she mistakenly believed she was pregnant and was, in her terms, "absolutely panic-stricken," an experience she describes as the "worst of her life." For religious reasons, abortion was not feasible. Determined never to have to repeat the experience, on her own initiative she arranged to be sterilized. Although she still keeps open the possibility of adopting a child someday, she has no definite plans to do so and expresses only satisfaction with the childless state.

In contrast to this couple, in the case of a journalist who later became a successful novelist, it was the wife who first opted for childlessness. While still in high school, she decided she was not suited to be a mother and was not interested in having children. Her husband, a successful lawyer, became aware of her feelings during their courtship and extended engagement. Although he liked children and had always assumed he would have them someday, he also was content not to be a father. In his reasoning, since the woman must bear the children, look after them and assume primary responsibility for them, the decision of

---

[2] Contrary to Marciano (1978), we did not find any suggestion that the influence of one spouse approached coercion, or that the husband was likely to exert a disproportionate amount of power. Although husbands presumably had more power than their wives in these as in other marriages, on this particular question the chauvinist advantage is more than offset by the general assumption that issues relating to children fall more within the feminine than the masculine sphere.

whether or not to have children should be left to her. If for whatever reason she should not want children, no one—not even her husband—had a right to coerce her into motherhood. The wife reports that their marraige of twelve years is a close one, and that both feel considerable satisfaction with their childlessness, their relationship, and their general way of life.

Commitment to Childlessness

The degree of certainty attached to the acceptance of permanent childlessness varied among the respondents interviewed. All of the persons who were early articulators, and who had demanded a childlessness clause in their marriage contracts, felt that not wanting children was an immutable characteristic of themselves. Together with some persons who were involved in the postponement process, they felt that "becoming a parent is not the right thing for me." Such persons are "independents" (Cooper *et al.*, 1978) in that they make their decision to parent or not independently of the attitudes of their spouse. In discussing the extent to which childless persons were committed to childlessness, and the extent to which that commitment did or did not relate to their current marriage, respondents were asked: "What would you do if you (or if your wife) got pregnant?" Most immediately protested that such a thing could not happen accidentally, but were then persuaded to consider the consequences if, hypothetically, the "impossible" did occur. As an illustration of the extent to which some persons are committed to childlessness as an immutable personal attribute, rather than merely as a decision reflecting their current circumstances, one young husband replied concisely:

> Well, in that case, my wife could have three choices. One, she could have an abortion. I hope she would do that, but I guess I couldn't make her do it. If not, two, she could have the baby and place it for adoption. Or three, she could have a divorce.

Childless persons who unambiguously see themselves as nonparents are likely to be in favor of sterilization and to seek it at an early age. In several instances where both husband and wife had personally rejected parenthood independently of each other or their marriage, both had sought sterilization. Such persons do not report adverse reactions to the operations, and consider it a private decision. In other couples where levels of commitment vary, one or the other may be persuaded to "volunteer" to be sterilized, a process often jokingly referred to as "getting fixed," "getting spayed," "having been to the vet" or even "having been sent to the vet." It seems likely that those persons most likely to experience adverse reactions to sterilization are those who did not really want to have the operation done, but who were somehow talked into it by "rational" arguments that failed to take into account the emotional level. Among the respondents, none of the persons sterilized expressed any regret. However, a number who had considered sterilization said that they had decided against it not out of ambivalence towards having children, but out of a squeamishness about the operation itself. One husband was quite explicit: "For me, the expression 'put your balls on the line' is going to remain just a figure of speech!"

In contrast to persons who characterize themselves as irrevocably childless by choice, more than half of our respondents related their decision not to have children to their present marriages. They acknowledged that, if they had happened to marry someone else, they might well have decided to have a child. Moreover, they often speculate that, if in the future they were to be married to someone who did want children, they might very well be persuaded to change their minds. Such persons feel that not wanting children reflects not their own nature *per se* so much as the situation in which they find themselves. After a period of negotiation, they and their mates came to agree that "becoming parents is not the right thing for us" or more likely "becoming parents is not the right thing for us right now." This does not imply a lack of consensus or a lack of satisfaction, but it does imply an openness to the potential for sometime living differently. One husband, who resisted the idea of sterilization, explained:

> Right now, I'm totally happy. We have a good marriage, we don't need kids. But who knows? Suppose we got a divorce. Suppose she got killed? I'd remarry, I know I would, and if my next wife wanted a baby, I would not automatically be opposed to it. That would be a different marriage, I'd be a different kind of husband married to a different kind of wife. If she wanted to be a mother, I'd be a father, I suppose. But now, here, for us? No way!

Moving from Stage to Stage: Some Factors Accelerating Commitment

Couples who know before they marry that they will never have children are not troubled by decisions, other than by choosing how they will avoid pregnancy. However, couples who remain childless through continued postponement, and who in doing so progress through four rather distinct phases, tend to have considerable variation in the ease and speed with which they move from one step to the next. Some circumstances tend to push couples rapidly on to the next stage; others tend to provide ample opportunity for continued delay.

Pregnacy scares

One traumatic event which may serve to accelerate a couple's movement from one state of postponement to the next is a pregnancy scare. When the wife's menstrual period is late, or even worse, when a period is missed entirely, the possibility of pregnancy may serve to crystalize hitherto vague and unrecognized feelings about parenthood. Irregular periods, or even amenorrhea, may have many causes other than conception, but for a sexually active woman pregancy is the explanation which comes most readily to mind. The abstract idea of a child is quite different in its psychological impact from the concrete idea of a child's forming and growing day by day. For example, in response to the question of when she first knew she did not want children, one woman replied very emphatically and precisely: "The first moment I knew, and I was absolutely certain about it, was the first moment I knew I was pregnant." In fact, although she "knew" she was pregnant, her menstrual period was simply delayed and started spontaneously ten days later. During that time, she had been involved in an intense search for a competent abortionist, a search which she described as discouraging and humiliating. She was greatly relieved to discover that she was not pregnant after all, but by that time, the decision had been crystallized, and she and her husband were weighing the relative advantages of vasectomy versus tubal ligation.

The husband of another couple in a similar position stated:

> When we thought she was pregnant we found ourselves desperately trying to look on the positive side of it—that it will be fun being parents—but we weren't fooling ourselves, though we *thought* we were being nice guys and fooling each other. When her period came, we knew we'd made our decision never to risk pregnancy again.

Aging and the decline of fecundity: the adoption alternative

One of the problems of opting for the postponement model is the biological fact that childbirth cannot be postponed indefinitely. As one recent book puts it, women who decide to postpone are literally *Up Against the Clock* (Fabe and Wikler, 1979). Three interrelated problems are involved. In the first place, fecundity is known to decline with advancing age. Although it is theoretically possible for a woman to bear a child until her menopause is completed, in actuality her fecundity tends to decline with each year, as to a lesser extent does her husband's. Couples who could have had a child in their twenties but who chose to wait until their thirties may find that their fecundity has declined, or has been lost, during the intervening decade and that conception is no longer possible. In the second place, many childless couples perceive that once the wife is in her late thirties or early forties, the chances of having a defective child are much increased and that it therefore would be dangerous to do so at that late date.[3] Third, it must be realized that a larger part of the definition of how old is "too old" to have children is social, rather than biological in origin (Rindfuss and Bumpass, 1976). When the mother's age is too advanced, it is believed that her tolerance of young children is reduced and that the family situation would not be "good" for the child. Moreover, since couples tend to associate with persons their own age, a late birth would place them in the unusual situation of coping with toddlers while their friends were coping with teenagers.

As a consequence of these three factors, as the age of the wife approaches thirty, the decision to postpone deciding whether or not to have a child becomes less comfortable. In order to avoid the stress of having to make an imminent decision, one strategy is to redefine the maximum age at which reproduction would still be safe and desirable. Interestingly, this age seems to recede in time, depending upon the age of the woman, with a tendency to leave a margin of about two years. Thus, women of twenty-eight report they feel they must make a decision by the time they are thirty; women of thirty-four say they must do

---

3 The increased medical risks associated with late pregnancies are more important relative to other women at younger ages than they are in absolute terms. For example, Down's syndrome is a congenital malformation which clearly increases in risk with advancing maternal age, especially after the age of forty. However, among births to women aged forty to forty-four, the incidence of Down's syndrome is less than one per cent (Nortman, 1974: 7). In other words, a childless woman of this age has a better than 99 per cent chance of not having a Mongolian idiot. "Clearly, in the absence of a personal history to the contrary, older women run only a small risk of producing a congenitally malformed child, although their risk is much higher than that faced by younger women" (Nortman, 1974: 7). The risk of congenital deformity is further attenuated if the woman has access to amniocentesis, a procedure for examining a sample of amniotic fluid for signs of Down's syndrome or other abnormalities. If the foetus is not normal, it can then be aborted and an attempt made to conceive again (Fabe and Wikler, 1979: 238).

so by thirty-six; and women of thirty-eight vow to make up their minds by forty. Although such stalling defers immediate pressure, it is inevitably a temporary solution. When a forced choice appears imminent, a more practical solution is to include the vague possibility of adoption as a satisfactory "out" should one be needed. One wife makes a typical comment when she trails off her discussion of children by concluding: "If we've left having children too late, we might adopt one." An ex-nurse of twenty-nine, who believes that if you are going to have children, you should have them before you are thirty, suggests that: "If at fifty we decide we did miss something after all, we will adopt an Indian kid, or maybe a homeless teenager."

When we examined our childless couples closely on this subject of future adoption, however, it became clear that, in most instances, talk about adoption is unlikely to be a precursor of actually becoming adoptive parents. Although many of the childless couples referred at least once to the possibility of someday adopting a child, their discussions of this eventuality were exceedingly vague. They had apparently given no thought to the kind of child they might like to adopt, not even in terms of such obviously important traits as sex, age, or race. They had no information regarding the conditions under which adoption would be possible or what steps it would entail. It is noteworthy that it apparently never occurred to any of the couples who discussed adoption that, if they wanted to adopt, a suitable child might not be available. Nor did it occur to them that, if a child were available, he or she might not be placed with them. Although adoption is seldom a pragmatic option for voluntarily childless couples, it does have considerable symbolic importance in that it allows postponers to remain indefinitely at the third stage of debating endlessly the pros and cons of parenthood.

Ambivalence towards achievement

Couples in the first stage of postponement, who hold out other goals as "excuses" for not starting a family, may find themselves feeling quite ambivalent when they do finally achieve their goals. Such achievement is intrinsically desirable and presumably satisfying, but at the same time, it removes one of the most readily acceptable reasons for avoiding parenthood. Thus, one can be happy about graduating from college or about getting a good job, and at the same time be apprehensive about the attendant responsibilities that may come with it. For example, one husband reflected:

> I remember we were out celebrating the fact that we would both be finished with school and would graduate from college a full semester sooner,

> but when it dawned on us that now we didn't have any excuses left to postpone a family, we got a sinking feeling inside. Neither of us wanted that now. We found ourselves agreeing that it wouldn't be a good idea to have kids yet. We still acted the same way, but after that, it was a lot harder to explain. It was like our days of grace had run out, like on a mortgage or something.

Similarly, if couples have postponed having children until they are "out of debt," or until they can "afford to buy a house," their achievement of these goals necessitates a re-evaluation of their parenthood aspirations. Thus, removing the once-perceived obstacles to "being ready" for parenthood accelerates the couples more quickly toward a resolution of their dilemma and their inevitable entrance into either parenthood or a childfree lifestyle.

The social import of pets

All childless couples are aware of the stereotype that childless people are supposed to be inordinately fond of pets of various kinds, and to treat animals like humans. Of the subjects interviewed, about one-third had no pets at all, about one-third had one pet, and about one-third had two or more pets. Statistics on the distribution of pet ownership in the general population are predictably difficult to obtain, but available data suggest that the fact that about two-thirds of childless respondents owned animals is about what would be expected among couples in general.[4]

For most childless couples, attitudes towards animals are irrelevant to their attitudes towards children. However, the presence of pets in a household does have some consequences similar to those resulting from the presence of a child, especially a baby. For those couples for whom the presence of animals was of some relevance for the childbearing decision processes, two antithetical processes were observed. In a minority of cases, pets served as child surrogates,

---

[4] The United States National Center for Health Statistics (1971) reports information on a national probability sample of over seven thousand noninstitutional children in the United States aged six to eleven years. Of these, sixty per cent are reported by their parents to own a pet. The actual proportion of all parental couples who have animals in the house may be expected to be somewhat higher than this, as some pets may be perceived as belonging to the parents and so not reported in questions concerning children. It is possible that the probability of pet ownership is somewhat different for the parents of very young children, or of teenage children, than it is for the parents of children aged six to eleven. No statistics are given on the kinds or number of pets, but some information on responsibility for pet care indicates predictably that in most cases (about 80 per cent) the pet owned by the child is usually cared for by the parent.

eliminating the perceived need for children. More usually, experiences with pets proved to be unsatisfactory, and reinforced a general reluctance to care for dependents, either animal or human.

The elevation of some pets from the status of animals to the higher status of substitute humans is apparently quite common, although there are no precise statistics regarding how often such anthropomorphism occurs.[5] It is due in part to generally increasing affluence (Szasz, 1968: 192), reaching the point where most of the goods and services available to human consumers have also been adapted for the canine or feline markets (Rice, 1968: 104). Under ordinary circumstances, pets have been recognized as useful outlets for affection and sources of companionship, especially for the very young and the very old (Levinson, 1972). Foote (1956) goes so far as to discuss the family pet as a "neglected member" of the family. We begin to be concerned about affection for pets only when it is expressed *instead of* rather than *in addition to* affection for humans.

Among childless couples whom we interviewed, a small minority openly admitted that their pets were child surrogates. The most extreme example involved a middle-aged couple. When they first acquired their puppy, Mary-Lou, a friend gave them a commercial baby book as a joke. Finding this amusing, they filled in the appropriate statistics as one would for a child, but then over the years continued to add items and photographs until even they saw that the "joke" was quite real. Another couple, who raised pure-bred dogs commercially, were very devoted to their hobby. The wife explained:

> Our pets mean an awful lot to us. I guess they are our children, they're as important as kids to us. People say this, but I just say "Pets aren't going to turn around and kick you in the teeth when you get older." Our ultimate aim is to live in the country and raise dogs. I think that's why I don't feel empty at the thought of not having children, because I love animals so much. We went to a dog show the other day and coming out Joe turned to me and he said, and he was serious: "Why do people have children when they can have dogs?"

For most childless couples for whom animals were a factor in their decision-making, the acquisition of a pet on a trial basis served much the same function as acquiring a baby on a trial basis, with the result that they were even less inclined towards the parenthood role. For example, one young nurse whose husband travelled extensively decided to get a puppy to keep her company, and to provide some protection

---

[5] For an extensive account of *The Social Role of Household Pets*, see Chapman (1978).

when alone in the house at night. The dog himself she found "extremely lovable", but she then went on to lament:

> He made me realize what having a small child would be like. I got very frustrated because that damn dog really intruded on my privacy and screwed up things I wanted to do. Alone with the puppy, and having to watch him constantly, I realized that having a small child would be like that too. Having a dog poses enough problems when we're going out at night, or for the weekend, and can't leave him alone too long. It would be even worse with a child.

Another young wife described her experience in a similar vein.

> We both always have liked animals, especially puppies; they're so cute, so we got this puppy. And he was cute, he was adorable. But havoc! The house was all turned upside down, he cried and fussed and had to be walked and bathed and cleaned up after, although he did get sort of housebroken quite soon. And if we left him alone, he'd howl and howl like his heart was breaking or we were beating him or something. Pretty soon we were feeling like we ought to stay home or take him with us and that was just ridiculous. And we said, if a puppy is this bad, think what having a kid must be like! So we got rid of the puppy finally, gave him to some people who live in the country. But you can't do that to a kid!

The stereotype that childless persons, especially those who deliberately avoid children, are inordinately fond of pets does, like other stereotypes, have some basis in fact. There are some couples for whom animals are obviously child surrogates. However, also like other stereotypes, it appears to be greatly exaggerated. Persons who call their dog "baby," refer to themselves as "mommy" and indulge in congruent baby-talk are more conspicuous, and more memorable than the childless couples who do not share this attitude. More typical of the respondents was a young husband who, after lamenting the "waste" of food and vitamins on "precious little pampered pets," went on to state strongly:

> I do not feel a need for pets. People who have pets seem to be making up for something else that needs to be added to their lives. They need to be needed, need someone to be glad to see them when they get home from work; that's pretty pathetic. I think that if people have pets that they make a big thing of, there must be something wrong with their human relationships.

Of the childless couples we interviewed, about a third did not own animals. Of the two-thirds who did, only a minority treated them as surrogate humans and indulged in excessive anthropomorphizing. In future research, it would be of interest to know how often persons with children regard the family dog or cat as, in effect, an additional child, and ascribe to it a number of human-like traits.

Insecurity about the marriage

A final factor in moving couples through the stages of postponement related to grave doubts about the future of their present marriage. This dimension was not frequently mentioned by our respondents, but it did surface in the course of some interviews. Marital insecurity often leads to a more immediate decision about having children, but does not necessarily mean that either parenthood or childlessness is the automatic choice. Folklore suggests, for example, that a child may be an effective solution to some kinds of marital problems. Family-life specialists have suggested that, although the effectiveness of this "solution" is at best questionable, the motivation of improving marital relationships may be a significant factor in fertility planning. It is possible that unhappily-married childless wives reject this solution for one of two reasons: either they do not accept its probable efficacy, or they do not want their "problem" to be solved. Simmel notes that there is a tendency for "cold, intrinsically alienated, unhappy spouses" not to want children, a phenomenon he attributes to the fact that:

> . . . it might unify them; and this unifying function would contrast the more effectively, but the less desirably with the parent's overwhelming estrangement. . . . They instinctively feel that the child would close the circle within which they would be nearer one another, not only externally but also in their deeper psychological layers, than they are inclined to be (Simmel, 1950: 146).

While this may well be so, it is difficult to elaborate in terms of the present research, since only a few of the couples interviewed reported markedly unsatisfactory and conflict-ridden marriages. In interpreting this fact, it must be remembered that a criterion for inclusion in the sample was a marriage duration of at least five years. For some, marital unhappiness may have been a major factor in both the decision to remain childless and the decision to get a divorce.

Chapter Three: CHALLENGING THE PARENTHOOD MYSTIQUE

Being able to reconstruct *when* childless persons made the decision to avoid parenthood is only peripherally relevant to the more basic question of *why* they did so. Throughout the interviews with childless couples, it was apparent that the motives for avoiding parenthood are at least as numerous, variant, complex, convoluted, and contradictory as are the motives for having children. Out of the nexus of competing and interrelated factors contributing to fertility decisions, it is difficult to isolate a single motive and to correlate it unambiguously with a single sociological condition. A more fruitful approach is to begin merely by seeking "motive antecedents associated with not wanting children" (Centers and Blumberg, 1954: 252). In-depth interviews with childless persons suggest, but by no means establish, several plausible motive antecedents associated with this atypical choice of lifestyle. In this chapter, we attempt to outline some salient background factors which contribute to the decision to avoid the parenthood role. Three sequential aspects seem to be involved: first, the questioning of the intrinsic desirability of parenthood; second, the phrasing of parenthood in "either/or" terms so as to preclude other options; and third, the perception that since parenthood is irrevocable, those other options are lost not only for the present but permanently.

It is important to emphasize at this point that our interviews relied heavily on retrospective perceptions which, of course, are significantly affected by one's current life situation. Thus, it is quite likely that our respondents' impressions of their formative years were guided, at least in part, by what had happened subsequent to those years. It is possible that some respondents may have overemphasized their "troubled" family life in order to justify their present childfree lifestyle, which radically differs from that of their own parents. *Post hoc* justifications of family size are difficult to interpret in terms of cause and effect.

> First, actions—even decisions—can be precipitated by fortuitous environmental or social conditions of which the individual is barely aware, or they may evolve from earlier commitments to a pattern of behavior. Second, attitudes, values, and even perceived incentives or constraints, which seemingly led to an action, might actually have followed from them. Action must be viewed as a potential *cause* of attributes, perceptions, and other actions, as well as an effect (Kiesler, 1977: 59).

Questioning the Inevitability of Parenthood

A large part of the moral imperative of parenthood derives from its apparent inevitability. The parenthood mystique in our society is so pervasive that it is doubtful if most married couples even consider the possibility of deliberately remaining childless. Once married, they do not decide to have children, in the sense of considering the pros and cons of parenthood and then opting to have a family. Rather, they become parents because it never occurred to them that they could or should do anything else. This does not mean that they are necessarily unhappy with their "decision," but rather that having children was so taken for granted that the question of their intrinsic desirability was never asked. There is continual reinforcement of the implicit assumption that most people will marry, and that once married, they will therefore want to have children. Couples do, of course, agonize and vacillate over some of the options open to them. They debate how many children they should have. They consider how soon after marriage they should start having children, and how closely the pregnancies should be spaced. If they could arrange it, they might like to be able to decide in advance if a particular pregnancy would result in a boy or a girl, often preferring that the first-born child be male (Williamson, 1978: 6). When they become parents, they analyze the pros and cons of having the wife-mother enter, or remain in, the work force. However, few persons seriously question the more basic alternatives of whether or not they should get married at all, or whether or not they should become parents.

Given that most persons automatically assume that they will, of course, become parents, how is it that some unusual persons come to challenge the inevitability of this assumption and to question its desirability? The parenthood mystique entails at least two related beliefs: first, that children are compatible with self-fulfillment; and second, that children are indeed necessary for complete self-fulfillment. Most persons in our society endorse these views, and whether or not they believe that children are necessary for happiness, they certainly believe that they make important contributions towards it. Persons who have opted for childlessness are unusual in that they have had early experiences which have destroyed, or at least discredited, their belief in the parenthood mystique.

One very suggestive question put to respondents was: "How do you think your mother's life would have been different if she had not had children?" Almost all of the voluntarily childless replied unequivocally to the effect that it would have been very different and much more satisfactory. One man gave a typical reply when he said simply: "Well, without children she could have been happy; with all of us, she never had a chance, and neither did my old man." Several components are involved in these kinds of observations. First, there is a perception that one's parents, especially one's mother, did not lead satisfying lives; second, there is the belief that their lives were unsatisfactory *because* of having children rather than for some other reason; and third, there is the implication that having children not only failed to bring happiness, but actually precluded satisfaction from other sources.

Whether or not the parents of our respondents actually had less satisfactory lives than most persons is beyond the scope of the present research. For our purposes, it does not matter if these perceptions are "correct." What is relevant is that childless persons come to believe that having children, instead of contributing to happiness, actually tends to detract from it, or even to preclude it altogether. When childless persons recall their youth, a number of patterns become apparent, occasioning serious doubts about the parenthood mystique and leading ultimately to a rejection of it. Such doubts result from their observations and interpretations of the impact of pregnancy, childbirth and child-rearing on their own parents, their brothers and sisters, or their close friends.

Raising the option of permanent childlessness does not automatically mean that parenthood will be rejected. Obviously, some persons who debate the pros and cons of parenthood decide that the ayes have it, and deliberately plan to become parents. However, it seems very likely that the simple fact of deliberating the desirability of parenthood, and thereby focusing attention on some of the disadvantages, may increase the probability of rejecting it. Questioning the unquestionable is a necessary first step in choosing permanent childlessness.

Childless Role Models

There are many facets of the adult role which we learn, more or less adequately, by identifying with our parent of the same sex. However, there are some role alternatives for which one's own parent is by definition disqualified as an example. Under usual circumstances, a parent cannot provide an identification figure as a never-married person. More importantly, our parents cannot provide an example of what it is like to be married but childless.

Since childlessness, voluntary or otherwise, is statistically very unusual in our society, there is a paucity of potential role models. Moreover, those who could provide the most appropriate models for emulation probably do not spend much of their time interacting with young people. When adult role models are presented in the mass media, such as magazines, fiction and movies, there is virtually no attention paid to the childless either as "good guys" or as villians.[1] The absence of role models of the childfree lifestyle may in part account for the low probability of ever questioning the inevitability of parenthood.

In some unusual cases, however, the choice of remaining childless is facilitated by the presence of at least one role model who has made a reasonably satisfactory life adjustment in spite of, or perhaps because of, never having had children. The construction of a social reality which condones rather than condemns an alternative to the moral career of motherhood requires not only that alternative definitions of its inevitability be learned, but that they be learned at the emotional as well as the intellectual level. The simple cognitive awareness that, somewhere in the world, there are people who do not want to be parents does not have much significance, unless the individual takes

---

[1] Other researchers have noted the lack of models of childlessness. Hardin (1971: 264) suggests that one factor in population control might be to provide some media stores aimed at girls in elementary school to teach them that: "It is not necessary for them to become mothers when they grow up" and that there are "alternative goals to marriage and parenthood."

the next step and develops an awareness that this alternative is also emotionally possible for oneself. For example, one wife's decision in her early teens never to have children coincided with her going to work for and to live with a childless divorcée, who became a major identification figure and source of emotional support. Although the woman never advocated deliberate childlessness, she did provide a working model of a woman who managed to be happy although unmarried and childless, an alternative her own mother had never intimated. She related:

> When I was fourteen, I went to work for an artist. I did not exactly work, for I was not paid, but I was her assistant, almost an apprentice. I went back for several summers. I was very shy and timid and couldn't do anything. She made me do all kinds of things: wait on people in the shop and sell things and write business letters and go to the bank and shop for lunch and make it. She was twenty years older than me, but she treated me with respect and took me seriously. I was a failure in my parent's world because I wasn't a social butterfly, pretty and flirty and flitting about, but I wasn't a failure with her. I learned to paint too. And I felt better about myself. I was so relieved to discover my parent's world wasn't the only one. I knew somehow I wanted to live like her. I didn't know then I'd actually be in the arts too. I still go back one or twice a year.

Another childless wife remembers brief glimpses of the glamorous and exciting lives led by two unmarried aunts who occasionally visited or sent presents, and who took a remote interest in her while she was growing up.

> My mother had two sisters who never married. One was an interior decorator or designer or something in New York. We never really knew why they didn't marry. They were really strong people, but pretty too. They had no patience with wishy-washy people. When other people in the depression were barely getting by, they had good jobs and entertained and travelled all over—Europe, the Orient, you name it. Sometimes they sent me cards. I wonder if they travelled with men? My father always put them down because they had not married, but I thought they had done better than he ever would. I thought even then they had a lot more fun than my mother did.

Occasionally, role models for childlessness are not family members or significant others, but are relatively casual acquaintances. One childless wife traces her decision not to be a mother to a cocktail party.

> I met a striking woman there and for something to say I asked her when she was going to start a family. I was really startled when she answered flatly: "Never." It had literally never occurred to me not to. I was so intrigued, I

got to know her better. We were never really close, but she started me thinking: if it was OK for her, why not me too?

Pregnancy Perils: Negative Definitions of Parturition

Questions about the intrinsic desirability of parenthood can occur on at least two different levels: childbearing and child-rearing. For some women, a preliminary challenge to the motherhood mystique came not from questioning the desirability of the role of mother *per se* but from the antecedent question of the desirability of pregnancy and birth. Negative definitions of parturition entail two separate dimensions: the association of pregnancy with illness and death, and the association of it with a loss of erotic appeal.

Pregnancy as illness

Pregnancy is often defined as an occasion for assuming the sick role (Rosengren, 1961, 1962). Maternal mortality is now very low, and few childless women believe that having a child would actually cost them their lives.[2] However, many believe that the state of being pregnant is at best unpleasant and that giving birth is a traumatic experience. In describing childbearing, they select adjectives such as sickening, repulsive, disgusting, repugnant, and loathsome. In anticipating how they might feel, they select terms like degraded, humiliated, embarrassed, and undignified. One woman makes a typical comment when she says:

> When my sister was pregnant, she really did disgust me. She kept insisting on showing me how much bigger she had gotten, as if it were an important

---

2 In recent past, childbirth was a major cause of death. For example, in the United States in 1935, among white women, the rate of death in childbirth was 530.6 per 100,000 live births. By 1976, this rate was reduced to only 9.0 per 100,000 (United States National Center for Health Statistics, 1978: 8). Mortality associated with pregnancy and childbirth does increase with age. In the United States in 1972–1974, the death rate from these causes for women in their early thirties was 24.9 per 100,000 live births, more than double that for women under thirty. In contrast, the rate for women in their late thirties or early forties was 44.0 and 71.4 respectively (Tietze, 1977: 74). While this appears to be a sharp increase, it must be remembered that all of these rates are now very low. Even in a high risk category, such as women in their late thirties, 99.4 per cent will survive their pregnancies.

> thing. The experience of pregnancy revolts me. In fact, the whole birth process is undignified. If I had to be pregnant, if for instance Ron wanted a baby, I would go away by myself to have it. I could not bear to have him see me like that.

Abstractions about pregnancy, which are learned when one first learns where babies come from, may be quite different in their emotional impact than the first few pregnancies to which one is personally exposed. A number of voluntarily childless women report that the pregnancies of women close to them have been unsatisfactory and dangerous experiences, quite apart from the consideration of the impact of the child on their life changes. In one extreme example, a nurse observed a series of undesirable consequences of all of the pregnancies of her mother, her best friend and her sister. Her mother had a series of nine miscarriages between the time of her birth and the birth of her brother thirteen years later. Her mother never verbally acknowledged her pregnancies, but the respondent understood what was happening at an early age, and remembers her mother repeatedly going to the hospital where she was very ill for a long time. On two occasions the mother was found unconscious and hemorrhaging at home and had to be rushed to hospital by ambulance. When the last child was finally born, it was considered a miracle that she was able to bring the child to term at all. She had a hysterectomy soon afterwards and for the rest of her life remained a semi-invalid.

The same respondent reports that when she was in high school, her closest friend became pregnant and was forced to marry. The girl's husband consented to the marriage with great reluctance, beat his wife and drank a good deal, and the couple were divorced after six months. Meanwhile the young wife had neglected to follow the strict diet prescribed for her and suffered from toxemia, resulting in a very difficult and unpleasant pregnancy. At the age of seventeen, the friend had dropped out of school, and endured a disastrous marriage and a traumatic divorce, and was left with a child to support and no resources or marketable skills.

The respondent's third vicarious experience with pregnancy was with her sister, who accidentally conceived three times very early in her marriage: once when she forgot her pill, once when her diaphragm proved ineffective, and once when her IUD perforated the lining of the uterus, resulting both in pregnancy and in emergency surgery. She suffered toxemia in all of the pregnancies, underwent difficult and prolonged labors, and bore each child several weeks prematurely. She expressed great relief when she was able to be sterilized during her last confinement. Her marriage deteriorated with each successive pregnancy, and her husband apparently blamed her for their excessive fecundity.

Because the respondent is a trained nurse, she is cognizant that her mother, her friend and her sister all underwent atypical experiences. However, before she had the benefit of medical training, all of the pregnancies which she observed and with which she was vicariously emotionally involved were complicated and difficult, and markedly changed the women's lives in undesirable ways. In spite of her knowledge of the objective medical odds, she perceives pregnancy itself as a dangerous venture. Although the fear of childbirth is not her primary motive in avoiding motherhood, she does not in any way regret missing the experience of pregnancy and birth, and concludes that in the unlikely event that she ever did want to have children, she would prefer to adopt.

Explicit attempts to resocialize childless women to believe that pregnancy and birth are positive experiences may have just the opposite effect. One woman reports that at a social gathering, a casual friend tried to "turn her on to motherhood" by giving her a minute description of her recent labor and delivery, which the respondent found "repulsive." Another reports seeing a film *No Blade of Grass*, which contained a childbirth scene apparently intended to convey the image of childbirth as natural and wondrous. It did make a difference in how she felt about the physical aspects of pregnancy, but not in the expected direction.

> Having seen labor once in all its glory with blood and everything—it turned my stomach. They showed you the actual birth and I had no idea there was so much blood involved until I talked to a couple of friends of mine who have had children. They said: "You'll see pictures in medical textbooks where it's very clean. Actually you think you're going to bleed to death." And it scares me.

This woman did not believe that if she had a child she would actually "bleed to death," but she did anticipate that the experience of childbirth would be undignified, bloody and painful. One wife expresses very clearly the distinction between expecting pregnancy to be dangerous and expecting it to be, literally, a "bloody bore."

> I'm not really scared of pregnancy. I mean, I don't think I'd die or anything like that. The rates of death in childbirth are really low, aren't they, not like it used to be when you really took a chance. No, I *could* do it all right, but who would *want* to? It's like—it's like having a tooth out or something. You can do it and it's not going to kill you, but why would you want to if you didn't have to?

Dilemmas of femininity: maternal versus erotic appeal

The dominant definitions of femininity in our culture contain an implicit contradiction. On the one hand, female sex role identity is associated with the general motherhood role: with fecundity, pregnancy and acting motherly. On the other hand, another important part of femininity and sex role identity is associated with erotic appeal which, for many people, is exactly the opposite of the motherhood role. If mothers are platonic, sex objects are erotic; if mothers are pregnant, sex objects are slim; if mothers focus on the child, sex objects focus on the male. Given these built-in cultural contradictions, it is understandable that some women may take the reasoning to its logical conclusion and may define remaining childless as contributing to the development and expression of one's femininity. To be feminine is to be sexually attractive to men, and in their worldview this requires, or is at least facilitated by, avoidance of pregnancy and the motherhood role.[3]

Although some people apparently define pregnancy as enhancing a woman's beauty rather than detracting from it, and as increasing her erotic appeal rather than decreasing it, such definitions are unusual, especially in the last trimester of pregnancy. For example, one feminist writer argues that:

> During pregnancy a woman's face may be radiant (and that belief is by and large a myth too), but what of her body?—the breasts swollen, the nipples brown, the belly distended and shiny with stretch marks, the belly button protruding. Are women beautiful then? And after pregnancy the breasts of millions of women collapse, the stretch marks remain, the belly sags, and the nipples stay brown (Stannard, 1971: 123).

Although this opinion is very strongly stated, the basic attitude it reflects is quite common. The main theme of the articles and advertisements which refer to pregnancy is "how to be sexy though pregnant," and the "solution" which they advocate is to minimize seeming pregnant at all. Maternity clothes are designed to hide, rather than to accentuate. A woman carries her pregnancy "well" if she happens not to show until well advanced, and then to remain relatively small.

---

[3] Even for married women who apparently want their children, pregnancy is often not the fulfilling period it is supposed to be. Thus, Loesch and Greenberg, after a study of first pregnancies, conclude:

> Pregnancy for nearly all of the group of married mothers—randomly selected and not consciously seeking psychiatric aid—was a period of mixed feelings with underlying moods of anxiety and depression. . . . We saw only intermittent flashes of the narcissistic bliss and self-contained dreamy comfort which has been described by others (1962: 632).

In addition to definitions of pregnancy as in itself being unattractive, there is considerable cultural concern regarding the long-term effects of childbearing on a woman's body even after the pregnancy has been brought to term. In most cases, a woman's figure is altered after bearing a child (and certainly after bearing several), and such changes are generally away from the cultural stereotype of what is currently defined as attractive and sexy. Such changes are not inevitable, especially if the woman is attractive to begin with and strongly motivated to minimize changes in weight and muscle tone as, for example, professional beauties—like actresses and models—might be. However, they usually occur among ordinary and not highly motivated or disciplined wives. The woman who is told, "You don't look as if you'd had kids," is being complimented.

There is an endless succession of books and magazine articles which assure the reader that having sexual appeal and sexual competence does not necessarily depend upon having a beautiful body. Variations on this theme find a ready and inexhaustible market, for they provide reassurance against the firm belief in most people's minds that sexual attractiveness depends upon a certain type of physical make-up. While the public buys and reads accounts discrediting the myth, it also buys and reads diet books and exercise books and how-to-stay-young books which advocate the cultural stereotype of the desirable woman's having a slim figure with relatively large breasts and long slim legs, and offer concrete suggestions as to how this ideal may be attained. A number of childless wives take very seriously these cultural themes, and have developed very strong definitions of pregnancy as reducing one's physical appeal. One woman related her "horrified" reactions to the physical changes she observed in her sister following the birth of her first child, describing in fairly graphic terms the alteration from having a fine figure to looking like a "sock full of porridge."

Some wives who do not themselves believe that pregnancy is unattractive may seek to avoid it because they believe that it does carry the stigma of a physical blemish (Taylor and Langer, 1977), and that many men find it unappealing.[4] There are numerous references to pregnant women looking like cows or barns, to their awkwardness when they waddle around, to their being bloated or swollen, and to their general weight gain. A number of our respondents reported remarks by their husbands or male friends to the effect that not only was the pregnancy

---

[4] Certainly some men feel this way and make their reactions to their wives quite explicit. Clarkson (1971: 13) reports that one of her respondents was so totally revolted by his wife when she was pregnant that he could not bear to sleep in the same room with her.

unfortunate but that the people deserving of sympathy were the husbands rather than their wives. For example, one husband often remarked when he saw a pregnant women: "Some poor bastard got caught with a bastard." Another sympathized with his friend when he reported resignedly: "My wife got herself knocked up." The facts that pregnancy itself may be defined as unattractive, and that pregnancy may have long-range disfiguring effects on one's appearance, take on additional meanings when associated with the importance of sexual appeal in keeping one's husband faithful, and with the common belief that the most likely time for a husband to be interested in extramarital sex is when his wife is pregnant. A number of childless wives expressed some variation of this theme, sometimes with references to their mothers' teachings and sometimes with reference to the behaviors observed in friends and acquaintances.

Dilemmas of Dichotomous Choice: This or That

One characteristic of voluntarily childless persons is their tendency to view parenthood goals as mutually exclusive from other important life goals, both present and future. For most persons, having children is something which is done in *addition to* doing other things. Childrearing can be more or less taken in stride, and the "needs" of children can be defined in ways commensurate with the resources available for their care. Men presumably find fatherhood to be less disruptive than women find motherhood, but most persons of either sex can usually manage to have and to raise children without making permanent or drastic alterations of their other priorities. In contrast, childless couples tend to define having children as something which can only be done *instead of* other things. For women, the choice is often defined not so much as, "Do you or do you not want to be a mother?" but "Do you or do you not want to be *only* a mother?" When parenthood is phrased in "either/or" terms, it very much increases the likelihood that remaining childless will be an attractive option.

Several interrelated dichotomous choices were apparent in the reconstructed careers of the voluntarily childless couples who were interviewed. Although not all such dilemmas were experienced by all deliberately childless couples, most had perceived that more than one of these factors contributed to their decision. The first and most important dilemma initially appeared to be the choice between full-time child-care *or* employment outside the home. A successful parenthood career was perceived as incompatible with a successful occupational career. Motherhood was associated with incompetence. The cost of having children was exaggerated by an unwillingness to go into debt. The choice therefore entailed either mortgaging one's future *or* being debt-free. In addition, parenthood was associated with marital dissatisfaction, with the additional handicap that divorce was perceived as possible for the childless but as unacceptable for parents. Consequently, having children was associated both with leading to marital maladjustment, and then with precluding the possibility of doing something about it. In general terms, childless persons tended to define parenthood as martyrdom, and to construe a choice between personal sacrifice *or* self-actualization.

Housewives versus working wives

A large part of the cost of children in both financial and emotional terms may be minimized by the wife's working. Gainful employment of the wife may make a dramatic difference in the couple's overall standard of living and in the woman's social and psychological adjustment.

During the past few decades there has been a trend toward greater involvement of wives in the work force.[5] Although there is some ambivalence about the desirability of working mothers, it is also apparent that it is becoming increasingly common and acceptable for mothers to work also, especially if their children are old enough to attend school.[6] It was initially expected that deliberately childless wives, having rejected a major requirement of conventional family life, would also reject lesser requirements and would be very tolerant of working mothers. However, a number believe that working mothers are not satisfactorily performing their duties to their children, and that alternative child-care arrangements are inadequate. Moreover, they resent

---

[5] For example, in Canada in 1961 only one wife in five (22.2 per cent) was in the labor force; by 1971, more than one out of three (38.6 per cent) worked outside the home (Veevers, 1977: 22). In the United States, the rates are even higher. In 1960, about one third (34.7 per cent) of married women were in the work force; by 1975, nearly half (44.4 per cent) of them were employed (Glick and Norton, 1977: 11).

[6] For example, in Canada in 1971, four out of ten (41.2 per cent) of all mothers with children over the age of six were employed, compared with only one out of four (25.2 per cent) of those with children under six (Veevers, 1977: 23). Similarly, in the United States in 1975, over half (52.3 per cent) of mothers with children over the age of six worked, compared with only one out of three (36.6 per cent) of those with preschool children (Glick and Norton, 1977: 11).

the fact that childless couples may be required to pay, at least indirectly, for the child-care facilities used by parents. One wife who made these concerns very explicit reflected a common attitude when she stated:

> I've always felt that if a woman is going to be a mother—well, then, she should *be a mother*. What's the point of having a child and then just foisting it off on a day-care center, where they treat it God knows how and where people without kids have to pick up the tab? If she wants to have a kid, fine, but then she should stay home and look after it.

Almost all of the mothers of the childless respondents interviewed were full-time housewives. Those mothers who had worked after marriage had generally stayed at home after the arrival of the first child and had returned to work, if at all, only after all of the children were grown. The few mothers who did work while their children were young did so only because of drastic economic necessity, and were employed in menial and expedient jobs rather than in professions selected for their intrinsic value. Although our childless couples rejected many aspects of their parent's lifestyle, they often retained commitment to the belief that a baby needs a mother's full-time attention. A girl whose mother works learns by first-hand example that having children can be combined with a career; the girl whose mother is a housewife is more predisposed to think in terms of a dichotomous choice of either working or having children. This forced-choice situation increases the probability of opting for the childfree alternative. Couples who feel that they can afford the direct costs of a child do not necessarily feel that they can also afford the loss of the wife's income. Women who feel that they would like to become mothers do not necessarily feel that they would like to become only mothers. Professional women who feel that they can afford to lessen their career commitments for a few years do not necessarily feel that they can drop out completely and still retain some measure of professional competence and recognition.

The perception that working mothers perpetrate an injustice on their children is sometimes reinforced for women who have occasion to interact with disadvantaged children in the course of their work. One elementary school teacher saw many children in her primary grades whose mothers were not at home when they got home from school or at lunch time; those children were apparently emotionally, if not physically, hungry most of the time. Another worked for some time as a social worker, and saw many examples of neglected and unhappy children required to manage on their own for most of the day.

Being a working mother serves to reduce significantly the costs of children in both financial and emotional terms. It requires, however, that surrogate child-care be available and that it be evaluated as adequate to fulfill the child's needs, both physical and emotional. If the mother-child relationship is otherwise satisfactory, there is no evidence to indicate that the children of working mothers necessarily suffer deleterious effects (Nye and Berardo, 1973: 280-284). However, many childless wives do not *believe* this to be the case. They remain childless, not because they reject children *per se*, but because they reject the role of full-time housewife and mother. They are unable to accept the alternative of day-care centers, nursery schools, baby-sitters, and other facilities of surrogate mothering.

Incompetence versus competence

In addition to the basic dichotomous choice of motherhood *or* a career, more than a third of our respondents perceived a parallel choice between being a mother *or* being a competent woman. In this instance, those who are childless by choice may be very similar to other low-parity women. Clarkson *et al.* (1970: 392) found that "women who reject in themselves the traits of the feminine stereotype implying low competence and immaturity have fewer children than women who incorporate these undesirable feminine characteristics." Although Clarkson *et al.* based their conclusions on a study of older women who were mothers of at least two children, the factors in their fertility motivation may parallel factors in the thinking of childless wives, who often perceive themselves to be very competent, and hold this attribute as an important part of their self-image. The voluntarily childless may represent an extreme case in rejecting the negative stereotype of femininity and incorporating attributes of competence and achievement.[7] The association of motherhood and competence has two closely related parts: first, the idea that motherhood is chosen by women because of a lack of competence in coping with other role alternatives; and second, the idea that even competent women become less competent after they have become mothers.

---

[7] Clarkson *et al.* view this rejection as having positive consequences:

> Although sex-role stereotyes assign greater competency to the masculine role and less com petency to the feminine role, competency can be conceived more broadly as a developmental a tribute toward which healthy adults of both sexes aspire. In fact, the items making up the com petency cluster have been judged by psychologists and psychiatrists as attributes of menta health. Incorporation by women of the male-valued stereotypic items, therefore, implies a enhancement of self-concept along a dimension of mental health, maturity, or self-actualizatio (Clarkson *et al.*, 1970: 392).

Incompetence leads to motherhood. One perception is that only or mostly incompetent women choose to become mothers, and that part of the reason for this choice is that they do not have the skills, intelligence or talent to do anything else. Childless wives may observe that their girl friends in high school dropped out and got married, not because they perceived this as a great alternative, but because they did not know what else to do or, too stupid to use birth control effectively, were "forced" to get married. When the childless encounter a woman who manages to be happy and productive as well as being a mother, they are not only impressed, but surprised. Generally, motherhood is perceived as a "cop-out" used by women who have flunked out, or would have done so in any case. To some extent this observation may be accurate, in that motherhood does certainly perform a "cooling-out" function for a number of women who have not found notable educational, occupational or erotic success (Goffman, 1952).

Motherhood leads to incompetence. A critical point in deciding to be voluntarily childless may be the observation of how parenthood affects not people in general, but one's immediate peers and contemporaries, who are in important ways perceived to be basically like oneself. Such effects are often reported in quite negative terms. For example, one wife who made her decision in her late twenties reported that:

> I had a couple of girl friends who really wanted to have children—they were all gung ho—and they each had them too. And they've become quite frustrated; they are really having second thoughts about what parenthood demands. I've only thought about this lately, watching them cope. Watching them *try* to cope! They've got so little time for themselves. A few hours to get their hair done is a big deal. Everything is a big deal, until it's not worth it, so they don't do much at all.

The same woman comments later that:

> I really can't say that I admire any women who do stay home all day with their children. They can be the brightest, most qualified women in their areas, but they get stunted in the head or something when they stay at home all the time.

The perception that housewives are or become "stunted in the head" is repeatedly made by the childless by implication, if not in such explicit and graphic terms. They may not be overly concerned with the intellectual competence, awareness or growth of most women, for most women are assumed to be uneducated and not very bright to begin with, and hence not people with whom one identifies. What is of concern is the perception that "bright," "heads-up," "with-it" women like themselves have been ruined by motherhood, and that they too would deteriorate if forced to have children and to remain at home caring for them all day. Women who become mothers are perceived as likely to lose some of their most attractive qualities through disuse and the distraction of other demands. In varying degrees, this diminution and dissipation of talent is perceived as inevitable for all but the most competent of women under the most conducive circumstances. Another wife, recalling an old girl friend with whom she has lost touch explains:

> I can remember one Sunday inviting some friends around with children. Well, we didn't say three words to each other, my friends and me, because it was constantly a squall squall here and a squall squall there, and she spent her whole afternoon chasing one child after another. She's a very, very intelligent woman, but she has three children under four, and her whole intellect—everything—she's lost it. She's just going to have to wait until those kids are able to look after themselves before she's going to be able to do anything, because her entire life and time and energy and biology is taken up with those kids. It's pathetic!

The association of motherhood with the deterioration of competence is, of course, most relevant for those childless women who do not approve of working mothers and so consider the alternatives in terms of either developing one's potential in a career or of being stultified and stupified by full-time housework and child-care.

The perception that motherhood is not "good" for a woman will be even more important if the mother in question is one's own. One girl the eldest of twelve children, looks at her mother's life and concludes that mothers in general are a mess. Although she occasionally feels sorry for her mother, there is nothing about her she admires, respects or wants to emulate.

> I like her more now than I did as a kid, she seems to have more personalit now—though she doesn't have too much. You can't be too aggressive whe you are having kids all the time. She's still sort of ineffectual. She worke in a bank once before she was married, but she wasn't too competent a that. She just doesn't know how to handle people. She's a poor manager s she's always in a mess. She doesn't know what it is to be happy. Havin children has turned my mother into a slave, a drudge. She can't think, sh doesn't read, she doesn't do anything. She's tired, she's always so—so ac cepting, you know.

Although childless men do not seem especially concerned with th issue of parenthood versus competence as it applies to themselves they frequently voice such concerns with regard to their wives. For example, one husband explained:

> Of course a woman's going to change after she's married. I expect that—I mean, ten years later she has to be different. But I don't want my wife to be *that* different from the woman I married. Some of my friends—they hardly recognize their wives after years of dropping out and having kids. They are so busy being mothers they are hardly women any more. My wife is still a foxy lady and I like her that way. She keeps up, she keeps fit, she's involved. When I talk to her, she still makes sense. My brother's wife used to be a winner but now—all she can talk about is what's wrong with the damn schools. She hasn't read a paper or had a thought since she had the baby—I don't know how he stands it.

Mortgaging the future: the intolerance of debt

Another dichotomous choice many childless persons contend they must make is deciding between having children and having money—or, more specifically, being out of debt. There is general agreement in our society that one should not have more children than one can afford. Such a norm is worthless in decision-making, however, since there is almost no way to determine what one can or cannot afford, or to determine what children do or do not need. Does it mean "afford" in the sense of providing a minimum of food, clothing and shelter? Does it mean "afford" in the sense of providing children with advantages, such as a university eduation and other kinds of specialized training? Does it mean "afford without simultaneously reducing one's own standard of living"? Finally, does it mean "afford now, or afford eventually over a life time"? Alternatives which greatly facilitate child-raising in our society with a minimum of personal sacrifice are a perception of children's "needs" in modest terms, and a willingness to go into debt to fulfill them.

The physical needs of children for material and consumer goods are difficult to specify. One perception which may keep childless couples in that state is that children need a great deal in the way of material advantages. In the same way that the childless may exaggerate the need for continuous parenting, they may also exaggerate children's need for physical comforts. For example, a number of childless couples explained that they did not think it was "fair" to have a child until they had a house in which to raise it. If you require a house before undertaking childbearing, and if your attitudes about debt are such that you cannot buy a house until you can "afford" one, then, of course, childbearing must be postponed for some time for all but the very rich. In contrast, many parents consider that children can be raised quite adequately in apartments, and of those who have houses, most also have heavy mortgages.

Whatever the physical needs of children are thought to be, if the cost of fulfilling them can be spread over many years, a couple can dramatically lessen the number of occasions where they must make a direct choice between spending on themselves and spending on their children. At any one moment, an employed couple with an established credit rating can "afford" almost anything if they are willing to mortgage their future to get it. The availability of credit minimizes the perception that the best years of youth are passing one by and that by the time one can "afford" to do things, one will be too old to bother. Within broad limits, going into debt is socially acceptable and is widely practised. This fact is of considerable significance to the question of whether or not a couple feel that they can afford to have a child. From one perspective, one can never afford it; from another, one can fairly readily maintain the initial costs and borrow the future costs if necessary. One of the traits apparent in a number of childless couples is a marked reluctance to go into debt for *any* reason.[8] Debt is defined not as a way of self-actualizing in the present, but as selling one's soul.

How does one come to acquire strong negative feelings about something as basic to the Canadian-American way of life as living beyond one's means? A number of childless persons had watched their parents struggle under a heavy burden of debt for years, and came away imbued with an abhorrence for interest and payments. A number of couples had themselves experienced excessive debt as a result of financing two expensive university educations, and once they were finally in the clear were determined never to experience it again. For some couples, such feelings resulted from first-hand knowledge about the pitfalls of casual money management. One husband was a very successful accountant, to whom cost-benefit analysis was a way of life. Two husbands had worked for short periods of time for commercial finance and loan companies and had accurate knowledge of the true cost of apparently low interest rates. In addition, in working to collect overdue debts, they had ample opportunity to review the financial resources of middle- and lower-class people who had over-extended their credit, and who typically were also burdened with large families to support. One wife, having worked in the office of a public housing

---

[8] In a large controlled study, Rice (1964) found that fewer childless couples used credit, but when they did the ratio of debt to income was not significantly different from that of parents.

corporation, had ample opportunity to review the case histories of individuals applying for low-cost subsidized housing. Many families were on relief and most combined low income with large families. In her opinion, there was no doubt that they were poor because they had children rather than the other way around. These kinds of experiences with family finances may serve to break down some of the pluralistic ignorance which leads to the conclusion that even though you and your family may have some trouble financing children, most people manage it just fine.

Unsatisfactory versus satisfactory marriages

People raised in the context of a happy marriage learn from first-hand experience that children do not necessarily disrupt the husband-wife relationship. They are predisposed to accept both the cultural belief that children enhance and strengthen the marital relationship, and the corollary belief that having children may even be necessary to achieve a happy marriage and to prevent its deterioration and disruption. Acceptance of the parenthood mystique may be expected to be more automatic among those from intact as opposed to divorced homes, since the latter have learned from first-hand experience that children are not an effective talisman against marital strife, and that they do not necessarily hold a marriage together. In addition, the childless person cannot completely discount the possibility that his or her parents were divorced not *in spite of* having children, but *because* of having them. In contrast to both these situations, those raised in the context of a very unhappy marriage which did not result in divorce may be expected to acquire different definitions of the nature of marriage and of parenthood, including a rejection of many elements of the parenthood mystique.

Social scientists often postulate that many kinds of social deviance and/or social pathology are associated with childhood disruptions of one's family life, especially with broken homes and with working mothers. It is noteworthy that, contrary to what might be expected on the basis of such hypotheses, nine out of ten childless respondents reported that their parents had never been divorced or separated, and eight out of ten reported that their mothers had never been employed outside the home. In spite of such conventional behavior, however, respondents felt that their parent's conformity had not led to happiness. Many perceived that their parents were trapped in unhappy marriages and unfortunate situations because children restricted their mobility to the point where it was psychologically impossible for them to move and to cope with the situation. This is especially likely if one or both of the parents makes it quite clear that they are enduring a miserable situation only "for the sake of the children." For example, one woman reported that her parents had a very unhappy marriage for over twenty-five years, during which time her father gambled, drank heavily, occasionally beat his wife, disappeared for days at a time, and provided only erratic support. Her mother was forced to work throughout her marriage at a series of low-paying, low-status jobs, and reports that she would have left her husband years ago except that she did not feel that she could support both herself and a child. The respondent's parents were finally legally separated a few weeks after her wedding, when her mother no longer felt responsible for her support. Another wife, who reported that her parents had been separated twice and had fought continuously for as long as she could remember, commented that:

> If it had not been for us kids, they might have been able to get along or have had a better marriage. Or even if they didn't, at least mother would not have had to stay with him all those years. She'd never have stayed if she'd been on her own, if it hadn't been for us.

The perception of childless couples of their own parents' marriages involves several elements beyond the simple observation that their union was unhappy. Not only are children perceived not to bring marital happiness, but they are perceived as actually directly contributing to marital conflict and discontent. In addition, the presence of children *per se* is perceived to preclude marital disruption, condemning the parents to a state of "holy deadlock" (LeMasters, 1959) where divorce is either impossible or very difficult. The childless tend to believe that if they become disenchanted with their marriages, they would be morally justified in seeking a divorce and would be psychologically able to cope with the divorce process. If they had children, however, they feel that it would be necessary for them to stay in the marriage regardless, "for the sake of the children." Morally, they have trouble justifying a divorce when there are children who might suffer as a result. Psychologically, the wives tend to feel that while they could, if need be, support and care for themselves, they would not be equally capable of supporting and caring for a child by themselves. In addition, being a divorcée with a child would put them in the double bind of either not providing support, or of providing it and therefore imposing on the child the double burden of the divorce trauma and of having a working mother. The husbands share the moral hesitancy of their wives. In addition, they perceive excessive financial restrictions if they had children. If they were to be divorced from a childless wife, the financial burden would be minimal, in that she would likely be employed. However, if they were to be divorced when they had children, and if they supported the ideology that mothers should not work, then they would be required to pay full support both for her and for the child—quite a different proposition indeed. From either perspective, the voluntarily childless perceive that if they were to have children, they would lose their freedom to divorce. The manifest message conveyed by parents who stoically endure very unsatisfactory marriages "for the sake of the children" is supposedly related to the sanctity of the family and of the marriage bond. The latent message, however, is that having children means permanent entrapment in a relationship which later may or may not prove to be rewarding. The childless tend to narrow their options, seeing that they can either stay childless and free to divorce, or have children and so lose the right to divorce.

Learning Child-Care Skills: Birth Order Variables

In talking with respondents, one component of their case histories which was taken as a matter of routine was their birth order. If one knows the distribution of families by size, it is possible to estimate the distribution of individuals who will occupy a particular birth order (Veevers, 1973f). When this was done, to our surprise several patterns emerged showing childless respondents to have atypical birth order patterns compared with the general population. In the first place, there was an unusually high number of first-born persons.[9] In the general population, about one person in three is first-born: among our respondents, nearly half of them were.[10] In the second place, among

---

[9] Other researchers have also noted that a disproportionate number of childless persons are first borns with at least one sibling (Barnett and MacDonald, 1976; Ory, 1978; Nason and Poloma, 1976; Kaltreider and Margolis, 1977; Thoen, 1977). However, one study of childless men (Magarick and Brown, 1976) failed to find such a pattern.

[10] Some researchers concerned with birth order have suggested that first-born persons may be over-represented among subjects who volunteer for experiments. Since the in-depth studies of the deliberately childless have depended very heavily upon persons coming forward and volunteering to be interviewed, there is a possibility of bias in the

those first-born respondents, a large proportion of them were also only children. In the general population, about one person in twenty is an only child; among our respondents, about one person in five was one. In the third place, among first-born respondents, more than would be expected were the first-born of large families.

Only children: child-care anxiety

Only children are unusual because they have never observed their own parents in parenting roles with anyone but themselves, and are, of course, unable to remember the care given to themselves as infants or toddlers. These persons express considerable concern about their ability to care for children, indicating that because of their lack of either models or experiences they are uncertain what to do with children, or how to act towards them, and therefore feel uncomfortable in their presence. Although only children may identify with their mothers, they have not had an opportunity to identify with their motherhood role. It has been suggested that only children have a higher propensity for childlessness because they want to remain children themselves (Toman, 1970). Whether or not this is so is difficult to assess, but the incidence of only children among respondents was clearly much higher than would ordinarily be expected.

The little-mother syndrome

In contrast to first-borns who are only children, first-borns who are the eldest of large families have few qualms about their competence at child-care. As far back as they can remember, they have been active in all aspects of child-care, from the feeding and diapering of infants to the supervision of school-age children. By the time they reach their teenage years, little about parenthood remains a mystery to them. As their own mother was increasingly worn down by a rapid succession of pregnancies (most of which were unplanned if not also unwanted), more and more of the burden of child-care passed to the oldest children—most often the girls. They believe from their earliest years that children are a limitation, and that many ordinary schoolgirl activities are forbidden to them because of their little-mother responsibilities. When little girls from small families play with dolls, their anticipatory socialization for the role of mother is idealized, glamorized

reports of a high incidence of first-borns. Later research, however, does not support the idea that persons who volunteer as research subjects are any more likely to be first born than are non-volunteers (Ward, 1964).

and totally unrealistic. The dolls never misbehave in unmanageable ways, they never pre-empt or preclude other activities, and when they become burdensome or boring, they can be readily, if temporarily, abandoned. The first-born of a large family has had much more realistic experiences regarding what it means to be a mother, and at an early age may become permanently disillusioned with the motherhood mystique. One girl, when asked about doll play, commented:

> I never played with dolls, I played with all those younger kids, ten of them all about a year apart, just one right after the other. Only it wasn't play, it was hard and we all had to help.

Similarly, a male respondent, the eldest of eight and the veteran of many fatherly tasks, ranging from nursing a kid brother's bout with the measles to teaching his kid sister how to dribble a basketball, reported: "My father had my children for me." For such persons, the evaluation of parenthood is realistic rather than romantic. A surfeit of experience with the realities of child-care at too early an age may establish one's competence to perform the role, while diminishing one's willingness to do so.[11]

Unsavory Children

It seems likely that the positive valence usually assigned to infants and children as interesting and attractive social objects draws its emotional import, not from pronatalistic propaganda extolling the charms of the young, but from actually having had positive experiences with young persons. Most childless persons interviewed were relatively disinterested in children and childish things; in some instances, however, passive disinterest had degenerated into active dislike.[12]

At some point in the interviews, respondents were asked outright: "Do you like children?" Virtually everyone, male and female alike, found this query difficult. About half of our respondents were insulted

---

[11] A similar relationship has been reported in studies of the etiology of maternal rejection. Figge (1932: 246) found that rejecting mothers were more likely than non-rejecting mothers to have assumed heavy responsibilities at a young age, often before they were teenagers, and often including the care of younger siblings.

[12] In an early study in Indianapolis among voluntarily childless couples, nine out of ten reported little interest in children (Pratt and Whelpton, 1955).

that the question had been asked, and expressed varying degrees of indignation at the imputation of what they perceived to be an abnormality. They said, in effect: "Of course I like kids! What do you think I am? Sick?" Responses on this order were typically followed by a series of tributes to children of whom they were especially fond. The intensity of these responses suggests that in our culture, it is more taboo not to like children in general than it is merely not to want to have any of your own.

The other half of our respondents who did not affirm an appreciation for children were also reticent to assert an overt rejection of them. Initially, they were evasive in their replies ("It depends on the child, doesn't it?" "Some ages are better than others." "I guess they have a place in society just like old people do." "Well, we have to have them around, don't we?"). After some hesitation, they eventually admitted that, in fact, they did not especially like children. Once the statement was made, it was then supported by specific instances of the dislike either of particular children or, more usually, of particularly childlike traits.

In English, there exist a number of special words to refer to special aversions: one who dislikes marriage is a misogamist; one who dislikes women is a misogynist; and one who dislikes humanity in general is a misanthropist. In the same vein, one who dislikes children can technically be designated a misopedist. One of the most visible spokesmen of misopedia was W. C. Fields, who offered the oft-quoted conclusion: "Anybody who hates children and dogs can't be all bad" (Cohen and Cohen, 1971: 73). How do some persons learn to dislike children? As with other aspects of rejection of the parenthood role, the seeds of the behavior are present in the dominant culture itself. Although there is generally a positive orientation towards children, the adjective "childish," which means "being like or befitting a child," also means "puerile, weak and silly." "Childish" has a negative connotation and "childlike" a positive one, but both adjectives refer objectively to the same behavior. Some childless persons have selectively focused on the negative aspects of this cultural ambivalence.

One facet of experience which may be salient for childless persons is prolonged and close contact with children who are not esthetically or emotionally rewarding. Despite homilies to the effect that all children, or at least all babies, are intrinsically appealing, it is clear that some are more lovable than others. The child who is too forward may be as obnoxious as the child who is backward and slow to learn. The child with a cranky, sullen disposition is quite a different kind of companion than the one with a sunny disposition. Indeed, some children are not only unappealing, but are actually unsavory, in the sense of being insipid, unpleasant, and vaguely offensive. "Dennis the Menace" is to some persons "cute" and "funny," but to others he is literally a menace, and a tedious one at that.

Exposure to unattractive children typically is of little consequence if it is a sometime thing. However, excessive contact with unsavory children can lead to the Hobbsian view of children as nasty, brutish, and short. Those adults who have been exposed to children they define as unsavory, and who have learned to dislike them, develop a lexicon of pejorative terms to express the nuances of their displeasure. The most common terms used by respondents included "brats" who resist directives, and who, if really recalcitrant, would be termed "spoiled brats"; the persistently demanding were considered "pests" or "varmints," and were usually depicted as being "underfoot" or as "tugging at one's skirts." Some of the more sophisticated referred to experiences with an *enfant terrible*. Aberrations of various kinds were included, such as "little demons," "mealy-mouthed monsters," or "demanding little devils." The terms relating to being small, such as "rug rats," "mites," "urchines," "small stuff," or "small change" did not have the affectionate connotation which usually accompanies the diminutive. The intensity of negative affect was often conveyed as much by the terms selected as by the actual content of what was said.

Experiences with unattractive children may not be an enticement to child-rearing, but they are still within the normal, everyday range of experience. A second kind of precursor to voluntary childlessness may be experience with children who are not only unsavory, but who are actually repellent and offensive. Some childless persons traced their rejection of parenthood to direct experience with the poignant personal tragedies it may entail. A considerable proportion of voluntarily childless persons had disruptive and debilitating experiences with child-care, such as having had in their home a severely retarded child, or one who was seriously ill for a long time. A number had worked in situations where they were exposed to an excessive number of children whom they found unattractive to the point of repulsion. For example, some had worked in homes for the grossly deformed or retarded, some had supervised hyperactive children with behavior problems, and some had nursed the terminally ill. The children were, in their parlance, "something only a mother could love." Although these respondents were sympathetic to the mothers and fathers and to the very real anguish they experienced over their unfortunate offspring, they also had a sense of, "There but for the grace of God go I." Fully aware of the realities of parental dilemmas *in extremis*, they had little desire to risk putting themselves in the same situation.

Parenthood as Martyrdom

To a large extent, voluntarily childless persons tend to perceive their own parents as living lives of "quiet desperation." In terms of their own decision-making, the significance of this belief is not merely the commonplace observation that some parents are unhappy. Rather, these respondents perceived that the advent of children altered their parents' lives in important, negative, and irrevocable ways. Critical to this perception is not only the observation that undesirable things have happened to some parents, but the corollary that undesirable things happened to those people *because* they had children, rather than for other reasons.

The anticipation that having children will be a rewarding experience is emotionally credible only to the extent that you perceive that you yourself have been a rewarding experience to your own parents. In many cases, parents were not exactly reticent in expressing the opinion that they had received very little satisfaction from their children, either when they were young or after they were grown. At least by implication and innuendo, their comments are reminiscent of the humorist's parody: "I love the dear silver that shines in your hair." "You ought to, my child—it was you put it there." The kind of mother who laments loudly and frequently over her unfortunate state has been immortalized in a number of contemporary satires, such as Greenburg's (1965) *How to Be A Jewish Mother*. The martyred mother has not only sacrificed greatly for her children but has found that sacrifice to be both unrewarded and unappreciated. David Steinberg, a television comedian, expresses this philosophy when he comments: "Fortunately, my parents are fine, intelligent people. They accept me for exactly what I am—a punishment from God!" Such parents would concur with another television comedian, Phyllis Diller: "Work your fingers to the bone for your children and what do you get? Bony fingers!"

The parents of the voluntarily childless do not directly instruct their children not to have children; rather, by their own obvious lack of satisfaction with the parenthood role and their apparent regret at being involved in it, they manage to convey by innuendo and by suggestion the idea that parenthood is neither inevitable, nor automatically advantageous. After years of hearing negative attitudes expressed, some sons and daughters take quite literally their parents' implicit advice not to have children themselves.[13] If you do not perceive yourself as giving satisfaction and consolation to your parents, it is quite logical to question the probability that your own children would be a comfort to you. One wife made a typical comment:

> I can't imagine what kind of solace my husband and I ever gave to our parents. I mean, kids aren't around when you're forty or fifty years old. We go our own way, move away, live our own lives, and they are there to go on their own way, just like people who never had kids. Which is how it ought to be, you have to live your own life. Sure, we keep in touch, but getting a letter or a phone call or even the odd visit doesn't make much difference in their lives now. Or in ours for that matter.

Many childless wives perceive that their own mothers endured considerable sacrifice in the rearing of their children. A common theme is that of a mother who had, or could have had, a promising career but gave it up to have children, a "mistake" she appeared perpetually to regret. For example, one wife explained in some detail the story of her mother's life, with which she was obviously quite familiar. The mother had worked as office manager for an insurance firm, a job she enjoyed and at which she had been quite successful, maintaining herself comfortably until she was thirty-five. When she married, she moved with her husband to the country, where her activities were much restricted and where she began having children almost immediately, bearing two daughters four years apart. Although regularly employed, the father did not make much money, and most of what was available went to care for the children. The daughter now reflects:

> My mother had a really hard time bringing up me and my sister. She had to struggle and scrimp and save for fifteen years, and she was never able to buy clothes or go anywhere or do much of anything. I think this may be the reason why I'm kind of hesitant to have children. It's because of my

---

[13] A dumpy little woman in one of Feiffer's cartoons delivers the following monoloque:

> Listen, if Khruschev wants a picture of America let him come to my home. If Khruschev wants to know how selfish your own flesh and blood can be let him have a conversation with my daughter. Take! Take! My husband will tell him. If Khruschev wants to know how not to do anything to help his family, let him talk to my husband. Or my son. Let him meet my son! Khruschev would get down on his hands and knees to me and beg my forgiveness that he should give me more worries with the kind of son I got. Listen, if Khruschev is coming for advice I could give him all he needs. It would solve all the world's problems. Just never be a mother (Feiffer, 1960).

> mother—she gave up so much and sacrificed so much for us. Though probably it wouldn't turn out the same for me if I had children. But what thanks do we give our parents? How do we pay them back?

Although somewhat sympathetic with her mother's situation, she is not at all grateful, feeling that parents ruin their children's lives and that her mother almost ruined hers. The best she can manage is the comment: "She hurt herself more than she hurt us." Another wife whose mother had twelve children comments:

> They [mothers] are not sexy or attractive or anything. They look as if they work hard and have their hands in dishwater all the time and scrubbing dirty diapers, which they do. Well, my mother did. There was just no time or energy left over. You got through the day as best you could and that was it.

There is nothing about this dismally hard and relentless role she now wants to emulate.

The deliberately childless perceive not only that motherhood means sacrifice, but that those sacrifices are not appropriately appreciated and rewarded. One respondent who did love and appreciate her mother nevertheless concluded that children in general are bad investments who will "kick you in the teeth when they get older." This women had always been close to her mother and shared a satisfactory relationship with her. When she was fourteen, her mother had an unplanned and unwanted menopause baby which left her physically exhausted for some time. The wife was intensively involved in all stages of care of her younger brother from the age of fourteen until she left home at eighteen. The child was not a source of gratification in the family. She reports that he was "spoiled and unmanageable" and a "tyrant whose every whim had to be catered to." Not only did the child interfere with the pastimes she would have preferred as an adolescent but he was not appreciative of the attention and effort given to him and did not respond with affection and obedience. He had temper tantrums and used to "just wear away at my mother on and on until she gave i just to get a little peace." In her words, she watched her brothe "literally sit on my mother all her life." Her experiences with this prob lem child, an "irritating and obnoxious beast of a boy," led to the con clusion in her mid-teens that children are generally liabilities who ar not worth the effort and emotion expended on their behalf.

A common occurrence which reinforces the idea of motherhood a sacrifice is the observation that one's mother's happiness and genera satisfaction with life increased when her children left home. To b relevant to questions of the desirability of childlessness, this correl tion must be interpreted in causal terms. The childless perceive that their mothers were unhappy because they had to take care of children, and that their lives improved over time because the children left home, removing this constant obligation. In a typical comment, a wife described her newly-emancipated mother:

> She's having a lot more fun now. She has gone back to work, she buys new clothes, she does whatever she wants to do. She and Dad get along a lot better too. They like to make jokes about how things were when we were all young, but they're not very funny. I mean, they try to make it sound funny, but you can sure tell the good old days weren't very good. Now, she's her own person again.

The voluntarily childless tend to exaggerate the social and emotional costs of parenthood by phrasing the consequences of having children in "either/or" terms. The choice then becomes one of either having children or working; having children or being competent; having children or being debt-free; having children or having a good marriage: in short, of having children or being happy. The tendency to define parenting versus other options in dichotomous terms is further reinforced by the tendency to perceive childbearing decisions as irrevocable. The "baby trap" is defined as a trap because it is felt to preclude other options, not only for the immediate present but also for the foreseeable future.

The permanent consequences of having children are also apparent in terms of lifelong options regarding the freedom to enter various careers, to change careers, or to abandon careers altogether. The permanent consequences of having children are especially apparent to women who believe that, to be a good mother, they should not also be employed. If marriage and motherhood do not prove fulfilling, there are no other sources of satisfaction to draw upon, and no options to seek new ones via divorce and/or re-entry into the labor market. For husbands, having children also has permanent consequences for careers, except in this case it involves not the right to work but the right not to. In this context, the meaning of debts is especially relevant. If one has no debts, one is relatively free to pursue a variety of interests. In contrast, if one is in debt, one must give priority to working to make payments. Being debt-free implies the right to quit. Among childless couples, the phrasing of childbearing decisions in dichotomous terms is closely associated with the desire to have whatever decisions one makes reversible. Depending upon future circumstances, one should be able to stay married or get a divorce, or to maintain a career or abandon it. The perception of freedom is a central focus of the childfree lifestyle.

Chapter Four: THE CHILDFREE LIFESTYLE

Most persons spend most of their active adult years in living situations which revolve, in varying degrees, around the needs and interests of children. Adult concerns and preferences are routinely modified to accommodate the demands of child-care. In contrast, childless couples are engrossed in an adult-centered lifestyle as opposed to a child-centered one. Involvement in the adult-centered lifestyle is, for most persons, predicated upon three conditions which must be achieved simultaneously: being accorded full adult status; being relatively affluent and successful; and being childfree. The actual content and concerns of the adult-centered lifestyle vary widely, according to backgrounds, occupations, and idiosyncratic preferences of individuals. The *modus vivendi* associated with childlessness, however, does revolve around a number of common interrelated themes of freedom, experience, and self-expression. If, by accident or by design, young couples happen to experience adult-centered living for a few years, then the desire to continue in this lifestyle may become an important motive in their desire to continue being childless. The present chapter is concerned with the ways in which childless persons organize their time and their priorities, and with the experience of the childfree lifestyle as a factor in postponing childbearing and in adjusting to permanent childlessness.

Disreputable Pleasures: For Adults Only

In our culture, the idea of a double standard of morality is usefully applied not only to discrepant expectations of sexual morality for men and for women, but also to differential expectations for adults and children. One of the privileges of adult status is the right to take responsibility for one's own actions, which includes the right to make one's own mistakes. Within reason and law, adults can follow their own fancies, ignoring the opinions of their neighbors as to whether or not their actions are prudent and wise. Adult status conveys the right to indulge in a variety of "disreputable pleasures" (Hagan, 1977) not congruent with a strict interpretation of conventional morality, but which are considered more or less acceptable for "consenting adults." Leisure-time activities which are designated "for adults only" may appropriately involve an element of calculated risk, and may appropriately be of at least questionable morality, such as smoking, drinking, drug use, and vicarious and direct sexual experience.[1] In contrast, children do not have comparable rights. Leisure-time activities which are designed as "family entertainment" are restricted to those considered to be safe, wholesome, and morally impeccable. Until children reach the age of consent, we endeavor to protect them from themselves, and to restrict their activities to the straight and narrow path of behaviors which in the conventional wisdom are deemed to be "good" for them, or which at least will do them no harm.

In our society, parenthood typically imposes two important lifestyle constraints: the perceived need to provide a suitable model for one's children, and the perceived need to include them in one's activities.[2]

---

[1] In this regard, it is noteworthy that not all adults are routinely given the right to choose disreputable pleasures. Any population which is institutionalized, such as the infirm, the insane, or the very old, will routinely be treated as children in that they are told when to get up, when to go to bed, and what to do. Access to tobacco is typically restricted, and access to alcohol is typically forbidden entirely, as is the expression of any form of sexuality other than masturbation.

[2] It is important to note that it is not necessary to be childless in order to participate in adult-centered living. Members of the upper class have always been able to maintain a childfree lifestyle if they choose to do so. Nannies, residential schools, and if necessary even a separate children's wing attached to the house can reduce the interference from children to a minimum. Some middle-class parental couples can also approximate this lifestyle, if they maintain some emotional distance from their children, and if they are willing to devote a large proportion of their incomes to the purchase of extensive surrogate child-care. It would appear, however, that very few choose to do so. For most, having children means becoming involved in a child-centered world, and thereby giving up more sophisticated adult interests, pleasures, and pursuits.

An important part of the parenthood role is to guide children in behaving "correctly." It is commonly believed that "parents should be more moral than non-parents" (Goode, 1968: 339), a perspective often shared by the childless. A disadvantage of having children may be the feeling that, as a parent, one is obligated to give up a number of minor vices which, although not seriously wrong in themselves, do not "set a good example" for the moral development of one's children. Parenthood may be defined as precluding, or at least drastically inhibiting, slightly immoral or naughty activities. The norms for parents, but especially for mothers, reflect more stringently puritanical expectations in a wide range of areas: smoking, drinking, or otherwise indulging oneself with other chemical supports; expressing oneself in the salty and salacious argot of the streets; or generally failing to sublimate one's sexual energies. Among people who marry young and who have children very soon thereafter, the moral constraints imposed by their parents because they were "too young" for adult pleasures may almost immediately be replaced by parallel constraints imposed by their perceived need to set a good example for their children.

The constraints involved in providing a suitable model for children are further exacerbated by the expectation that parents will not only live with their children but will spend most of their leisure-time with them. This expectation of "togetherness" restricts the extent to which one's activities as an adult can be separated from one's activities as a parent. To the extent that parents remain committed to the idea that they should spend all or most of their leisure-time with their children, children will both know what their parents do and will share the same experiences. If one is also committed to the idea that only certain kinds of activities are possible or suitable for children, then opportunities for new experiences are drastically limited. Once babies are out of their infancy, and are old enough to participate in family interactions, activities tend to be structured in terms of the lowest common denominator of competence of the youngest member of the group, thereby insuring that all members present can actually become involved in the interaction. The intellectual content of conversations tends to be restricted to the level of understanding of the youngest family member participating. Recreations and entertainments tend to be selected by whether or not children will be interested in and enjoy them, and by whether or not they are "good for" or "suitable for" children. A place to live comes to be selected in terms of its access to proper schools and playgrounds, and by whether or not it is a "good" place to raise children, which is to say one which is relatively "safe."

Most people marry for the first time at such a tender age that they have been considered adults for only a short period of time, if at all, before they become husband and wife.[3] Marriage marks a final coming of age, and with their newly ascribed maturity they begin for the first time to be treated as full-fledged adults. Having married, most people then begin to have children almost immediately, usually within the first two years. Consequently, they experience a rapid escalation of events from becoming adult to getting married to becoming parents which permits at most a peripheral involvement in adult-centered pleasures and recreations. Full enjoyment of the adult-centered lifestyle requires more than merely being an adult: it also requires the time, and the financial resources, to take advantage of implicit opportunities. At the time of their first marriage, most people are at the beginning of their occupational careers and have demonstrated only marginal financial competence. While they are in one sense free adults, they are also poor and struggling, relative to their own aspirations, and relative to the status they will later achieve. Full participation in adult-centered living tends to be postponed while "getting on one's feet," a process usually involving getting out of school and achieving a modicum of financial security.

Those few individuals who somehow avoid this pattern, either by getting married relatively late, or by postponing childbearing for several years, are inadvertently exposed to quite a different set of circumstances. The cinderella complex of having to be home by midnight to conform to one's parents' curfew does after all result in the same behavior as having to be home by midnight to relieve the baby-sitter. Once one has participated fully in the lifestyle of adults who are accountable only to each other, and whose behavior may therefore be as risky and risqué as they choose, there may be a real reluctance to return to the child-centered world of wholesome movies, polite vocabulary, and safe and educational pursuits, all of which are already excessively familiar from one's own safe and wholesome childhood.

The Quest for Experience

In the worldview of the voluntarily childless, being childfree means in part being free to seek out and to enjoy new experiences. In discussing lifestyles, the use of the term child*free*, rather than the more neutral

---

[3] In Canada in 1971, the median age for first marriages was 24.9 years for grooms and 22.6 years for brides (Veevers, 1977: 6). In the United States, it was even younger, being only 23.1 for grooms and 20.9 for brides (Scanzoni and Scanzoni, 1976: 135).

and more ubiquitous term childless, is not incidental, in that freedom in its many manifestations is a central theme in the lifestyles enacted by childless couples. The concern of childless couples with the amorphous concept of "freedom" is, at first glance, paradoxical. Although they refer to freedom often, and maintain that it is an issue of central concern, their daily round of activities does not seem substantially more free than that of many parents. Like their more conventional counterparts, most are bound by the constraints of a monogamous marriage, a nine-to-five job, and a limited amount of time, money, and imagination. However, the childless still report that they *feel* free. The absence of children is perceived as the key to a plurality of opportunities which would otherwise be denied them—opportunities which are defined almost exclusively in terms of options and the maintenance of options. Upon investigation, it becomes apparent that this feeling is not so much focused upon the experience of freedom as upon the potential to experience it. Implicitly and explicitly, having children is associated with permanently surrendering one's freedom. Being childfree means that the constraints which are accepted are accepted voluntarily, and so do not feel like constraints at all. Options may be exercised seldom, if at all, but their very existence is crucial to maintaining the contented perception of potential freedom, and therefore of potential self-actualization.

Spontaneity: the avoidance of routine

For many childless couples, the quest for experience first manifests itself in a delight in novelty, and in a concerted effort to act spontaneously, and to avoid routines. Again and again, childless wives refer to the fact that full-time housewives with children have so much of their time pre-empted by the necessity of performing daily and repetitive tasks that they have no opportunity to seek out novelty, to have new experiences, or to develop themselves as persons. The needs of the child provide a constant source of non-negotiable demands to be fed, washed, put to bed, amused, and generally taken care of; in contrast, although a spouse may also "need" to be cared for, his or her demands are less urgent and more flexible. When asked the general question, "Can you describe for me what you typically do in a day, besides work?" the childless often find it difficult to do so, in that they have quite deliberately avoided establishing set routines, or as they would see it, falling into the "trap" of repetitive experience. With only two persons to please, the preparation of meals can be quite casual, with eating out a ready and affordable alternative. Mealtimes and bedtimes can and do vary with the whim of the moment. Shopping can be done whenever the stores are open. Participation in activities outside the home requires no special arrangements other than co-ordination with the mate's timetable, which is also flexible. Consequently, even quite elaborate plans and arrangements can be made at the last minute. Much more than parents, the childfree can structure their leisure-time mainly in terms of the hedonistic question, "What do we feel like doing right now?" Although the activities may occasionally be quite exotic, usually they are quite mundane and conventional. For example, one lower-class wife, reflecting on her husband's attitudes towards parenthood, commented:

> I think that it would be very much of a shock to him if we were to have a child now, because he is just the type of guy who wants to pick up and go to the Dairy Dell for an ice cream when he wants to go. He likes to be organized but he does not like to have to go through the rigamarole all the time of getting things ready.

When this woman talks about the joys of being free to travel, she means free to drive fifty miles out of town for a picnic. What is important to her is not the nature of the experience in objective terms, but the potential for spontaneously taking advantage of opportunities for new experiences should they arise.

Novel delights

The quest for experience also incorporates a desire to experience new things directly, and to learn about new things. A minority of couples made a point of seeking new experiences which, although not exactly unique, are not entirely typical of suburban routines of middle-class couples. For several, the search for new experience meant joining a nudist camp and tentative experiments with swinging. Others were or had been involved with the drug culture, and their quest for new experience included the extensive use of a wide variety of drugs. A number of others reported transitory experiments with drugs, mostly marijuana, to see what they were like and whether or not they would produce unique sensations. Some who had no drug experience mentioned lack of opportunity, and that given a chance they would want to experiment.

Interest in new experience may lead to some ambivalence about pregnancy and birth. Women may wonder what being pregnant would feel like, and may be fascinated by natural childbirth as a wondrous and miraculous experience, while considering the child produced to be of somewhat secondary importance. Thus, one woman confessed her favorite fantasy in this regard:

> I've always thought it would be great to be pregnant and to watch my body change and my breasts get big and then actually to do it—to produce a child and see it being born and think: I did that! I'd like to look at my child and count its fingers and toes and then say to the doctor: "That was very interesting. Thank you very much for a great experience. Now here is your baby back!" If only I could just have a kid, without having to keep it!

The attitude of sensation-seeking reflects an acceptance of relatively high-risk situations. Some of these directly involved physical risk, such as racing motorcycles or sport cars, or simply enjoying high-speed driving. One couple were enthusiastic sky-divers; another planned an expedition to go ballooning, another had twin kayaks for running white-water rapids. The acceptance of high-risk situations can also be expressed less directly in terms of seeking unusual social contacts. Thus, some apparently "straight" couples expressed considerable fascination in the marginal street-culture of the slums, and were on occasion involved in it as participants as well as observers. Their recountings of the various predicaments which had resulted from such interests were manifestly tales of fortunate narrow escapes, but implicitly came through as tales of exciting adventures. Many inconveniences and trials are retrospectively justified by being able to say: "Well, that was certainly an unusual experience! That was different!"

The search for novelty is further reflected in a marked enthusiasm for learning new things, even when the acquired knowledge has no particular use or significance. The roles of teacher and of pupil—of the person who informs and the person who is informed—are complementary, and everyone routinely enacts both of them. Nevertheless, individuals may have a distinct preference for one or the other. A preference for teaching is closely related to what Erikson considers to be "generatively . . . an interest in establishing and guiding the next generation" (1963: 276). One component of the childfree lifestyle is a distinct lack of generativity, and a clear preference for learning over teaching.[4] Such inclinations lead to a tendency to gravitate to people who are defined as superiors, or at least as peers. As one husband reflected with a wry grin: "The main trouble with children is they are

---

[4] The preference for learning over teaching obviously was not characteristic of all our childless respondents, some of whom were teachers by profession and appeared to perform their role competently and with satisfaction. However, for these persons, the interest in teaching and in other forms of generativity was quite adequately fulfilled during the work week rather than after hours, and with other people's children rather than with their own.

so immature." Given such attitudes, considerable emphasis is placed upon being competent, and upon utilizing one's abilities to full capacity. The lack of interest in children is paralleled by a lack of interest in other people who are considered to be intellectual inferiors, and who are therefore not considered especially challenging, stimulating, or helpful. In the adult-centered environment, what holds one's interest is not reviewing things that are already known, but learning new things. One wife expressed this directly:

> Child-raising is a bore, because you are always going over the same things. I do not have any teaching instincts at all. I don't like to deal with people who know less than I do. I like to deal with people who know more than I do. I might learn something. At least I'm not bored.

Another related her disinterest in children directly to her disinterest in having to teach or otherwise cope with uninformed persons.

> Look, let's face it, nobody ever says it, but children are stupid. When a six-year-old has an I.Q. of 120, that means he is very smart *for a six-year-old*. But compared to even a slow grown-up person, he is stupid. I guess I like kids as well as I like other stupid people. I mean—I know it's not their fault, but all the same, I don't want to spend much time talking with them. And even bright people may be ignorant. Teenagers are as smart as adults, but they haven't lived long enough to know much. They are smart, but they are not informed. I like people who are both—and I guess that always means adults. I've always preferred people older than me.

In keeping with their preference for learning rather than teaching, many childless respondents reported consistent and deliberate efforts at developing their skills and potentials. They tended to view education as a lifelong process, rather than an end state. Many were involved in some form of adult education, and often talked about someday returning to university. Others were concerned with developing their facility for self-expression by writing, painting, drawing, sculpting, or even arranging flowers! A general orientation regarding competence stressed a maximizing of one's own competence, while expressing considerable impatience for the incompetence of others. In fact, among respondents, levels of competence and ability varied considerably, but many stressed a common value on self-improvement and on the intrinsic value of the learning situation.

Wanderlust: the importance of travelling

Consistent with these themes, most childless couples expressed great enthusiasm for travelling and perceived that one of the major advantages of being childless is being able to enjoy longer and more frequent trips than they could otherwise manage. A considerable part of their conversation was concerned with recapitulating past travels and with planning future ones.

Some childless couples have managed to do a considerable amount of travelling, avoiding the short and superficial tours offered to the usual tourist. For example, one young wife recently returned from a hitch-hiking trip with her husband around Canada and the United States. The previous year they had spent some time on a walking tour of Morocco, and were making plans and saving money to return to Africa the next fall, where they hoped to take a month-long trip by camel caravan across the Sahara. An older couple spend at least two months a year travelling in Europe or in the West Indies, and during the rest of the year make many weekend trips to New York, Boston or other large centers in the northeastern states. One young wife accompanied her geologist husband on excursions to the Arctic, and another frequently managed to be included in zoological field trips. Several couples aspired to even more extensive travelling, hoping to take a year off and to circumnavigate the globe. Rather than considering this possibility as something which might be done "eventually," perhaps after retirement, they were making specific, albeit tentative, plans and stringently saving the required money. The feasibility of such plans presupposes either a casual attitute towards one's work, or an occupation in which leave can be arranged. All couples reiterated the impossibility of even considering such adventures if children had to be taken into account.

Although some childless couples do manage long and exotic trips, in most cases, the travel plans must be arranged in terms of the requirements of two jobs, leaving the childless with not much more holiday time than parental couples. However, an important characteristic of the childfree lifestyle is that travel is less likely to be restricted to one or two weeks a year formally designated as vacation time. In comparing childless and parental couples, the discrepancy in amount of travelling is probably greater for the wives than for the husbands. Childless wives are able to travel as their work demands, and some deliberately seek employment with such opportunities. In addition, considerable emphasis is placed upon the value of short-term excursions which can be spontaneously arranged any weekend. In contrast, most mothers with an intense interest in travelling manage to do so for only a few days a year and then only after extensive planning. On most occasions, the typical pattern is for the husband to travel alone in connection with his work, while the wife stays at home with the children. Even if child-care for long periods of time were not prohibitively expensive, and even if the cost of travelling were not high, most couples would find the alternative child-care arrangements unsatisfactory, and the logistics of transporting the entire menagerie too complex. The childfree alternative provides both the money and the opportunity for both husband and wife to travel extensively. The extent to which this is a decisive factor in childlessness is difficult to determine. On the one hand, it is unlikely that many childless couples avoided parenthood primarily because they wanted to travel; on the other hand, once they have become accustomed to these and other advantages, such practical considerations may become important factors in their continuing to avoid it.

Earning a Living: Childlessness and Work

Married couples who remain childless for a number of years find themselves in notably different circumstances than do their more conventional counterparts who become parents, in that they are often able to experience considerably more personal freedom. The fact of being relatively free is of course of little consequence, and provides little incentive or compensation, if one shares the opinion expressed in Kris Kristofferson's famous aphorism: "Freedom's just another word for nothing left to loose!" Not all childless persons necessarily consider freedom a worthwhile advantage.[5] Being free may for some be equated with being lonely, or rootless, or generally anomic. However, those childless persons who do learn to define their unusual situation in terms of opportunities rather than deprivations often come to savor their sense of freedom both as an end in itself and as a means to other ends. The actual ways in which such potential freedom is used, and the kinds of experiences which it affords, vary widely. Although the discrepancies between child-centered and adult-centered lifestyles are perhaps most apparent with reference to leisure-time activities, it is important to remember that childless adults, like other adults, must also spend a major portion of their lives earning a living. Discussions of their lifestyle only in terms of their after-hours pursuits are one-sided, and have a misleading connotation of frivolity. Of the childless

---

[5] For example, Blood and Wolfe (1960: 137) asked childless women in the Detroit area to list some of the good things about not having children, and found that over a third of them were not able to think of any advantages at all.

respondents we talked with, all of the men and almost all of the women were either employed or were full-time students. Although they perhaps gave their recreations more salience than do many parents, by and large they were serious and industrious people. To employ the folklore metaphor comparing the character of the grasshopper and the ant, we did find some grasshoppers, but we found many more ants.

Conventional sex roles dictate quite clear norms regarding the appropriate division of labor within a marriage. The woman, who is typically a mother as well as a wife, is expected to be primarily engaged in expressive roles, and to remain at home devoting herself to housework and to child-care. The man, who is typically a father as well as a husband, is expected to concern himself with instrumental roles, and to work to provide for his family as well as possible. If being childless is valued because it is felt to increase one's freedom, the question remains: if one has freedom, what is that freedom to be used *for*? Among the respondents, many considered that a major advantage of being childfree was freedom to modify conventional sex roles. In terms of the question of work, the nature of freedom was quite different for women than for men. Stated as concisely as possible, for women childlessness was often significently associated with the right to be involved in or even devoted to instrumental roles, as reflected in one's *freedom to work*; for men, childlessness was often associated with the right to be involved in or even devoted to expressive roles, as reflected in one's *freedom from work*.

Freedom to work: career commitment

Although virtually all of the childless wives encountered were employed, only about half of them had a career, in the sense of being intrinsically committed to a demanding profession. For employed women who are not content with the relatively routine jobs traditionally assigned to women, and who aspire instead to success in the kinds of absorbing careers usually reserved for men, childlessness is a critical factor in their professional achievements. The usual accouterments of the wife-mother role may be satisfying, but their demands on time, attention, and energy function to exaggerate the traditional sex role disadvantages faced by women who presume to compete with men. In this context, childlessness is indeed the "ultimate liberation" (Movius, 1976) in facilitating career involvement.

Of the childless women who had careers, some were in the arts or the humanities, working as writers, sculptors, singers, decorators, or artists; others were in the professions, working as physicians, professors, lawyers, or scientists. Their ambition to succeed—indeed to excel—was exceedingly high. Being childless was viewed as an important if not also a necessary condition of excellence. For them, being childfree meant being free from responsibilities and demands of time and energy which they felt would detract from their careers. Their levels of achievement were high, but their aspirations for achievement were higher still. Having children would have meant having to give up, or at least to modify, their aspirations; being childfree meant being free to achieve to their full capacity. Such women were typically married to men who were equally high achievers, usually in a related field. Occasionally, couples worked together as a team, but more often they were engaged in parallel endeavors. They worked long hours with demanding schedules, but reported that they found their work exciting and generally satifying.

There can be little doubt that being a mother adversely affects the probability that a woman will achieve marked success in her professional and occupational endeavors. Whether or not motherhood significantly affects a woman's general competence and ability at the average level is a question for debate, but there is clear evidence that it significantly affects the probability of extraordinary achievements. Many case histories are available of remarkable women who have managed to have very successful careers while being married and raising large families. However, while such examples do suggest that a combination of many roles is possible for some exceptional women they do not alter the fact that a woman's potential for professional success is greatly enhanced by avoiding the motherhood role.[6] Certainly among women who make outstanding achievements, such as the eminent women who appear is *Who's Who*, rates of childlessness are much higher than for the general population.[7] If motherhood makes a signifi-

6 For example, in a study of women scientists and engineers, Perrucci (1970) found tha childlessness was more common among the career-oriented and the successful tha among the non-career oriented and the less successful. Sells (1975) examined the rate of completion of degrees among Woodrow Wilson fellows in the United States, control ling for sex, marital status and childbearing. Among this very select group of excep tional students, drop-out rates ranged from twenty-six to sixty-six per cent, dependin on the field of study and a number of personal factors. In the humanities, the differenc in drop-out rates for those with and without children is only two per cent for men an thirteen per cent for women, a pattern not markedly different from that in the socia sciences, where the difference is three per cent for men and eleven per cent for women However, in the physical sciences quite a different pattern emerges. In this field o study, having a child decreases a man's chances of completing his degree by only on per cent, but reduces a woman's chances by thirty-one per cent.

7 In 1926, of all ever-married women listed, over half (fifty-four per cent) did not repo having had children (Cope, 1928). The proportion of childlessness declined to forty-thre

cant difference for women known to have exceptional ability and motivation, it might be assumed to make even more difference in the professional careers of women of average or below-average ability who are not as highly motivated in the first place.

The childless wives interviewed have not yet made what might be considered "outstanding contributions" in their different fields, and except for their decision to be childless are not innovative. However, their average age of twenty-seven is still too young to have made "outstanding achievements" and their life plans and degree of expressed motivation would indicate that their potential for innovation is relatively high. For example, one wife is doing original research as a post-doctoral fellow in biochemistry; two are completing doctorates in the physical sciences; and one novelist and one artist are just beginning to achieve some professional recognition after years of apprenticeship.

Many voluntarily childless wives perceive that their varied career and professional interests occupy much the same place in their lives that children occupy in the lives of mothers. However, the question of who is compensating for what is open to a variety of interpretations. The relationship between childlessness and career achievements is complex and probably reciprocal. As childless women become more successful in their careers and are increasingly rewarded for their achievements, they become more committed to remaining in their careers. A number of childless wives are seriously concerned with the extent to which having children would disrupt otherwise promising career prospects—a concern well justified by the fact that children do in many cases constitute a major disruption of professional development, much more so for women than for men. Conversely, it seems probable that when women are not experiencing success in their careers and are not finding them rewarding, becoming pregnant may be a convenient and an acceptable way out of an unpleasant situation. If some women do not achieve professional recognition and success because they become mothers, it is also possible that others become mothers because they do not achieve professional recognition and success. In the worldview associated with the parental lifestyle, the high achievements of childless women are considered to be attempts to compensate (usually unsatisfactorily) for their "failure" to achieve

---

per cent in 1948 (Kiser and Schacter, 1949) and thirty-nine per cent in 1962 (Frank and Kiser, 1965) until, in 1970, only twenty-four per cent of the women listed did not report children (Miller, 1978). In contrast, among ever-married men in *Who's Who*, rates of childlessness were slightly lower than in the general population (Kirk, 1957; Sly and Richards, 1972). In 1970, only eight per cent of the males listed remained childless (Miller, 1978).

motherhood. In the worldview associated with the childfree lifestyle, motherhood is designated as neither a significant achievement nor an especially creative act. It is contended that it is equally plausible that for some women a baby may compensate for the book they never wrote, the picture they never painted, or the degree they never finished. Several voluntarily childless wives reported that the one time they had seriously considered having children was when they had suffered some substantial career setback, such as failing a major examination, conducting an expensive but useless scientific experiment, or being unable to find suitable employment.

Freedom from work: the right to quit

In contrast to the dedication and the ardor of career-oriented childless couples, some respondents were satisfied with not having children, not because it left them free to pursue a career, but because it left them free not to! In assessing our respondents, we found paradoxically that whereas voluntary childlessness for women was often associated with relatively *high* career involvement, for men it was often associated with relatively *low* career involvement. For some male respondents the "deviance" associated with being childless included not only being minimally involved in the emotional rewards of child-rearing (as are many fathers), but also being minimally involved in work outside the home.

In contemporary definitions of masculinity, the role of family provider is pervasive, especially when it is incorporated into the associated role of father. By implication it is not enough for a father to be employed to support his family; it is also implicitly incumbent upon him to be as well employed as possible, in order to support his family in as much comfort as possible. Conventionally, a responsible family man takes as the "best" job the one that pays the most. Other considerations, such as preference for another kind of work or a preference for earning less money but working less hard, are supposed to be secondary to considerations regarding the welfare of one's family. If others are dependent upon you, then you are in a "job trap," in that the onus is on you not only to provide as adequately as possible but to insure that the income you provide is as secure and as steady as possible. A number of childless men perceived that being childfree meant being free from the necessity of working continuously throughout one's adult life, so as to earn as much money as possible. It also meant being free to take chances, either in accepting a position which was not particularly secure, or in investing assets in something less than blue-chip ventures.

Unlike fathers, the childless man does not have to work for the sake of his children, now or in the distant future. Unlike most husbands, childless men generally do not have to work for the sake of their wives, who are themselves employed and self-sufficient adults, rather than dependents.

Voluntarily childless men are characterized by a high degree of job satisfaction, but not necessarily a high degree of job success, as measured by conventional means. They are more likely to have a varied career history, perhaps having changed jobs several times after the generally acceptable trial period of the early twenties. They perceive themselves to be "released" from the sole responsibility of earning an income for a household. When they compare themselves with men who are fathers, childless men see themselves as being relatively free to take any kind of job they want, and to accept a trade-off of relatively low pay for relatively pleasurable work. Should the work cease to be pleasurable, they see themselves as free to change jobs as often as they like, and even to quit work entirely for as long as they have the minimum resources to support themselves. None of the childless men interviewed were unemployed, and very few had even had extensive periods of unemployment. From their point of view, the significant point was not that they did quit work, but that they *could* if they wanted to. With the option of escape at any time, they did not feel trapped. The perception of the potential freedom to "quit the system" offers considerable comfort even to those couples who continue to work steadily and conscientiously year after year.

The importance of freedom from work is dramatically illustrated by those few childless couples who have actually exploited their potential freedom. One man began his career in a very conventional mold. At the age of twenty-three, right after graduation with a B.A., he went to work for the same pharmaceutical company that employed his father. By twenty-nine, he had been promoted from a mere salesman to the manager of the regional sales office, and was well established in the bureaucratic hierarchy, making more than $40,000 a year with good prospects for more. During the early years of his marriage, he had postponed having children until he felt "settled," by which he meant settled on what he was going to do for the rest of his life. In a kind of early mid-life crisis occasioned by his thirtieth birthday, he suddenly realized that he really cared nothing for cosmetics, prophylactics, or suppositories. He quit his job and went back to school, taking an M.A. and than a Ph.D. in fine arts, which finally qualified him for a one-year limited-term appointment as a university lecturer, making one-third his former income. The modern "executive image" suburban home was sold, and they moved into a modest apartment near campus where they still live. Now, surrounded by art, music, and "people who are at least literate," he is very happy, his ulcers have healed, and he never has to wake up "wondering how to make it through another gray week."

At the time of this man's "liberation" his wife was twenty-eight. Although she had been ostensibly supportive, it was only under duress. She remembers:

> Once I decided he was really serious about dropping out, I only had two choices. I could go along with his madness—which was how I thought of i then—or I could wave him good-bye. It seemed pretty obvious that he was going to do it—go back to school I mean—one way or the other. Well, you know he *did* ask me, but I knew if I refused he would do it anyway. So figured, what the hell, five years of marriage down the tube, I'll try it Maybe by thirty I'll have a crisis of my own. But you know, I liked it once we got started. And I liked him a lot better when he liked what he was doing We worked it out.

What his wife liked about the new arrangment did not include bein poor. The extent to which this couple were able to "work out" a nev understanding reflects the considerable flexibility of a childless mar riage between androgynous people. Although she had not married he husband for his money—at the age of twenty-four he had very li tle—she had grown accustomed to the "good life" and was reluctant t relinquish it. Summarizing her reasoning, she explained:

> Well, I told myself, if he leaves you or vice versa, what are you going to d then, little lady? You are going to have to pick up *all* of your own expense and you won't get any luxuries. But if you stay, he'll help some, and you ca buy your own frills. So, that is what we did. We figured out how we coul live if he paid for half. And that is how we decided how much to spend fc rent and stuff, and we each paid half. My salary was then a lot more tha his, so I had some extra. And with that extra, I bought the rest of the stuf wanted. Lots of clothes, which he can't understand. Sterling silver, airlir tickets, and baubles—like I just got a microwave oven which I love and l thinks is a rip-off. But we figure, he wants to work less at stuff he likes, he works less and makes less and spends less. Me, I work a lot, not alwa at what I like, but I have money in my purse and I spend it any way I lik That seems fair, it works for us, but it sure seems weird to our friends. Li last year, when I bought a $2,000 fur coat, or took myself to the Caribbe last winter, and Jessie repapered the living room while I was away. I dor live as well as I did when he was working too—at a real job I mean—bu live a lot better than if I were on my own and I'm a lot happier. If I want st more, that is my problem. I'll go out and earn it.

This couple is unusual, in that the husband remains unperturbed the fact that his wife makes a lot more than he does. Part of his securi stems from the fact that he once "made it in the straight world" and so knows that he could do it again. He commented:

> I'm supposed to feel threatened, whatever that means. Sure, she makes more than I do, but not nearly as much as I could if I wanted to. Remember, I was there, I did it. Six long, dreary years, but I did it and I could always do it again if I wanted to. You know that line from—Eliot or Lawrence or somebody—earning your living while your life is lost. Well, that's how it was, but at least it was a good living. I don't know if I'd have the guts to live like I am and feel good about it if I had not done that first. Say, if I had been fired or something. But I quit. Those poor bastards with kids and a mortgage and a spongy wife. Lots of them feel like I did but they can't quit, not till they are sixty-five. By then who cares?

The stability of this new arrangement is still to be established, as it has been in effect only a couple of years. After thirteen years of marriage, however, both husband and wife report they have never felt closer. With the wife now thirty-five, it is very unlikely they will ever have children.

The association of childlessness with the right not to work was not usually as significant for childless women as for men, in that once a woman is married, she is almost automatically granted the right not to work unless she wants to. However, it must be remembered that although (almost) all wives were employed, only about half of them could be described as career-oriented. The remainder worked primarily for extrinsic rewards, such as money and the satisfactions of interacting with others in the job situation. This is not to imply that the latter group was necessarily dissatisfied, since most reported that they liked their work, but only that the particular job with which they worked was not a source of identity or of significant intrinsic fulfillment. This relatively casual orientation towards the occupational sphere is illustrated by the description offered by a young bank clerk regarding how she came to her present position. After a seasonal job ended, she was working for an employment agency for temporary office help.

> I was working there as a stats. clerk and they started a Teller Training Program and they called me up to see if I wanted to be a bank teller, and I said: "Well, of all the things I wanted to grow up to be, that's probably the last one." And they said: "Well, you're making $1.85 an hour, how would you like to make $2.03 an hour?" And I said: "I wanna be a bank teller, I wanna be a bank teller." So I took their training course and worked on a temporary basis like that for about six months, and then the program sort of decayed. So I quit and joined the Royal where I am working now, it's just—sheer luck, you never know what you'll wind up doing.

For those who are not intrinsically involved in their work, the impor tant component of the childfree lifestyle is the fact that they are (o feel) free to move from one job to another, or even to quit wor altogether. Having children increases the possibility of bein "trapped" in a job which one no longer likes, but which is necessar because of one's responsibilities. One woman stated it very simpl "When you've got children, then you have to be security-conscious." I contrast, the childfree lifestyle allows one the freedom to change job to take a more interesting job for less pay, to go back to school, or i other ways to remain mobile within or outside of the occupation structure.

The Good Life: Financial Consequence of Childlessness

Part of the uniqueness of the lifestyle of childless couples rests up the simple fact of their relative affluence. If couples are matched terms of the husbands' salaries, the childless have many times mo resources for optional spending than do their parental counterpart The magnitude of these differences is considerable, and results fro the interaction of several factors. First, a childless wife is much mo likely to work outside the home than is a mother. When she does wor she is more apt to work continuously and to be career-oriented, there tending to be more successful and to have a higher income. Second, t salary of the childless wife is almost all profit, in the sense that only very small proportion of her income (if any) is needed to buy servic compensating for a lessening of her participation in housework a cooking tasks. In contrast, a high proportion of the salary of a mother immediately designated for surrogate child-care and household he Third, even when the total family incomes are comparable, t resources of parents are committed to the direct costs of children a to other essential expenses, leaving the parents with a relatively l proportion of their income free for optional spending. With the exc tion of the very rich, these factors operate at all class levels to produ substantial discrepancies in the standard of living of parental and childless couples.

The value judgments of social scientists concerning the desirabil of children are so pervasive that until very recently the simple and vious question of the financial cost of children to their parents had even been posed, much less adequately researched. Goode make classic understatement when he concludes simply that: "Economically, children must be classified as a loss" (1963: 52). Udry is one of the few authors who does not mince words on the issues of the cost of children:

> For the individual deciding on parenthood, the fact cannot be avoided that *every decision to have a child means a decision to accept a lower standard of living in return for the satisfactions of parenthood.* If parenthood were strictly a rational economic matter, few of us would have been born. (Udry, 1971: 391)

Recent studies make it possible to estimate the approximate economic costs of raising a child (Epenshade, 1977). To do this, two components have to be taken into account. **Direct maintenance costs** include the actual money outlays for food, clothing, shelter, education, and other out-of-pocket expenses directly incurred by children.[8] Estimates of direct costs must take into account variations in family income, in region, and in rural-urban residence. **Opportunity costs** include the loss of income which the mother would have earned if she had been employed full-time in the labor force, rather than staying at home and caring for children. Most of the opportunity costs accrue to the first child, with subsequent children making less and less difference.

Estimates of the direct costs of raising a child spiral upward with inflation. The United States Bureau of Labor Statistics estimated direct costs in 1959 to be about $20,000; this figure increased to $40,000 in 1969 and to $70,000 in 1977. Since then, the figure has probably risen to between $80,000 and $100,000 (*The Family Planner*, 1979: 2). An alternative way to express the direct costs of child-rearing, which may be more meaningful than astronomical grand totals, is in terms of the total resources the family has available. The Institute for Life Insurance suggests that the cost of a child varies between three and four times the family's annual income (Sohn, 1971).

Opportunity costs vary directly with the education of the mother. The Commission on Population Growth and the American Future estimated in 1972 that the indirect costs associated with one child

---

[8] Estimates of the direct costs of raising children occasionally have unusual applications. *The Windsor Star* (November 25, 1971) carried the following news item:

> A drug firm that filled a faulty birth control prescription for a woman will have to pay forty-two thousand dollars in expenses to raise her unexpected child. The decision was handed down by a Superior Court in Los Angeles to a forty-six-year-old who was given sleeping pills instead of the requested birth control pills, became pregnant, and gave birth to a son who is now six. The money is that which should cover the costs of raising him until he is twenty-one.

were, on the average, about $40,000. However, if the mother wa university educated, the costs rose to about $55,000, and if she had fiv or more years of university training, they were estimated at $69,00 (Reed and McIntosh, 1972).

After reviewing and evaluating recent research, and taking into ac count a multiplicity of variables effecting the direct and indirect cost of raising children, Epenshade (1977: 27) comes to a concise and rel vant conclusion.

> In summary, estimates indicate that direct maintenance costs and oppo tunity costs are roughly of equal magnitude. Assuming that the bett educated a wife, the higher her husband's income, and adding direct an opportunity costs together, we obtain a total economic cost confrontin American families in 1977 that varies on a per child basis from abo $77,000 at the low-cost level to approximately $107,000 at the moderat cost standard.

The cost of children can also be assessed in terms of their impact o the overall standard of living. On the average, the first child absor more than thirty per cent of the family's total yearly income (*The Fan ly Planner*, 1979: 2). Put somewhat differently, if one were to consid two husbands of the same age, one with a wife to support, and one wi a wife and two school-age children to support, the childless husba would need to earn only sixty per cent of the father's income to mai tain his family at the same standard of living (Espenshade, 1977: 3 The *Commission on Population Growth and the American Future* (197 notes that for some educated women: "Having a child will not on mean giving up one lifestyle for another but also potentially giving one standard of living for another."

The preliminary efforts to estimate the actual cost of children ha not yet inspired any attempts to assess how many of what kinds people think in these terms, and what social determinants affect t kinds of estimates they are likely to make. Since most people are n future-oriented enough to consider the consequences of any behavi which will not be manifest until later decades, it seems likely that ve few people ever think of children in terms of their total financial c over twenty years. In addition, given the strong cultural values children, most parents and would-be parents are reluctant to consid directly the financial liabilities associated with childbearing, mainta ing that children are "worth it" whatever they cost.[9] It is hypothesiz

---

9 A typical comment on this question is that made by Cavan (1959: 424) in which she cludes a brief discussion of the cost of children with the observation that most par

that the voluntarily childless are more likely than parents to have considered the total cost of children over a lifetime, and that having done so, they are likely to make higher estimates, holding constant other relevant variables such as annual income and rural-urban residence. If these hypotheses are sound, and they have yet to be demonstrated, the importance of financial concerns in the childfree lifestyle is still problematic.

The Autonomy of Motives

Back in 1937, Allport suggested a useful concept for the description of motivation, namely the "autonomy of motives." The reasons for beginning a behavior may be quite autonomous and separate from the reasons for continuing it. For a number of childless persons, the inital decision to postpone having children was made for reasons which had little to do with the childfree lifestyle *per se*. However, once they had incidentally become conversant with the advantages and options of adult-centered living, the desire to continue to enjoy them then became significant. The principle of relative deprivation is firmly established and extensively documented in sociology. Its import in decision-making about childbearing is aptly illustrated with reference to the question of money. Many people could have been quite content on incomes substantially lower than the ones they now possess, as long as they had never become accustomed to greater affluence. However, once a high standard of living is achieved, they are much less content to forego it. The parental couple who follow the usual patterns of having children almost immediately after marriage very early become accustomed to dividing the husband's salary among three or more people; in contrast, the couple who postpone having children have the opportunity to become accustomed to dividing two incomes between two people. In considering children, they must also consider the prospect of a marked drop in standard of living. During the early years of marriage, a not uncommon pattern is the continued escalation of appreciation and use of increasingly expensive consumer goods and services, an escalation encouraged by the general materialistic values in our opulent society which are cleverly and continually exploited by effective advertising.

---

would not give up their children for any amount of money. True enough, perhaps, but childless persons could pose another question: how many cases do we have of parents being offered the alternative of a hundred thousand dollars in cash?

What a couple "need" to be "modestly comfortable" tends to be consistently magnified. One could not realistically say that such couples decided not to have children in order to have more money to spend on material goods. However, once accustomed to a high standard of living, they may well continue to remain childless in order not to have to revert to a lower standard of living.

The autonomy of motives also applies to other aspects of the childfree lifestyle. A successful professional woman may have initially intended to dabble in a career before settling down to marriage and motherhood. The experience of success in the career may later make her reluctant to give it up—or to suspend it—in order to have a child. A couple accustomed to spending a month every winter basking in the southern sun may never have made the considered judgment that they would rather travel than have children. Nevertheless, giving up one's annual sojourns later comes to constitute a real "cost" to be considered when debating the pros and cons of parenthood. As Wrong reminds us in his discussion of the over-socialized conception of man: "The fact that material interests, sexual drives and the quest for power have often been over-emphasized is no reason to deny their reality" (1961: 191). The desire to savor the childfree lifestyle may not have been of central concern when couples were making the initial decision to postpone having children: however, the desire to continue to enjoy adult-centered living may become a major factor in the desire to continue to be childfree.

Chapter Five: PERENNIAL DYADS: MARRIAGE WITHOUT MOTHERHOOD

For most couples, the roles of husband and wife are inextricably confounded with the complimentary roles of father and mother. In contrast, childless couples face a singular situation, in that they perennially interact with each other on a one-to-one basis. In most families, the marital dyad is only one pair-bond of many pair-bonds. In contrast, in childless families, the marital dyad is *the* pair-bond on which all else depends. Ordinarily, the man-woman relationship *per se* tends to be the primary focus of attention in a family only during the courtship and honeymoon stages, where it is evaluated largely in terms of what it portends for later relationships involving children. In contrast, the man-woman relationship of childless couples is always the primary focus of attention in the family, and is evaluated not as a precursor to later roles, but as an end in itself. Childless marriages *are* different from parental ones, in that they are based perennially on a single dyad, unmitigated and unrelieved by other relationships.

Childless respondents were asked to tell the story of their marriage, from the first encounter with their spouse to their present scenario. They were encouraged to describe the current nature of their relationship, to evaluate it, and to reflect on how it had evolved over time. Telling the story of the marriage often occupied a considerable proportion of the interview time. The richness and complexity of the resulting data are difficult to convey. The shifting ephemeral interactions and ex-changes over the span of years, which in their totality constitute the warp and woof of the husband-wife relationship, must eventually be summarized in concise phrases and that reduction, although necessary, inevitably means that some essential meanings will be distorted and some subtle nuances will be lost. Objectively, deliber-ately childless marriages have much in common with sterile marriages, or with honeymoon couples, or with those elderly parents whose children have grown and gone. Subjectively, however, the meaning of childlessness differs, depending on whether it is a state deliberately sought, or one accepted with resignation. One couple, left alone, may see themselves loose in an "empty nest," presumably having lost wha was intended to fill it. Another couple, equally isolated, may be quite content in a "spacious nest" which was designed in the first place fo only two persons. Our model for assessing childless marriages was th seminal work by Cuber and Haroff on *Sex and the Significan Americans* (1966). Among our respondents, three repetitive patterns i their marriages seem worthy of note and will be discussed in som detail: the intensity of their relationships; their generally high level o marital morale; and their preference for egalitarian roles. Evidenc concerning the relationship of childlessness to divorce will be re viewed, leading to the general conclusion that whatever correlatio does exist is likely to be spurious rather than causal.

Dyadic Intensity

The most salient feature of childless marriages compared with pare tal ones relates to the basic and incontrovertible fact that relationship which are confined to a single dyad are more intense than are relatio ships which encompass a larger group. Most couples entering ma riage experience a "honeymoon phase," wherein their primary co cern is expected to be with each other, and wherein their levels mutually focused interaction are very high. The claim of a bride or groom for exclusive access to their mate's time, attention, or affectio is recognized as having priority over almost all other relationship Typically, the primary disruption of the intensity of the honeymo period comes, not from intrusive relationships with other adults, b from the birth of a baby. In discussing this phenomenon, Slater (196 469) observes that:

> The advent of the first child itself tends to weaken the exclusive intimacy the dyad, first by providing an important alternative (and narcissistic) c

> ject of cathexis for each member, and second, by creating responsibilitie and obligations which are partly societal in nature, and through whic bonds between the dyad and community are thereby generated.

The shift from a dyadic relationship to one including children in volves both quantitative and qualitative changes in the nature of the man-woman relationship. With the onset of parenthood, neither husban nor wife can automatically continue to presume foremost rank in the other's interface of affections and obligations. Responsibility for and t the child takes precedence over responsibility for and to the mate. The child pre-empts the emotional saliency of the spouse.[1]

> Parents of any normally loquacious children will know how much perseverance may be needed to sustain a conversation with each other at mealtimes; leisure pursuits are commonly built around the family and even sexual life may be curtailed. Apart from added demands on the couple's time, child-rearing introduces a new set of stresses and an area of potential conflict from which those without children are spared (Humphrey, 1975: 276).

Generally, interaction between parents tend to be diluted by the existence of children, as well as by their direct presence.[2] In contrast, a couple without children can continue to be preoccupied with each other, and apparently a number of them do so. Their emotional energies are less dissipated by other relationships, and so remain more concentrated in the marital dyad.

If it is true, as we have suggested, that childless couples generally do attend to each other in more intense and focused ways than do parental couples, it is not clear what effect this may have on marital adjustment. According to folk wisdom, increased communication and contact

---

[1] Balchin, a father of five, describes this process with humerous resignation:

> Children . . . are destructive of the emotional life of the average man. A man getting married may realize vaguely that he will one day have a family, and even desire it. What he certainly doesn't realize is the change in his relationship with his wife that the coming of children will involve. He married a woman, and as a man he had first call on her duties and affections. But within a few months he finds that he is now married to a mother, which is something quite different. Their first duties are no longer to each other but to the Sacred Calves—their children. . . . Yesterday he was a racehorse (with a pretty filly at his side). Now he is shut between the shafts and bidden to pull the family coach (Balchin, 1965: 11).

[2] For example Rosenblatt (1974) observed that the presence of children tends to disrupt adult touching and talking, and by implication, to interfere with adult communication. In a comparative study of mothers and childless wives, Ryder (1973) found that although the birth of a child was not correlated with marital dissatisfaction, it was correlated with the wife's perception that her husband was not paying enough attention to her, a variable he somewhat uncharitably designated "lovesickness." As he notes, it is unclear whether this correlation can be attributed to decreasing interest on the part of husbands or increasing demands on the part of wives, or both.

are supposed to have a benign effect on marriages. However, it seems more likely that the intensification of relationships which seems to occur in childless marriages is a two-edged sword. On the one hand, positive relationships have a chance to develop fully, and there is a potential for maximization of the man-woman relationship; on the other hand, negative relationships have a chance to develop as well, and to enter a downward spiral, becoming worse and worse. The resulting dyadic warfare has been dramatically illustrated in Edward Albee's *Who's Afraid of Virginia Woolf?* (1963) in which, according to one interpretation, the couple invented a mythical child as a focus for their animosity (Humphrey, 1975: 276). The lessening of interpersonal intensity which occurs with the coming of a child may be to the detriment of good marriages, but it may constitute a welcome or indeed a necessary relief in unsatisfactory ones. Theoretically, the intensification of the marital relationship which is associated with childlessness might be expected to lead to a polarization of levels of marital adjustment, resulting in disproportionate numbers of couples who report either exceptionally negative or exceptionally positive relationships.

Among the couples interviewed, we observed a full range of marital relationships as described by Cuber and Haroff (1966), ranging from conflict-habituated ones to those reflecting virtually total preoccupation of husband and wife with each other. Although the general distribution of kinds of marriages is not known, we were left with the distinct impression that the couples interviewed were indeed happier than most. The high levels of marital morale which were observed are less likely to typify childless couples in general than to reflect two systematic kinds of bias. In the first place, by interviewing only couples who had survived a minimum of five years of marriage, the least satisfactory marriages tended to be weeded out by desertion or divorce before the end of the five-year period. In the second place, it seems likely that those persons most apt to volunteer to be interviewed, and to submit willingly to extensive analysis, are also those persons most likely to see themselves as happily married. Generally, the less content may be more reticent. In this area, therefore, our tentative generalizations must be phrased with double caution. However, our data do suggest two counter-intuitive findings. First, by whatever criteria one wishes to use, at least some voluntarily childless marriages are exceptionally rewarding to the husbands and wives. Second, as far as we could determine, some successful childless marriages are rewarding not *in spite* of not having children, but *because* of not having them. At least for some, the intensity associated with remaining childless appears to maximize the potential for the man-woman relationship.

Dyadic Withdrawal: Commitment to Intimacy

Whether or not childless marriages are generally more or less happy than parental marriages is a question beyond the scope of the present research. However, our interviews with childless couples did establish that many of them *believe* childless marriages to be happier. Moreover, for a number of childless couples, their desire to continue to enjoy a good marriage is a direct and primary reason for their desire to continue to be childless.

A dominant component of some childless marriages is their commitment to the ideal that a married couple should be a self-sufficient unit in which each spouse looks to the other for the satisfaction of most—if not all—of their social and psychological needs. Berger and Kellner (1970) argue convincingly that, at least in our culture in the middle class, one's spouse constitutes the main significant other in the construction of social reality.[3] Although a couple begin their relationship as separate individuals with separate and largely unknown biographies, during the development of the marriage they begin to construct a third reality. This involves incorporating both of their worldviews with modifications, and adding a third perspective which is new, and which is developed during the course of the marital dialogue. One dynamic in the construction of a new social reality is the gradual exclusion of others, who are relegated to positions of less and less significance in the social world, eventually to be either disregarded entirely or accorded only minor roles. Such processes are not necessarily either deliberate or recognized, but they constitute a necessary step if the marital relationship is not to be endangered. Among some childless couples, such processes are carried to their logical extreme, and the couple see in each other *a reference group of one*. Such couples approximate the pattern of total involvement outlined by Cuber and Haroff (1966), including a high level of communication and a great degree of *communis opinio*.[4] They relate to each other not only as man and wife, but also as lovers and best friends.

---

[3] For a comprehensive account of this approach, see *The Social Construction of Reality* (Berger and Luckman, 1965).

[4] Van Keep and Schmidt-Elmendorff (1975: 37) compared 75 infertile couples with a matched control group of 75 couples with children. They found that the childless couples had a higher level of communication, and greater consensus on a wide range of topics.

The intensity of some childless marriages can be illustrated by a brief description of two case histories: one of a woman working in an ordinary job, and one of a woman deeply committed to a career. Two of our respondents were a secretary and a draftsman who had been married for seven years. During that time, they had been separated for only three days, when the arrangements of changing jobs and moving from one city to another made it unavoidable. The wife leaves for work half an hour before her husband, who uses that time to clear away breakfast and start preparations for supper. At noon, they talk on the phone to discuss the morning's events. The wife gets home from work about an hour before her husband, during which time they usually talk on the phone again and she finishes preparing the evening meal. Except for the periods five days a week when they are actually working, they spend all their free time together and are never out of contact with each other for more than about three hours. Every event, every idea, every nuance of feeling is discussed in detail. They report that they never quarrel because:

> If we do disagree, which is not often, we just keep talking until we work it out. Sometimes it takes all night, but we always find a way of looking at things that both of us can buy.

This couple live a routine, conventional life, puncutuated by occasionally entertaining mutual friends, and by rather elaborate vacations. Comparing their marriage with others, their predominant emotion is one of smugness. They stress total intimacy and sharing, what they refer to as "real quality loving," something they consider only possible if you are childless, if you keep working at it, and if you are very lucky.

Another couple committed to a total relationship were two artists, who had a prenuptial agreement not to have children. The wife met her husband-to-be in art school, and was immediately impressed. She reports:

> The first thing we noticed about each other was that we liked to work together. Even before I fell in love with him, I knew I would like to share a studio with him. Art is first inspiration, but then a lot of hard work. Our styles are quite different but we do help each other. We are a working team.

This couple are unusually fortunate, in that a timely inheritance allows them to live modestly but comfortably without being employed. The initial legacy allowed them to buy land and to build their own home. Annuities, plus the occasional sale of paintings, provide for the rest of their expenses. Life in their home is organized around a large studio which, although divided into separate work spaces, does let them see and speak to each other while working. Some days, they spend eight to ten hours there, working independently and offering each other criticism, praise, and encouragement. They take turns serving each other breakfast in bed. Neither enjoys work in the home, but they split it: she does the cooking, he does the housework, and they do the dishes together. In their fourteen years of marriage, they have been apart only two nights. When they are not working, they spend most of their time alone, entertaining each other with apparently endless conversations. Except for a few friends also in the art world, they have few social contacts. Looking back, the husband reflected: "We are even happier now than when we started out." For this couple, pragmatic as well as interpersonal reasons dictate that the entire way of life they find so satisfactory is predicated upon remaining childless. If they had a child, they would have to supplement their annuity and their sporadic sale of art work with a regular income from a conventional job. Neither would consider a position which would separate them during the working day. Being childless, they share all aspects of their lives. They envisage that, if one of them were to "sell out" by working at a mundane job, they would be in danger of becoming like other couples, whom they describe as typically consisting of "an over-demanding wife, with an over-burdened husband, with nothing in common."

Couples involved in such intense dyads tend to see a child as a threat who would disrupt, and perhaps destroy, their rapport. One wife stated flatly:

> A child would come between us. I wouldn't be able to be as close to my husband if I had a child because a child is so helpless and needs so much attention. I'd have to give to it what I want to give to him, and I'd resent it a lot. And if I didn't give him as much, he wouldn't give me back as much after a while, and then I'd really resent it. I just don't want to share him.

Unilateral commitment to a strong and exclusive dyad is perceived to be dangerous, in the sense that one's emotional vulnerability to the existence and concern of the spouse is very great. Although such danger is recognized, the rewards of such an intense and exclusive relationship are perceived as worth the risk. For example, one woman comments that "you have all your emotional eggs in one basket," but views this exclusive commitment as a positive thing with which children would interfere, rather than as a frightening thing. She goes on to comment that "if you have children, then not all of your emotional involvement would be with each other anymore and you would have lost something."

It is sometimes suggested that one impetus to parenthood is t perception that a problem exists, and that having a child might co stitute to some degree a solution to that problem. For example, the are frequent allusions to the idea that childbearing may solve or least diminish husband-wife tensions, or that motherhood may provi fulfillment where other sources of fulfillment for the woman, such marriage and/or a career, have failed (LeMasters, 1970; Udry, 197 One characteristic which distinguishes some childless couples fro some parental couples may be that they do not perceive serious pro lems in their lives, and so do not seek parenthood as a solution to the Satisfaction with the present is associated with a desire to preser the status quo. As long as a childless marriage is rewarding, the may be serious hesitation to introduce any change and hence possib threaten that desirable state. Many of the wives interviewed wou agree with Michels (1970: 14) when she explains: "Life is so good rig now that we hesitate to change it in any way."

Wanting to maintain the intensity of commitment to the man-wom relationship by avoiding distractions and deflections from the dy may reflect not so much a rejection of parenthood as an exception commitment to ideals of how marriage should be. In discussing t causes of divorce, Berger and Kellner (1970: 69) contend that:

> Typically, individuals in our society do not divorce because marriage h become unimportant to them, but because it has become so important th have no tolerance for the less than completely satisfactory marital a rangement they have contracted with the particular individual in questio

In the same way, some individuals in our society may avoid paren hood, not because they consider marriage unimportant, but becau they consider it of such primary importance that nothing else should b allowed to interfere with it. The purpose of marriage has become ma riage as an end in itself, the quality of the dyad being something to b preserved at all costs.

One of the paradoxes associated with reactions to childlessness the possibility that those childless couples who have the "best" ma riages are the most likely to encounter hostile responses from others. a childless husband and wife are antagonistic toward each other, an apparently have an unsatisfactory relationship, the observations their interaction simply confirm the beliefs of parents that such is to b expected among those without the benefits of children. Moreove since the mutual involvement of the husband and wife is minimal, the potential for interaction with the community at large is still hig whether or not they share others' concern with children. However, if a childless husband and wife have a close and intense relationship, their apparently successful marriage represents a double threat. On the one hand, their very existence challenges the folk wisdom that children are necessary for a happy marriage; on the other hand, their preoccupation and satisfaction with each other minimizes their interest in the community at large and lowers the probability of their involvement with it. Although it is always hazardous to generalize from small groups of respondents, the data indicate that the childless couples least likely to be greeted with hostility are those who have a mediocre or even a poor relationship, and who maintain extensive interests in and involvements with the greater community.

Sexual Interaction

One component of the negative stereotype of the voluntarily childless is that they tend to be, in one way or another, sexually incompetent and maladjusted. The dominant cultural definitions of the meaning and purpose of sex assume a close association of sexual intercourse with reproduction. The birth control revolution has served to weaken this association. Most couples do not desire to conceive a child every time they have intercourse, nor do they desire intercourse only when conception is possible and desirable. Nevertheless, it is still true that for many people: "children . . . are signs of genital success in the unconscious mind of the woman and proof of potency to the man" (Simpson, 1966: 427). Not having or wanting children is often equated with not having or wanting sex. The childless may be assumed not to be having intercourse at all,[5] or to be having it only very infrequently. Thus, a couple may be jokingly advised: "Keep practicing and you are sure to get it right soon." Husbands may be queried: "Hey Joe, haven't you figured out how it works yet?" Infrequent intercourse is in turn explained by the implication of frigidity, impotence, homosexuality, or some other kind of sexual inadequacy. The stereotypic beliefs concerning the sexual behavior of childless couples are, like other stereotypes,

[5] In some atypical instances, this assumption is apparently warrented. Blazer (1964) and Friedman (1962) have done case studies of married virgins. While they cannot provide an estimate of the incidence of unconsummated marriages, their work does suggest that it cannot automatically be assumed that all married couples have sexual relations with each other.

inconsistent. Occasionally, the childless are viewed as having too much sexual activity rather than too little, and their separation of sex from procreation is interpreted as leading to "loose" standards of sexual morality, and perhaps to promiscuity.[6]

The association of childlessness with atypical sexuality is more of a problem for men than for women. The meaning of fatherhood for most men seems to be more as a mark of sexual identity than as a fulfillment of emotional needs (Humphry, 1977: 747). Having a child, especially having a son, is a way to prove one's manhood. In some definitions of *machismo*, the more children that have been sired, the more masculine the father is assumed to be. Sanctions against childless men may take the form of "friendly" teasing—verging on ridicule—which impunes their masculinity with reference to impotence or homosexuality. The childless men interviewed were well aware of these views, but found them more amusing than threatening. All appeared very secure in their own definitions of masculinity. Before hazarding any guesses as to the generalizability of this finding, it must be remembered that the respondents were all volunteers. Presumably, only childless men who felt secure in their masculinity would come forward to be interviewed about it—especially when the interviewer was a woman. Presumably some of the childless husbands who do not want to be interviewed do find that the absence of progeny is an incipient threat to their masculinity.

In spite of the so-called sexual revolution, serious discussions of one's personal experiences with sex still remain in the area of "sensitive" topics. Although all respondents managed to convey the gist of their sexual interaction with their spouse, they varied greatly in the directness or the obliqueness of their descriptions. The range of satisfaction also varied, but in general sexual adjustment *per se* did not seem problematic. At the same time, neither did it seem to be of great significance. Typically, respondents reported that sexual feelings were less intense than they had been in the past, and that intercourse was less frequent, and expressed the typical confusion as to whether a loss of feeling led to a decrease in frequency, or vice versa. If sexuality was not a major source of gratification, neither was it a major source of complaint. In interpreting these findings, it is important to remember that respondents were self-selected in terms of hav

6 This belief is consistent with data on premarital sexual standards. Reiss (1967: 14 found that married couples without children are slightly more permissive abou premarital sex than are couples with young children, and a great deal more permissiv than couples with teenage children.

ing stable marriages, and that those marriages were of relatively long duration, averaging nearly ten years. The fact the sexual pleasures with the spouse were not intense, and that sexual intercourse was not particularily frequent, is what would ordinarily be expected under such circumstances.

One theme that did come through in the interviews, especially in interviews with wives, was a concern not with sexual gratification *per se* as much as with the emotional rapport it expressed, or in some cases failed to express. For example, one women who had been married for twelve years offered the following description:

> We spend hours just cuddling each other, especially on the weekends when we don't have to work, we spend half the time in bed. But it's not a wild orgy, at least not anymore. We make love maybe once or twice a week, maybe less, which is not that often is it? How long do orgasms last anyway, a few seconds. But the other parts are just as important, the hugging and talking and kissing and maybe reading awhile and all. Fred had to teach me to be sensual—body rubs and long baths and all that. When we were first married, we spent a lot of time doing what makes people pregnant. Now we do a lot of what makes love.

The level of satisfaction which this woman is reporting could be accurately recorded with the concise description that she "has intercourse once a week and always has an orgasm." However, this would fail to convey the concern with making love as a *process*, rather than with having intercourse as an exercise with orgasm the end *product* to be achieved.

In the course of telling the story of the marriage, many respondents alluded to sexual infidelity as an issue, or at least an incipient issue, in their relationship. Many reported extramarital encounters, ranging from one-night stands to serious affairs lasting a number of years. Liaisons outside the marriage were considered peripheral to the marriage itself, and were not described as presently being contentious issues. The significance of these encounters is difficult to assess without knowing how common extramarital sexual experience is among middle-class couples who have been married ten years. Since involvement in extramarital sex is known to be associated with low religiosity and with other unconventional attitudes, presumably rates are somewhat higher among childless persons than among others. Although respondents perceived that their feelings about childlessness were directly linked with their feelings about marriage and about their mate, none made even an indirect connection between their sexual fidelity or lack of it and their attitudes towards childlessness *per se*.

Egalitarian Relationships

Among the childless couples interviewed, husbands and wives appeared to have more egalitarian roles than is usually the case, even among upper-middle class couples. Although the typical discrepancies in authority, power and perceived competence were still there, and still operated in the expected direction, the magnitude of the discrepancies between men and women was greatly attenuated. This effect may be partly due to selectivity, in that persons oriented towards childlessness may also be oriented towards liberal sex-role ideologies. More likely, however, the fact of not having children makes more feasible the enactment of egalitarian ideologies. Even among the involuntarily childless, husbands and wives appear to be more equal than do fathers and mothers.[7] In ordinary families involved in child-rearing, the coming of children tends to accentuate the biological sex differences, and to buttress conventional sex role expectations.[8] For example, in an intensive longitudinal study of the impact of the first child on couple relationships, Cowan *et al.* (1978: 310) found that regardless of the type of division of labor the couple had at first, after the birth of the baby there was a shift toward a more traditional division of roles.

> The shift was most marked in the household tasks, and least in the baby care items. Even couples who expected to share night feedings or calls to the pediatrician tended to find that, within several weeks after delivery, the woman took on these chores, regardless of whether she was breast-feeding or employed. Similarily, the initiation of sexual activity fell more to the men where previously both partners had taken this role . . . Despite the current rhetoric and ideology concerning equality of roles for men and women, it seems that couples tend to adopt traditionally-defined and more differentiated roles during times of stressful transition such as around the birth of the first child.

---

7 For example, Carr (1963: 5598) compared with marital adjustment of a matched sample of infertile and fertile marriages and found that "the dominance pattern reported by the infertile couples was more likely to show a democratic pattern and less likely to display disagreement" than that of the fertile couples.

8 Some anthropologists have contended that a significant part of the division of labor by sex is predicated on the definition of women as primarily responsible for child-care (Brown, 1970). Evidence from the study of primates, and from pre-literate societies, suggests that: ". . . activity distinction is more realistically a distinction between childless adults' work and childbearing adults' work rather than between male work and female work" (Williams, 1973: 1725).

In contrast, the roles of the childless husband and wife can and do remain more interchangeable, and hence more equal. Without the constraint of child care, men and women have a more realistic opportunity to approximate egalitarian sex roles.

Egalitarian role relationships are often perceived, both by laymen and by social scientists, as having come about as a result of a power struggle between husband and wife, in which the wife "won" in her desire to become more emancipated, and the husband, having "lost," reluctantly extended additional privileges to her. However, in a number of marriages studied, the initial impetus for the wife's emancipation appears to have originated with the husband, who not only tolerated her outside interests but actively encouraged them. For example, one of our respondents had dropped out of high school just before graduating to escape an unhappy home situation. She had drifted from one unsatisfactory, low-status job to another, working as an usher in a movie theatre, as a clerk in an office, and at other similar occupations. At the time of her marriage, she was working in a dead-end job with a local periodical, helping with the art layouts, a considerable discrepancy from the career as an artist of which she had dreamed as an adolescent. The husband actively encouraged her idea to take a fine arts degree. The wife was not confident of either her ability to do university work or her artistic talent, and went for some time without any concrete action. The husband found out the conditions under which adult students could be admitted to university without the final year of high school, brought home the application forms to be completed, and actually made the appointment for her to take the required aptitude test. She reports that she needed the stimulus of his encouragement, and that she would never have been able to graduate without her husband's help. Another wife commented that her husband does not admire helpless women, and that the few occasions on which they disagree come about when he tries to push her to do too much. Rather than the stereotypic kind of conflict where the wife struggles to assert herself against a dominant and reluctant male, this husband is unhappy with the idea of being married to "just" a housewife. As he explained:

> I don't want a childlike wife for the same kinds of reasons I don't want a child. Both are too dependent. The best relationships are with independent, grown-up people who know themselves and what they want and go after it.

He urged his wife to go back to school, and later encouraged her to take a prestigious but demanding job as an administrator.

A partnership of peers

Among the childless couples interviewed, the tendency towards egalitarian marriage was reinforced by the fact that all of the wives were gainfully employed. Compared with other dual-career families, however, the childless had a greater potential for negotiating equal partnerships, in that their incomes were less dissimilar than is usually the case. In most households in which both husband and wife work, the husband's income is perceptibly higher than his wife's (Glick and Norton, 1977: 11). The discrepancies are consistent and large. For example in Canada in 1961, wives who worked tended to earn about one-third of the family income, while the husband earned the remaining two-thirds (Veevers, 1977: 27-29). In spite of many changes in the employment of women, this ratio remained unchanged in 1971. Several factors contribute to the discrepancies. Some invole the mating gradient, in that couples tend to sort themselves out so that husbands are generally older and better educated, and hence can command a higher wage. Apart from the fact that male work received higher remuneration than female work, husbands are more likely to have stable and continuous employment histories, whereas wives are likely to have unstable ones interrupted for child-rearing.

When both husband and wife are employed outside the home, both may like to think of themselves as equal partners who contribute equally to the marriage. However, in a situation where the husband earns two-thirds of the income and the wife only one third—or to put it more directly, where he earns twice as much as she—it is predictable that the husband will tend to assume the role of *senior partner*, leaving the wife in the supportive role of *junior partner*. In evaluating the relative significance of their two careers, his tends to be considered more important, partly because in objective terms it *is* more crucial to the family unit. Among childless couples in dual careers, the male-female discrepancy in income is not eliminated: it is, however, greatly attenuated. Although, as expected, the husband is typically older than his wife by several years and is more educated, he is not much more educated. More importantly, both are likely to have had continuous employment since before they were married, and to have applied themselves to their work with equal diligence. As a result the disparity in their earning capacity is greatly reduced: generally, the husband makes about 55 per cent of the earned income, compared with his wife's 45 per cent. While this still reflects a male "edge" in terms of power, the discrepancy is small enough to maintain the fiction that it does not exist. One wife, to whom financial parity was very important, explained her concern with reference to many other areas.

> Look, most women go to their husbands and say: "Look, let's make a deal, let's pretend that my job is as important as yours." And the men go along with it. I don't have to get him to pretend that my work is just as important for us: it *is* just as important! And that makes all the difference in the balance between us, and the balance in other couples.

Androgynous roles

Although the childless couples interviewed tended to have egalitarian marriages in the sense of following a policy of more-or-less equal division of work, money, and power, they were not necessarily also androgynous, in the sense of incorporating both masculine and feminine personality traits (Bem, 1974, 1975). Most childless wives were interested in typically feminine pursuits, and most husbands were interested in typically masculine ones. However, in addition to conventional interests, the childless seemed to demonstrate a considerable freedom from sex-typed behavior repertoires. Some men were active in such "feminine" interests as sewing, gourmet cooking, and flower arranging; some women enjoyed woodwork, hunting, automechanics, and competitive track and field. Sex-role flexibility is becoming increasingly acceptable, especially among the well-educated upper-middle class, and especially when the wife is gainfully employed. In addition, the childless may have greater propensity for androgyny simply by virtue of being relatively non-religious and unconventional. However, the rejection of motherhood and fatherhood may be associated with the rejection of other behaviors typically thought to be necessary for the definition of feminine and masculine roles. It seems plausible that voluntary childlessness is associated with sex-role emancipation, including androgyny. If future research establishes that such is the case, two noteworthy questions arise. To what extend does androgyny lead to childlessness? Alternatively, to what extent does remaining childless facilitate the expression and development of androdynous sex roles?

Childlessness and Marital Morale

Interaction in childless marriages seems to be systematically different from interaction in marriages in which there are children. However, it is not clear which kind of union is most satisfactory, from the point of view of the participants. Almost all childless couples interviewed believed that, in general, childless marriages were happier than those with children. Whatever level of satisfaction they had in their own marriage, they tended to believe it was better than it would have been if they had become parents, and that remaining childless would maximize rather than diminish their chances for future marital satisfaction. These views are in direct contrast with those of the general public, who tend to consider children to be contributors to marital morale (Centers and Blumberg, 1954; Blake, 1978). The ultimate resolution of these two discrepant views is still unclear, as the actual overall relationship between childbearing and marital morale is yet to be established. Marital satisfaction in general is known to follow a U-shaped curve, being highest during the early years of marriage, declining during the middle years, and then increasing again during the later years (Rollins and Feldman, 1970; Renne, 1970; Rollins and Cannon, 1974). This pattern coincides with the periods of childlessness, of active childrearing, and of the "empty nest," with the result that the effects of the advent of children are difficult to distinguish from the more general effects of the "corrosion of time" (Blood and Wolfe, 1960: 263).

There are some data to support Bernard's (1972: 61) contention that childlessness has a "benign effect" on marital adjustment.[9] However, other studies have suggested that the relationship between adjustment and number of children is curvilinear;[10] and still others have failed to find any systematic relationship at all.[11] In considering this question,

---

9 For example, the Indianapolis fertility study reported a decline in marital satisfaction with increasing family size (Reed, 1947). In a British study, Slater and Woodside (1951) found that childless unions were among the happiest in their series. The supposed "crisis" of the first child has been found to be associated with subsequent *post partum* dissatisfaction with the marriage (Feldman, 1971). In a more recent and comprehensive study, Renne (1976) surveyed a large sample of Californians and found that in general childless couples were more likely to report being happily married than were post-parental couples, who in turn were happier than couples actively engaged in parental roles. The differences were largest for young marriages of less than two years' duration and for established marriages of more than twenty years' duration.

10 For example, Farber and Blackman (1956) found that couples with no children or with four or more children exhibited more marital tension than did those with one to three children. Blood and Wolfe (1960: 262) found that couples with one to four children were more satisfied with their marriages that were couples with no children or with five or more.

11 For example, Terhune and Pilie (1974: 162-168) reviewed over twenty research efforts over the last thirty years which have been concerned with the seemingly simple question of the effects that children have on the husband-wife relationship. In many instances, the available data failed to indicate any systematic differences in the adjustment of childless couples compared with parents (Terman, 1938; Michel and Feyrabend, 1969; Ryder, 1973; Figley, 1973; Magarick and Brown, 1976; Silka and Kiesler, 1977; Bram, 1978: 386). Such data, however, are not conclusive enough to justify the conclusion that therefore no relationship exists.

simple comparisons of childless and parental couples are of dubious value, in that they do not differentiate between involuntary and voluntary childlessness. The many special kinds of unhappiness due to sterility are not taken into account, not the least of which may be the absence of a sense of self-determination of one's marital lifestyle. Equally important, the parental group is not homogeneous either, being composed of some persons who were effective contraceptors, some persons who experienced errors of timing and/or excess fertility, and some unfortunate persons who did not want to be parents at all. The crucial variable in maintaining marital morale may be the ability to have as many children as one wants to have, whatever number that may be (Reed, 1947; Christensen and Philbrick, 1952; Burgess and Wallin, 1953; Christensen, 1968). In this perspective, one would expect to find the lowest level of marital happiness among those couples who failed to achieve their ideal family size, either because they were subfecund and were not successful in having children they wanted, or because they were too fecund, and had an excess number of children.

Childlessness and Divorce

It is widely believed that children tend to hold a marriage together (Heath, Rober, and King, 1974). The folk wisdom on the positive relationship between childlessness and divorce has been supported by sociologists and demographers. A superficial analysis of official statistics indicates that, in the past, divorce rates for childless couples do appear to have been substantially higher than for couples with children (Jacobson, 1950: 244; Chester, 1972). Except in very unusual circumstances, childlessness *per se* is not considered grounds for divorce.[12] However, childlessness may contribute to the divorce decision in a number of ways. At least three hypotheses are possible. First, couples who are unhappy and who are therefore divorce-prone may manifest that unhappiness by not having, or not wanting to have, children. If the marriage seems precarious, they may deliberately remain childless to facilitate the expected dissolution (Cohen and Sweet, 1974: 92). Second, couples without children, who miss the benefits of the parenthood experience as a common focus of interest, may be less

[12] In traditional societies, sterility is often grounds for divorce (Rosenblatt and Hillabrant, 1972). In the western world, sterility *per se* is not considered a just cause, although concealment of known sterility may constitute fraud. In some instances, deliberate childlessness may become grounds for divorce it can be construed as cruelty (Chester and Streather, 1972) or as injurious to health or as desertion (Goldstein and Katz, 1965).

happy than parents, and consequently more prone to divorce. Third, couples who are unhappy for whatever reason may feel more free to get a divorce for whatever reason if they are childless than if they are parents. It is this hypothesis which is most often mentioned by the childless themselves, who feel that by having children, parents have forfeited their right to easy access to divorce.

Since staying married or getting a divorce, and having or not having a child, are public and highly visible events, the relationship between childlessness and divorce can be addressed by an examination of divorce statistics.[13] The general conclusion suggested is that what relationship does exist is spurious rather than causal in nature. Most of the relationship between childlessness and marital stability appears to stem from the fact that most divorces occur in the early years of marriage, before children are born in any case. The association between childlessness and marital stability depends upon other variables, such as the duration of marriage, race, family size, and child density (Figley, 1973).[14] When empirical findings contradict firmly-held conventional beliefs, social scientists, like the laity, are remarkably resistant to them. In 1955, Monahan provided a convincing illustration of the statistical spuriousness of the alleged relationship between divorce and childlessness, summarizing his major article with the conclusion that: "Marital instability, in the final analysis, may have no general relationship to childbearing" (Monahan, 1955: 456). His contention, although widely cited, was not widely accepted. Twenty years later, after extensive work on the topic, Chester must still take pains to point out that we advance our understanding in recognizing: ". . . that the alleged relationship between divorce and infertility is largely a procedural artifact, and that it cannot be used to imply that children contribute to marital stability" (Chester, 1976: 124).

---

13 Like many other problems in social science, this apparently simple approach turns out not to be simple at all. Legal statistics are confounded by varying definitions of what does or does not constitute a "child of the marriage"; primary marriages are often grouped with remarriages; and the duration of the marriage is differentially defined as the time until separation or the time until the official decree of divorcement (Monahan, 1962; Chester, 1972).

14 In a recent study, Thornton (1977) attempted to sort out the relevant variables systematically. Among white couples married 4–12 years, the childless had higher rates of marital dissolution than did those with children. However, among couples married 12–16 years, their rates were not as high as couples with "large" families of three or more children. Among nonwhite couples married 4–8 years, rates of dissolution were higher for the childless than for those with small families, but lower than for those with large ones. Among nonwhite childless persons married more than 8 years, no consistent pattern emerged.

Chapter Six: MAINTAINING A VARIANT WORLDVIEW

The voluntarily childless couples we talked with were uniformly aware that their rejection of the parenthood mystique was very unusual, and that most persons would dismiss their views on parenthood as inaccurate and incomplete. Moreover, given a basically pronatalist society, they were also aware that most persons would consider their worldview to be morally offensive and would strongly disapprove of their rejection of parenthood. However, in the face of pervasive disagreement and disapproval, the childless persons we talked with were remarkably free of doubt concerning the rightness of their choice. At least among those voluntarily childless couples who have been married for a minimum of five years and who were mutually supportive of the childless option, the perception of others' disapproval of their lifestyle was paradoxically met with equanimity. Although aware of extensive and intensive social disapprobation, their reaction was more one of indifference than of concern.

In spite of pervasive pronatalism, some voluntarily childless couples manage to find support for their variant values and to render nugatory concerted social efforts to persuade them to have children. For childless couples to manage to remain virtually impervious to pronatalist "propaganda," they must solve two separate but related problems. First, it is necessary for them to find evidence which they deem to support their unusual worldview, and thereby to minimize anxiety and doubt concerning the rightness of their decision. Second, it is necessary for them to learn to deal with explicit and implicit social sanctions and thereby to minimize the negative consequences of having a deviant identity. The next two chapters are concerned with the pervasiveness of pronatalism and with the strategies which serve to counter its cognitive, evaluative and behavioral components.

The Pervasiveness of Pronatalism

The existence of pronatalist norms, which advocate that married persons should have and want children, is inevitable in almost all societies. Pronatalism incorporates beliefs, attitudes, and actions which are directly or indirectly supportive of parenthood. The cultural complex consists of three separate but related components: cognitive, evaluative, and behavioral. The **cognitive** component involves beliefs about the consequences of having or not having children, and supports the contention that parents are in a number of ways significantly different from nonparents. The **evaluative** component involves judgments concerning these perceived differences, with favorable attitudes towards the positive consequences believed associated with parenthood, and negative attitudes towards the unfavorable consequences believed associated with nonparenthood. Finally, the **behavioral** component involves the translation of beliefs and attitudes into overt actions. Stereotypic beliefs about the nature of childless couples, and unfavorable attitudes toward them, become manifest in negative sanctions of them. Some of these sanctions are purely expressive, but others are intended to persuade childless persons to become parents.

Fertility norms draw considerable impetus, support, and legitimation from the fact that all of the major religious groups interpret procreation as a moral obligation necessary for fulfillment of the religious ends and purposes of marriage. The religions of Moses, of Mohammed, and of ancient Rome went so far as to interpret sterility as a mark of divine displeasure (Berkow, 1937: 17). The dominant religious groups in North America all expound definitions of parenthood couched in terms of moral and religious responsibility, and all support to varying degrees the Biblical imperative to "be fruitful and multiply."[1]

---

1 Westoff and Potvin (1967: 93) examined the fertility goals of 1,500 university women. In response to the question: "Having children is the most important function of marriage," more than half (57 per cent) agreed or strongly agreed. Presumably a number of the remaining 43 per cent would have agreed that having children was *one* of the very impor

The most explicit statement of fertility obligations is found in Roman Catholic doctrine, which asserts that the only marriage that is valid in the eyes of God is one that is a permanent union *for* the procreation of children.[2] For the devout Catholic, the alternative of voluntary childlessness can never be reconciled with religious obligations. Jewish doctrine also requires that persons marry and have children.[3] Protestant groups are less vehement in their assertions. However, although virtually all Protestant theologies endorse birth control, they do not reject the traditional definitions associating marriage with procreation. The decision as to the number of children a couple should have is generally left up to them, but, except under extreme circumstances, it is assumed that it is a privilege and a responsibility of a Christian marriage to have children and to raise them in the faith.[4]

---

tant functions of the family. Among certain religious groups there was even greater consensus. For example, among Mormons more than 65 per cent agreed with the item, and among Catholic women attending Catholic universities, the proportions agreeing with the statement ranged from 74 per cent to 85 per cent. Westoff and Potvin (1967: 93) also asked subjects to react to the more extreme statement: "If people do not intend to have children, they ought not to get married." Of the entire sample, more than a quarter (27 per cent) agreed with this extreme view. Again, agreement varied with religious commitment. Among Catholic women attending Catholic universities, the proportions agreeing with the statement ranged from 39 per cent to 61 per cent; among atheists, Jews, and Protestants attending nonsectarian universities, less than 5 per cent agree.

2 The Catholic church firmly endorses the position that a marriage contracted with the intent of being childless is not valid in the eyes of God (McFadden, 1961: 44). The intention of defeat one of the purposes of marriage—namely, that of procreation—by refusing each other the right to uncontracepted intercourse constitutes fraud, and invalidates the marriage. The marriage could also be annulled on the grounds that true consent to the marriage was never given (Karwoski, 1955: 60-61). The judgment on the validity of voluntarily childless marriages applies to non-Catholic marriages as well. "For example, a Catholic may marry a previously divorced non-Catholic who intended childlessness at that earlier marriage, which is considered, therefore, never to have taken place" (Pohlman, 1970: 7). The law further indicates that:

> . . . should both parties actually bestow on each other the right to proper marital intercourse but mutually agree to have only contractive relationships with each other, their marriage is valid but gravely sinful. Their marriage is valid because they have mutually granted true marital rights, even though they intended to violate these rights. Their marriage is sinful because they have professed a determined intention to engage in an immoral act throughout their married life" (McFadden, 1961: 45).

3 For example, traditional Jewish law explicitly states the obligation of the individual to marry and to propagate the race. "A man has performed the Biblical precept to 'be fruitful and multiply' if he has had at least a son and a daughter; yet he should seek further to augment his natural increase beyond his minimum duty" (Jakobovits, 1959: 155). Strict interpretation of the law not only would allow divorce on the grounds of childlessness, but also would in some instances require it (Falk, 1966: 117).

4 For example, in describing *A Christian View of Sex and Marriage*, Eickhoff (1966: 155) notes that:

The cognitive and evaluative components of pronatalism entail beliefs and attitudes endorsing a positive evaluation of parenthood, and a correspondingly negative evaluation of nonparenthood. Popular culture abounds with "baby commercials" which implicitly reiterate and reinforce pronatalist values (Peck, 1971). A very commonly stressed theme in fiction is the unequalled fulfillment women experience when they have children, and the desolation they experience when they do not.[5] Even in nonfiction, as for example in supposedly objective textbooks on marriage and the family, a distinct pronatalist bias is often found.[6] While it is beyond the scope of the present work to document directly the existence of pronatalism, it is relevant to point out that it does exist, and that perceptions of it are something other than a kind of paranoia on the part of childless couples. Four studies

---

> Protestant Christian advocates of planned parenthood state that the decisions are essentially those of the parents. The primary determinant is whether the planning is within a Christian framework and if it is done within the spirit of Christian love. If the decision is one that is directly to maintain selfish ends, then it is contrary to the Christian imperative of unselfish love. If a couple choose to have no children, for example, so that they can enjoy all their material advantages without sharing with anyone, even their own possible children, it would be an immoral decision. Another couple, because of fear of transmitting hereditary defects to their children might quite legitimately decide not to have children.

Eickhoff (1966: 154) also notes that: "Some mothers have no difficulty in bearing and caring for many children; others are unable to cope with the problems of more than one or two." It is noteworthy that he does not acknowledge the possibility of some couples whose mentality or economic assets are such that they are unable to cope with the problems of even one child.

5 For example, Franzwa (1974) examined short stories appearing in three women's magazines: *Ladies' Home Journal, McCall's,* and *Good Housekeeping.* She concluded that:

> Traditional women's magazine fiction is definitely pronatalist. In those stories in which the woman started out single, the ending was either an engagement or a wedding (only five of sixty five young, single females in the entire sample did not get mated by the end of the story). The stories that featured married women glorified housewifery and motherhood, and the stories which featured "spinsters" bemoaned their empty, childless lives" (Franzwa, 1974: 75).

In a similar vein, Peck (1974) looked for pronatalism in soap operas on television, and found that pregnancy was depicted as a wonderful experience which superceded all other events, and that only cold and unattractive persons were less than enthusiastic about childbearing. She also noted that television commercials tend to present idealized vignettes of family life, and so implicitly "sell" parenthood at the same time they are manifestly selling products.

6 For example, Pohlman (1968) documented ways in which family life textbooks systematically misrepresent data concerning the relationship between having children and marital adjustment. Similarly, Cox (1974) notes a number of instances in which home economics textbooks perpetuate pronatalist views by assuming that parenthood is inevitable, and by either failing to acknowledge the existence of childlessness or by treating it as problematic.

are especially relevant: Rainwater's (1960, 1965) studies of fertility norms among blue-collar workers; Griffith's (1973) study of social pressure and family size; Polit's (1978) study of stereotypes of childlessness; and Blake's (1978) survey of opinions of the consequences of childlessness.

Rainwater (1960, 1965) was one of the first persons to document the negative traits attributed to persons who do not have children. From his study of ninety-six working-class men and women, he concluded that both childlessness and the one-child family met with disapproval. "The woman who wants only one child is condemned. . . . emphatically for being a bad person, for going against nature—and the woman who wants no children is beyond the pale, she should never have married at all (Rainwater, 1960: 55). The basic fertility norm, almost axiomatic among his respondents, was that "one shouldn't have more children than one can support, *but one should have as many children as one can afford*" (Rainwater, 1965: 150). Voluntarily childless persons were stereotyped as neurotic, cold, selfish, self-centered, self-involved, and generally sick.

Griffith (1973) asked a large sample of married couples to imagine they were childless.[7] Three-quarters of them felt that parents or other close relatives would urge them to have a child, and two-thirds felt that close friends would. Nearly half felt that people would say they were selfish. About a third of the men and nearly half of the women felt that they would feel out of place when they got together with relatives or with other married persons. Griffith found that pressures to have children were generally greater for women than for men, especially among the college-educated. Contrary to what might be expected, there were no major differences in pressures to have children depending upon the couple's age or religion. Employment status did not make a substantial difference either, suggesting that working does not insulate women from pressures to become mothers.

Polit (1978) provides significant evidence supporting the contention that our society is basically pronatalistic. The positive orientation towards child-rearing and family life is reflected both in the behavior

---

[7] Giffith (1973) surveyed a national probability sample of persons living in the continental United States. Data were collected from three hundred and eleven men and four hundred and twelve women who had been married and who were from eighteen to thirty-nine years of age. The wording of the question to respondents was: "I'd like to ask you now about some things that might happen if you had different numbers of children. Some of these may really have happened to you, some may not, but please try to imagine what each would be like. First, try to imagine what it would have been like if you had been married for quite a while and did not have any children."

of individuals and in their evaluations of others.[8] She concludes that "Parenthood—and being the parent of the 'right' number of children—is the behavior expected of all competent, well-adjusted and 'normal' married adults" (Polit, 1978: 114). As would be expected Polit found that the most positive attitudes to voluntary childlessness were found among persons who were relatively young, who did not have a Catholic background, who were highly educated, and who themselves had relatively few children.

Polit also provides noteworthy evidence of the discrepancies in the social meanings attached to voluntary as opposed to involuntary childlessness. The voluntarily childless were stereotyped as: ". . . more socially undesirable, less well adjusted, less nurturant, more autonomous, more succorant, and more socially distant than individuals of other fertility statuses" (Polit, 1978: 108). Compared with persons who wanted or had children, the childless person was viewed as ". . . more independent, . . . rebellious, wholesome and good natured" (Polit, 1978: 111). For the most part, voluntarily childless men were described more favorably than their female counterparts. In contrast, the involuntary childless were actually regarded *more* favorably than were parents. "Contrary to expectations, the person who could not have children was perceived to be extremely well adjusted and socially desirable" (Polit, 1978: 108).

Blake (1978) presents data from seven Gallup Poll questions concerning the advantages and disadvantages of childlessness (Table 2). Although respondents in general tended towards pronatalist beliefs, some were notably more pronatalist than others. Favorable attitudes towards childlessness were more likely to be found among the young than among the old; among the married or widowed than among the single or divorced; among Protestants than among Catholics or Jews; among nonbelievers than among believers; and among well educated persons than among less well educated persons. A major finding of Blake's research is the surprising fact that men are significantly more likely to regard childlessness as disadvantageous than are women.

---

[8] Polit (1978) mailed questionnaires to persons in Boston to test systematically the extent to which stereotypes or socially standardized perceptions of individuals are associated with the number of progeny, and to identify the characteristics of those who hold these stereotypes. Randomly selected subjects were sent a packet of materials and instruments to be completed and returned to the experimenter. They were asked to read four different biological sketches of fictitious persons (either male or female) who represented one of six possible family-size descriptions (no children, voluntarily or involuntarily; and one, two, four, or eight children) and to complete an adjective checklist and a social distance scale for each of the four persons described in the sketches.

Table 2. Opinions Regarding the Consequences of Childlessness

Question	Percent Agreeing[1]
Advantages of Childlessness:	
It seems to me that childless couples are the ones who are having the best time in life.	14
Having a child gets in the way of the closeness and intimacy of a couple's relationship.	13
Disadvantages of Childlessness:	
People who are childless are more likely to be lonely in their older years than persons who have children.	64
Childless couples are more likely to lead empty lives than couples with children.	44
If you have never had children, you are more likely to have a hard time financially when you are older.	15
Childless marriages are more likely to end in divorce than are marriages where there are children.	34
A woman is likely to feel unfulfilled unless she becomes a mother.	45

Source: Blake (1978)

Gallup poll questions asked of a random sample of 1,600 Americans in February, 1977.

This would seem to reflect the fact that the opportunity costs in childbearing still impinge more heavily on women than on men.

The general ambience in favor of reproduction is of little consequence unless it is translated into actions, and unless those actions then have undesirable consequences for the persons directly involved, and perhaps for society in general. The political protestations against pronatalism are not against the encouragement of reproduction for *most* persons, but against the perceived insistence of reproduction for *all* persons. Thus, Hollingworth (1916-1917) notes, and protests, not all devices encouraging motherhood, but those "impelling" women to have children. Half a century later, Blake (1973) is concerned not with pronatalism as such but with that which is "coercive." Russo (1976) laments the existence of a "motherhood mandate" for all women.

For some childless couples, manifest disapproval of their chose lifestyle is undoubtedly a cause of considerable distress. In a unknown number of cases, such harrassment leads to tensions ar recriminations which ultimately break up the marriage. In anothe unknown number of cases, the pronatalistic pressures do indee become coercive in that they actually lead couples to have childre primarily to gain or regain social approval and acceptability, rathe than for other motives and anticipated benefits (Rainwater, 1965: 14 Flapan, 1969: 409).[9] It is not known to what extent pronatalist pressure intended to encourage childbearing actually does so, or wh the outcomes of acting on such motivations are likely to be. Even if pr natalistic pressure is resisted, its existence may be injurious to pe sons remaining childless. It is ironic that while the study of childle couples does document clearly the existence of social pressure i tended to persuade people to have children, it simultaneous documents the fact that, for from five to ten per cent of the populatio such efforts are not successful.

Pluralistic Ignorance

Many qualitative aspects of family life in our society are considere both secret and private, with the result that people tend to be unawa of what is happening in their neighbors' marriages, and thus a unable to compare them to their own. This pluralistic ignorance especially significant for the voluntarily childless. The tabo associated with challenging the parenthood mystique are so strong a so pervasive that many childless couples, especially older ones, do n express their deviant opinions and do not expect others to share the Deliberate childlessness has existed for decades, but public expressi of such attitudes is only just beginning to emerge. As a result, almost a of the childless couples we talked with reported that, at the time th they had made their decision not to have children, there was almost social support for being childless. In addition, once the decision ha been made, they found only minimum social support from others. In th absence of social support, how then were they able to go ahead wi their unusual decision, and to feel comfortable doing so?

---

[9] For example, Pohlman (1970: 9) points out the possibility that:

> If it becomes common knowledge in the culture that the experts think childlessness and mala justment are often associated, this knowledge itself becomes part of the cultural pressu toward parenthood and may drive people who did not want children to have them anyway that they will not be labelled as disturbed.

Among the persons we talked with, by far the most important source of support was their husband or wife. In the absence of a peer group, childless persons may still have the minimal requirements for the maintenance of a comfortable worldview, namely a *reference group of one*, which, under intimate conditions in a close marriage, may serve the function as well as a larger unit. It has often been noted that married couples tend to form a subculture of their own: among the voluntarily childless husbands and wives studied, their mates provided the main—if not the only—source of consensual validation.

Faced with the undeniable fact that childlessness is statistically unusual, and therefore is inevitably going to be considered somewhat deviant, the childless have two choices of basic coping strategies: the strategy of rejection-of-difference and the strategy of acceptance-of-difference (Kirk, 1964). In coping by rejection-of-difference, the childless assert that, except for the incidental fact of not having had children, they are just like other people. In coping by acceptance-of-difference, the childless acknowledge or occasionally even accentuate their differences from parents but define those differences in positive, or at least neutral, terms. Whatever strategy the childless select, to feel comfortable with not having children, they need reassurance in answering two essentially unanswerable questions: first, am I really sure this is what I want; and second, am I really sure this is what I will *always* want?

Deviance Disavowal

Although the voluntarily childless are generally considered to be a deviant group, and hence to be systematically different from "normal" people, some childless persons systematically disavow the legitimacy of that deviant status. They insist, in effect, that except for the incidental fact of happening not to have children, they are "really" just like everyone else. The psychology involved in denial-of-difference is such that the childless state is defined as being as normal as possible. For example, one woman reported that when someone asked her, as they frequently did: "When are you going to start a family?" she always replied: "But I have started one. My husband and I started one when we got married." For many couples who retain familistic values while rejecting children, it is important to define a married couple as constituting a family in their own right. The disavowal of deviance typically takes at least two forms. The most obvious is to deny that present childlessness is an indicator of permanent childlessness, and thereby to claim the more acceptable status of someone who is merely postponing parenthood rather than foregoing it. A second form of deviance disavowal is to acknowledge that one is indeed childless but to deny that being childless necessarily implies the negative stereotype usually associated with it.

The symbolic import of adoption

A recurrent theme with many voluntarily childless couples was the possibility of eventually adopting a child. When such couples were questioned closely, however, it became apparent that in spite of their positive verbalizations, it was very unlikely that they would ever actually adopt a child. Adoption was discussed in general terms, but little serious thought was given actually to procuring a child by this means. For example, most couples who mentioned adoption had not considered even such elementary questions as whether they would prefer a boy or a girl, or whether they would prefer an infant or an older child. With few exceptions, the couple had not made even preliminary inquiries regarding the legal processes involved in adoption. Those few who had made some effort at least to contact a child placement agency had failed to follow through on their initial contact. None had investigated the issue thoroughly enough to have considered the possibility that, even if they should decide to adopt, a suitable child might not be immediately available to them.

For voluntarily childless couples, the significance of adoption appears to lie not in its feasibility as a pragmatic alternative but in its symbolic value. This symbolic importance is twofold: the reaffirmation of normalcy, and the avoidance of irreversible decisions. A willingness to consider adoption as a possibility communicates to one's self and to others that in spite of being voluntarily childless, one is still a "normal" and "well-adjusted" person who does like children and who is willing to assume the responsibility of parenthood. It is an effective mechanism for denying the possibility of considerable psychological differences between parents and nonparents, and legitimates the claim of the childless to be just like parents in a number of important respects.

The possibility of adoption at a later date is also of symbolic value in that it prevents the voluntarily childless from being committed to an irreversible state. One of the problems of opting for a postponement model is that eventually one must confront the fact the childbirth cannot be postponed indefinitely. The solution to this dilemma is to include the possibility of adoption as a satisfactory "out" should one be needed. While one may be sure that one does not want a child *now*, one cannot be equally sure of not wanting a child *ever*. The hypothetical possibility of adoption is comforting when faced with the important but unanswerable question of how one will feel about being childless in old age.

The denial of stereotypes

Even if a couple acknowledge that they are going to be permanently childless, they can still follow the strategy of rejection-of-difference if they deny that any socially devalued traits are associated with that status. By describing the attributes imputed to the childless as a "stereotype," one conveys the implicit connotation that the profile is somehow untrue. A valid stereotype is an oxymoron. Unfortunately, attempts to disavow a deviant identity by denying that the childless are stereotypically different from parents are usually ineffective. The negative image of childlessness is pervasive, and those individuals who do counter it may, at best, succeed in convincing some persons that they are exceptions to the rule. As one disgruntled husband put it: "Sure, I convince them that I'm a regular guy. All that means is they can say 'Some of my best friends are childless!' " Such contingencies, however, do not prevent some childless persons from trying to convey as positive an image as possible. Two aspects of the stereotype which are particularly sensitive are their assumed selfishness and their assumed dislike of children.

A recurrent component of the stereotypic view of the childless is that they are selfish. Since all persons are to some extent self-centered, and since this adjective is almost impossible to define, this trait is especially difficult to descredit convincingly. In trying to deny its legitimacy, childless persons may deliberately go out of their way to put their best altruistic foot forward. In trying to offset this presumed negative image, they cast about for good works which will meet with approval. For example, one couple said that any time they get criticism about how "selfish" they are and how much money they are saving by not having their own children, they refer to the hundreds of dollars they spend each year for orphans in Africa and Asia. If time and patience permit, they pull out their album of photographs, as they did for us, of the children they have "adopted" financially. Similarly, a young executive believed it prudent to give excessively to welfare drives. He explained:

> I always make a point of giving big to the United Appeal when they come around at the office. The guy next to me has six kids—he shrugs and smiles

> and says "Hell, they should be giving to me," and that's all there is to it. But I know if I didn't give, they'd make a big deal out of it, so I shell out even though I don't believe such charity does much good.

A second stereotypic attribute which many childless persons find offensive is the allegation that they do not have children because they hate kids. In the interviews, the childless were at some point asked directly: do you like children? Virtually all respondents found this question upsetting. About half of the men and women replied in the affirmative and expressed varying degrees of indignation that we had the nerve to ask such a question. The remaining half were manifestly uncomfortable and evasive, and eventually but reluctantly admitted that, in fact, they did not like children very much. Apparently, not wanting to have children of one's own is much less of a social sin than not liking children in general. Unfortunately, other than by becoming a parent, it is very difficult to "prove" to another's satisfaction that one does truly like kids. Persons who work with children, such as school teachers, had a ready out, although it was not obvious to us that such professional child-care workers were necessarily especially fond of their charges. One strategy widely used was to volunteer to work with children's groups. Thus, one husband spent a number of evenings coaching Little League because, he reported, he "got sick and tired of people carping on the idea that the stock market was more important to me than a family."

Protestations that one does, in fact, like children can sometimes backfire in terms of the social message which is conveyed. Thus, one young husband reported:

> For a few years I went out of my way to show how much I loved kids and that my not wanting my own had nothing to do with my enjoyment in playing on the floor with a three-year-old. But the response I got was: "See what a wonderful father you would make!"

On the issue of the intrinsic attractiveness and appeal of children, persons who deliberately have not had them are soon made aware that in order to be acceptable, they must be *more* conforming to the dominant norms than persons with children. Although persons can complain loudly about the inadequacies of children and the thanklessness of parenthood, the childless learn very quickly that voicing similar sentiments tends to reinforce the notion that they hate children under any circumstances. Goffman suggests that with stigmatized persons: ". . . we may perceive his defensive response to his situation as a direct expression of his defect . . ." (Goffman, 1963: 6). When the voluntarily childless express dislike of children, or of disinterest in them, this justification of their position is taken as further evidence of their abnormality. For the stigmatized, ". . . minor failings, or incidental impropriety may . . . be interpreted as a direct expression of his stigmatized differentness" (Goffman, 1963: 15). The voluntarily childless must be very careful not to express even minor reactions of annoyance or impatience with children, although these are in reality quite common among all adults. When articles such as "Children Are a Waste of Time" (Balchin, 1965) are published, they are inevitably prefaced by a statement of the large number of children the author himself has. As a parent, he is allowed to express opinions which would be taboo for the nonparent. Similarly, several couples noted how they go out of their way to appear delighted when friends tell them they are pregnant. A school teacher in his mid-thirties stated:

> Friends and acquaintances who tell us they are pregnant seem almost apologetic about it. Hell, if they're happy, I'm happy. But what I find myself doing is acting overly happy and effusive, just in case they *think* I am not happy for them.

Rejecting the Rejectors: The Superiority of the Childfree

Persons who follow the strategy of acceptance-of-difference readily admit that being childless is different from being a parent: these differences, however, are defined as advantages. The deviance avowal of such couples involves the development of a worldview which is essentially the obverse of the parenthood mystique, and which defines having children in negative rather than in positive terms. Although outnumbered twenty to one, they are able to maintain a counter-ideology which contradicts and contravenes many of the principles around which other married couples organize their lives. This worldview successfully protects the childless against a negative self-image, and serves to neutralize, or at least to minimize, social pressures toward parenthood.

A preliminary step in advocating the superiority of being childfree is to present deliberate childlessness as an "alternative lifestyle." This term, which sounds neutral, is actually a legitimating description, implying free choice after the rejection of other less rational alternatives.

By implication, this option is as good as or better than other optic (Marciano, 1978: 108). The processes involved in defending a tinatalist ideologies in a pronatalist world are essentially similar those employed by other minority groups who try to maintain a devia belief system which will neutralize the disapproval of others.[10] Defe sive strategies include, among other things, selective perception of t consequences of parenthood, the use of a pejorative vocabulary, the terpretation of disapproval of envy, and the structuring of "test" situ tions so as to reaffirm commitment.

Selective perception of parenthood

> The joys of parents are secret, and so are their griefs and fears; they c not utter the one, nor will they utter the other. Children sweeten labors, b they make misfortunes more bitter; they increase the cares of life, but th mitigate the remembrance of death (Bacon, 1854).

If the childless do acknowledge that they are different from other pe ple, it then behooves them to define those differences as advantag The worldview of the childless, which defines having children negative rather than in positive terms, can be readily formulate maintained, and bolstered by the careful selection of supporti "evidence" and the equally careful denial of contradictory data. T processes of selective perception are especially apparent regarding topic like parenthood, which is the subject for so much cultural a bivalence, and for which the criteria for assessing almost any aspe are very subjective and difficult to measure. In evaluating the con quences of marriage, one has at least a recognized "failure" catego that of divorce or separation. How does one formulate a comparab category for "failure" regarding the consequences of parenthood? the absence of standard criteria, both parents and nonparents are fr to select the ones that are most compatible with their own belie Selective attention to the consequences of parenthood enables t childless to document numerous negative sequelae of childbearing.

If one starts with the premise that "most people who have childr think it was a good decision," one can select from an endless array testimonials on the joys of parenthood. Any selection of contempora

---

[10] For example, Simmons (1964) described similar processes among Espers, a grou religious mystics. Relevant discussions are presented by Turner (1972) and by P (1975). For a detailed review of how deviants can disavow deviance by "rejecting rejectors" or by various accounts and evasions, see Rogers and Buffalo's (1974) disc sion of models of "fighting back" against deviant levels.

women's magazines, like *Good Housekeeping, Redbook, McCalls*, or *Woman's Day*, would produce a plethora of articles and stories to that effect. Conversely, if one starts with the premise that "if people really admitted the truth, they would agree that children are more often a nuisance than a pleasure to their parents," one can also select equally convincing evidence. There is a minority of women whose "murmur of maternal lamentation" is public and continous. For every poetic Mother's Day-type tribute to the sustaining influence of the "hand that rocks the cradle," there is a lament on the number of frustrated and frustrating unhappy mothers, whose indifference or hostility leaves lifelong scars on their offspring. "There is already a very strong cultural basis for the rejection of childrearing" (Lott, 1973: 575). To support their position, all the voluntarily childless have to do is to concentrate on the evidence concerning parents who are unloving and unloved.

The childless believe that many parents either conceived accidentally, or succumbed against their better judgment to the general cultural press towards parenthood. They tend to dwell on the unfortunate repercussions of unplanned and unwanted pregnancies, and rejected and rejecting mothers. Moreover, they tend to perceive that whether or not parents initially wanted children, they obtain little gratification from them. The physical and psychological costs of children are enumerated to illustrate that children are emotionally and financially draining, and generally constitute "bad investments" in the light of probable future returns. In this vein, we were struck by the number of respondents who spontaneously commented at some length on the now infamous Ann Landers survey. In response to the question: "If you had your life to do over again, would you have children?" 70 per cent of readers who wrote to Ann Landers said, "No."[11] Since doubts about lifelong satisfaction with childlessness are difficult to quell, such "evidence" is readily garnered to support the contention that having children is not necessarily satisfactory, either.

Selective perception also colors the interpretation of the ways in which parents interact with their children, and the things they say to them and about them. Even the most devoted and enthusiastic parent

[11] Landers received over 10,000 responses to her query, 80 per cent of which were from women. She reports four categories of negative responses: young persons concerned with global problems of war and overpopulation; parents who felt children had ruined their marriages; older parents who felt children had required too much sacrifice for too little return; and parents with teenagers in trouble. Although the survey is based on a self-selected sample and is therefore inconclusive, the large numbers of participants make it convincing "evidence" for persons wanting to believe it (Landers, 1976).

occasionally gets tired, or resentful, or angry. The task of child-rearing is difficult. Wanting to do it may make it easier, but even the most positive attitudes cannot make it easy. Although most parents undoubtedly love their children, at the same time they are continually faced with the high cost of that loving.

> The truth is—as every parent knows—that rearing children is probably the hardest, and most thankless, job in the world. No intelligent father or mother would deny that it is *exciting*, as well as *interesting*, but to call it "fun" is a serious error . . . it involves tremendous responsibility; it takes all the ability one has (and more); and once you have begun you can't quit when you feel like it (LeMasters, 1970: 18).

When the childless observe parents being hostile toward their children, or expressing the anger and resentment they inevitably feel occasionally, they conclude that, just as they suspected all along, parents do not "really" want or love their children, but are making the best of a bad situation because of social pressure to be responsible and respectable. One of the ways of sanctioning voluntary childlessness is to deny the integrity of the belief system and to assume that, no matter what the childless couple says or does, deep down they "really" want to be parents like everyone else. The childless use the same kind of reasoning in denying the rewarding aspects of parenthood by assuming that parents had children first and learned to put up with them second, and that deep down they "really" would prefer to be childless. One couple, for example, share an "inside joke" about public displays of parental frustrations. When they observe a scene in which a child is throwing a tantrum or being a general pest, one turns to the other and says, "The joys of parenthood." This ritual seizes on particularly negative parental experiences, and so reaffirms the couple's commitment to a childless lifestyle.

The importance of selective attention in terms of the parent-child relationship is aptly illustrated by the extreme example of child abuse and neglect. Some deliberately childless persons, in discussing the consequences of having children, dwell excessively on the specter of the battered-child syndrome, and on other facets of maleficent parent-child interactions. During the past decade, there has been increasing publicity concerning child abuse. Some childless persons focus on this evidence, and interpret it as a direct consequence of coercive pro-natalism, which forced persons who did not want to have children to have them anyway, with disastrous results. In their opinion, for every parent who actually beats his child seriously enough to make the newspapers, there are a number of others who abuse them in less visible ways, and many others who feel like beating them, but do not acually do so.

The tendency for childless persons to zero in on evidence concerning child-beating serves to support their worldview in at least two ways. First, avoiding children is partly justified by the implication that the dislike of children is more common than is usually supposed, and that he preference for childlessness is therefore not dramatically deviant. Although child abuse and neglect may well be more ubiquitous than the official figures suggest, the childless often choose to ignore the fact hat most children are reasonably well cared for, even if they were not planned or wanted, and even if they are not especially loved. Second, focused concern on child abuse serves to justify childlessness in terms of a lesser-of-two-evils model. Even if deliberately not having children may have some undesirable consequences, they are clearly not as undesirable as forcing men and women to have children whom they ater abuse or neglect. Several persons who discussed these concerns openly acknowledged that, under different circumstances, they could imagine themselves as child-abusers. Others implied that such a cenario had occurred to them. For example, one wife made this point explicitly:

> There'd be a lot less child beating if people sat down and thought about it before they went ahead and had babies. Someone sticking a kid's hand on a stove because they ran out of patience, it makes me sick. There should be some kind of course where you could find out if you're suited to have children. I know I'm not, I just get terribly irritated when I'm around children.

The power of pejorative

Having focused attention on problematic aspects of pregnancy and parenthood, the next step in defending the superiority of childlessness is to reinterpret these aspects in as negative a way as possible. If, as has been suggested, people tend to stereotype the childless, there can be little doubt that the childless also stereotype parents in general, and housewives and mothers in particular. Their expressions of superiority onsist of three related themes: one, that parenthood does not reflect ny special talent; two, that parenthood precludes other activities; and three, that parenthood is itself of minimal significance. These themes re indirectly conveyed through the use of a pejorative vocabulary.

The idea that parenthood does not reflect any special talent is emphasized by excessive reference to the biological aspects of it. For example, one woman referred to the psychological satisfactions of pregnancy as just as much "bovine belly-watching," and another referred to pregnancy as a "festering uterus." The use of terms usually employed with reference to animals is intended to be degrading. For example, the childless may refer to the process of giving birth as "whelping," or "folding," or even "hatching." A woman indiscreet enough to have more than one child may be called a "breeder," and her offspring may be referred to as a "litter" or a "brood." Closely spaced pregnancies often evoke a reference to persons who "breed like bunnies."

The idea that parenthood precludes other activities is reinforced by reference to women who are "*merely* baby machines." Thus, one wife expressed her reluctance to be "*just* an incubator," and another railed against women who were "*only* brood mares." Parenthood is also made less attractive when it is viewed as not involving choice. There were, therefore, many references to the accidental nature of pregnancies which occur to "fertile Myrtles," "planned parenthood flunk-outs," and even "recidivists."

The women who become special targets for disdain are those who elect to stay home as full-time mothers, in which case they may be called "frustrated hausfraus," or "the diaper set," and are assumed to be concerned only with "prams, pablum and poo-poo." Almost any housewife, but especially one who takes her occupation seriously, is designated as a "typical Susy Homemaker." If women are preoccupied with child-care and, worse, discuss it and debate the advantages of different methods, they are in danger of being considered "militant mamas," and their children are facetiously referred to as "protegés."

Disapproval into Envy: a Reinterpretation

Some childless persons assemble a worldview of the consequences of parenthood which allows them to believe that persons who react to them with apparent scorn, hostility or pity are, in fact, secretly jealous of the freedom and other advantages which the childless enjoy. The redefinition of disapproval into envy allows the childless to disregard the advice offered to them by parents, and to assign their motivations not to an unselfish concern for the best interests of the childless, but to a sense of disinterested punitiveness. Thus, one childless wife reflected:

> I think almost half of the people who raise the question of not having children, and who try to pressure us one way or another, are just sort of jealous, although they won't admit it right out. I mean, there they are, struggling to pay mortgages, and we are planning a trip to Europe. Or we just take off for the weekend if we feel like it with no fixed plan, or nothing special on. And they—I know married men who have the whole weekend mapped out with all the chores they must do. And the wives are worse. Even if they could get a babysitter, they would be too busy with stuff to do to go, or too tired to want to, or they can't afford it. So they just trudge along, and then there we are flitting about and having fun, and it doesn't seem fair. And they're the ones who keep harping on what we're missing by not having kids. Huh! They say we're selfish, but what they mean is that they want us to be in the same situation they're in.

A husband indicated that apparent envy and jealousy of childless couples are sometimes expressed quite openly:

> One guy said to me right out, as a joke, "What right have you to the joys of marriage without the responsibility and misery?" I think there was more truth to that than he was letting on, it was more than a joke on him.

LeMasters (1970: 19) draws an analogy between parenthood and military service.

> Often parents refer to married couples who have no children as draft-dodgers. The sentiment is similar to that which veterans of the armed forces have towards able-bodied men who somehow escaped military service in the last war. The veteran feels that military service is a rough experience but one that has to be endured for the sake of the country: his feeling toward men who did not have this experience is ambivalent: in a sense he resents their escaping what he had to go through, but in another sense he recognizes that there may have been valid reasons why they were not in the armed forces. Parents are also ambivalent towards nonparents: since children represent the future of the society, it is reasonable to expect that all of us would make some contribution to that future, and that of course nonparents have not done, but there is also a sense in which parents envy the nonparents their freedom, their less strenuous way of life, their lack of responsibility for another human being's welfare.

To pursue the analogy, if parents view the childless as "draft dodgers," the childless tend to believe that most parents are "draftees" or even "conscripts" who did not volunteer for parental duty, but who were pressed into service just the same. Under these circumstances, it seems plausible that parents would indeed envy the childless.

The psychology of reinterpreting disapproval as envy is aptly conveyed by Ann Landers' sarcastic comment on childlessness:

> There is nothing sadder than a childless couple. It is heart-breaking to see them stretched out, relaxing around the swimming pool, sun-tanned and miserable, trotting off to Europe like lonesome fools. What an empty life! Nothing but money to spend and time to enjoy it.
>
> They miss all the fun of doing without for the children's sake. How selfish they become, buying what they want and doing as they please. Everyone should have children. No one should be allowed to escape the rewarding experiences that accompany every stage of parenthood. Those all-night vigils, the coughing spells, drunken babysitters, saturated mattresses, midnight rushes to the hospital, separating little brothers and sisters when they try to kill each other.
>
> I pity the couple without children to brighten the cocktail hour. The little darlings have a way of brushing the martini from your hand and massaging the potato chips into the rugs. And what fun when they fight you for the olive! The little scuffles in the presence of guests make a well-rounded life. And an early breakdown.
>
> The real satisfactions come later. Those thoughtful discussions when the report card reveals your prodigy is one step below a nitwit. Then the hours of arguing. You try to pin it on his side of the family. He tries to pin it on your side of the family.
>
> But children are worth it all. The warm feeling the first time you take the boy hunting. He didn't mean to shoot you in the leg. Remember how he cried? He was so disappointed when you weren't a deer. The limp is with you to this day.
>
> Nothing builds character like practising self-control. And what better practice than watching the warm smile of a lad with the sun glittering on $500 worth of dental braces—ruined by peanut brittle.
>
> The childless couple live in a vacuum. They try to fill the lonesome hours with golf, bridge, trips, civic affairs. Sometimes the tranquility and extra money is enough to drive you crazy.
>
> All you have to do is look at these empty, unfilled shells to see what the years have done to them. He looks boyish, unlined and rested. She is slim, well-groomed and youthful. It isn't natural. If they had kids like the rest of us they'd be beat-up, gray, wrinkled and nervous wrecks too.

This ironic note conveys very well the feelings of many of our respondents, and each time the column is reprinted, they make a point of clipping it.

There is no concrete evidence as to whether parents actually do or do not envy the childless their atypical lifestyle. Very little work, theoretical or otherwise, has been done concerning the phenomena of envy and jealousy. One exception is the work of Ranulf (1964), who provides a brief theory of resentment. Ranulf notes that for the middle class, commitment to a middle-class morality of hard work and restraint is in fact necessary for the maintence of a middle-class way of life. He then suggests that resentment, and the disinterested punitiveness associated with it, are most likely to occur when individuals are "forced, either by the material conditions or by the moral rigorists among whom they are living" to follow the traditional morality, and when they "have generally felt their lives to be unsatisfactory or even miserable."

> The disinterested tendency to inflict punishment is a distinctive characteristic of . . . a social class living under conditions which force its members to an extraordinarily high degree of self-restraint and subject them to much frustration of natural desires.

Ranulf is concerned with the resentment by the middle class of others in different strata of society, but his analysis is equally applicable to any group forced to follow a moralistic position while observing other less moral groups reaping a disproportionate amount of social gains. Such an extreme description does not usually apply to voluntary parents who chose to have children and who are gratified by them, but it may apply to those who became parents against their wishes or their better judgment, and who are now constrained by their parental obligations to sacrifice many of their "natural desires" for the sake of supporting, supervising and guiding their offspring. Be that as it may, it is important for childless couples to *believe* such is the case. Reinterpreting disapproval as envy appears to be an important mechanism in maintaining a worldview supporting deliberate childlessness.

Testing Commitment: The Borrowed Baby Syndrome

In spite of selective attention to the negative consequenes of parenthood, and in spite of systematic reinterpretation of disapproving responses as envious responses, childless couples may still experience some doubts as to the rightness of their decision. When parents challenge them with the assertion that "if you actually had children, you would feel different," they pose a real dilemma. Such an assertion is, of course, plausible. The only conclusive way to know what one's reactions to parenthood would be is actually to have a child, a somewhat drastic course given the irreversibility of the decision. Couples who are ambivalent towards parenthood sometimes contrive to "test" their commitment to childlessness by borrowing a baby and temporarily assuming parenthood roles. The strategy of trial parenthood is ostensibly intended to approximate the parenthood experience, and therefore to provide additional data on the pros and cons of having children. For example, with these ends in mind, one young husband and his wife offered to baby-sit with a friend's three-year-old so they could attend an out-of-town wedding. He reported:

> You know the ad: "Try it, you'll like it." Well, we tried it. God, it was the longest weekend of my life. The kid cried half the first night, the neighbors must have thought we were sticking pins in him. Then, I was trying to give him a bath and he knocked over the shampoo, a glass bottle, and there was glass all over. Everything was slippery and he slipped and cut his knee and was crying again. The place was a swamp. In fact, by Sunday night the whole apartment was a shambles and Joan and I were nervous wrecks. I suppose you get used to it or something, but it'll be a while before we volunteer for that again.

"Experiments" such as this one are almost certain to fail, in that unintentionally they are "fixed" in such a way that the interlude is unlikely to be a gratifying experience. Three factors contribute to the likelihood of a negative outcome.

First, when childless couples borrow a child for a weekend, they tend to do so not only in response to their own interests and inclinations but also in response to some special circumstances in the child's home. One of the parents may be writing an important examination, or feeling ill, or responding to a death in the family. The childless offer free baby-sitting to help out with a family crisis, therby combining their own interests with the opportunity to assist their friends at a time when assistance is most needed. The problem with this very rational approach is that at the time of a family crisis of whatever nature, even a very young child is often aware that something is wrong. This stress is aggravated by a disruption of routine, and by taking the child out of its familiar surroundings and placing it in a new, and hence often threatening, environment. In these circumstances, even a placid and obedient child may be agitated and disobedient. The strange and stressful circumstances of the visit insure that caring for the child will be more difficult than usual and that the child itself will be less lovable than usual.

A second impediment to the successful evaluation of trial parenting is the simple factor of time. From what little we know of "parenthood as crisis" (LeMasters, 1957a; Jacoby, 1969; Hobbs, 1968; Russell, 1974), it is apparent that for most couples it is a transitory crisis, and that after a period of time, the adjustment of the husband and wife to the child, and to their new relationship with each other, improves. The childless who borrow children for an evening or a weekend are trying to make in a few hours or days the kind of adjustment other couples may take weeks or even months to achieve.

A third aspect of the failure of trial parenting is the physical environment in which it occurs. Typically, when childless couples borrow a child for a weekend, they move him or her into their own home. The homes of the childless are designed for the comfort of adults. Consequently, they are not particularly suitable to the comfort and safety of children. There are stairs to fall down, sharp corners to bump into, poisonous and toxic substances left on low shelves, and many other hazards. Compared with his own home, the child is in more danger of being hurt, and to insure that that does not happen, he requires much more anxious supervision and attention than does the child with access to a non-hazardous playroom.

Children in a house are trouble not only in terms of their own danger, but also in terms of how much they disrupt and destroy adult environments. Persons with children tend to "child-proof" their homes gradually over a period of years, in stages roughly concomitant with the growing child's increasing proclivity for exploration and destruction. When a borrowed baby is brought home, the house has not been "child-proofed," or has been altered in only a cursory manner over a few days. The surfaces are not stain-proof and washable, the scattered objects are neither unbreakable nor out of reach, and the areas of seclusion in the home (such as the master bedroom or the study) have not been adequately closed off from childish interference. Consequently, children are much more trouble and bother in the childless couple's home than in their own.

The experiment of borrowing a friend's child and playing parents, under circumstances in which the experience is almost certain to be unpleasant, does much to assuage a childless couple's doubts about whether or not they are doing the right thing in avoiding parenthood. Such experiments may be repeated every few years as doubts arise, usually with consistent results.

Chapter Seven: COPING WITH PRONATALISM

> An odd feature of the aura of sentiment surrounding marriage and parenthood is that one who enters either state immediately joins the great conspiracy to induce others to take the plunge . . . Married persons . . . try to get their friends married, and parents extol the joys of parenthood (Waller and Hill, 1951: 388).

The reactions of outsiders to childless couples is seldom one of indifference or of disinterested curiousity. If childless persons can manage to defend their worldview as a valid alternative lifestyle, and to satisfy themselves as to its desirability, they can successfully defend themselves against the cognitive component of pronatalism, which predicts that childlessness will lead to unpleasant consequences, and against the evaluative component, which views it in unfavorable terms. However, they may still be faced with behavioral consequences, in that many persons presume to sanction the childless for their actions. The present chapter is concerned with the way the childless protect themselves against unpleasant encounters. Their vulnerability varies according to the stage of the life cycle, and to the kind of sanction which is encountered. Coping with sanctions tends to follow two basic patterns: either taking evasive action to avoid confrontations, or endorsing an emergent counter-culture to justify the childfree alternative.

Pronatalist Pressure: Life Cycle Effects

The amount of social pressure exerted on childless couples, and the amount of discomfort they experience as a result, depend on two factors: the duration of their marriage and the stage of their commitment to permanent childlessness.

Childlessness is, of course, not always a disapproved state. Couples are rewarded, not punished, for remaining childless for the first several months of marriage, thereby negating the possibility that they were "forced" to get married. After the minimum of nine months has passed, there is a short period of time when the young couple is excused from not assuming all of their responsibilities, or are perceived as having had intercourse for too short a period of time to guarantee conception. The definition of how long childbearing may be postponed within conventional expectations is difficult to determine, and apparently varies considerably from one group to another. In most groups, the first two years constitutes an acceptable period of time.[1] After the second year, the pressure gradually but continually increases, reaching a peak during the fourth and fifth years of marriage. However, once a couple have been married for six or seven years, there appears to be some diminution of negative responses to them. Several factors figure in this change: the increased ability of the childless to cope with negative and hostile responses, making the social pressures of the early years only seem more intense in retrospect; the increased ability of the childless to avoid those who consistently sanction them; and an actual change in the behavior of others. After six or seven years, family and friends may give up the attempt to persuade the reluctant couple to procreate or to adopt, and resign themselves to the fact that their intervention is ineffective.

Childless persons, especially men, who were early articulators, and who decided before marriage never to have children, are the least vulnerable to pronatalistic pressure. Other persons, however, who

---

[1] It is noteworthy that it is apparently the length of marriage, rather than the age of the wife, that is of primary importance in childless couples' being defined as deviant. Thus, one wife reported that when she wanted to get married when she was only seventeen, she met with considerable resistance and disapproval from her parents and others who insisted she was "too young" and should wait until she was at least twenty. She went ahead with her marriage plans, but was somewhat bewildered when, two years later at age nineteen, the same people who would have said she was "too young" to assume the responsibilities of marriage were then urging her to assume the responsibilities of motherhood as well.

come to be childless through a series of postponements, are more vulnerable at some times than at others. During the first years, when childbearing is being postponed for a definite period of time, childlessness is relatively easy to explain, and social pressure to have children is relatively easy to resist. However, during the stage where the couple are debating the pros and cons of parenthood, and coming to grips with the interpersonal, political, and philosophical implications of being childless by choice, they are easily provoked by critics of their lifestyle. It is a period in which, in many ways, they are attempting to convince themselves as well as others that the choice they made regarding parenthood was a correct one. Women are more affected by pronatalistic pressures than are men, and those most vulnerable are women who have been married four or five years and who are in the process of debating whether or not to have a child. This vulnerability is accentuated if these two circumstances coincide with the wife's approaching her thirtieth birthday, generally perceived as a now-or-never point for childbearing.

Once couples have settled down to a firm commitment never to have children, they often have little concern for others' evaluations, positive or negative. At this point the couple have truly accepted the fact that they will never have children, and that they will always be viewed as a little odd by others as a result. Our discussion of the strategies which couples use to combat pronatalism, and defend their variant lifestyle, is primarily germane to the initial stages of adjustment to voluntary childlessness, though some strategies may be used on occasion for the rest of their lives.

Accounting for Childlessness

An ubiquitous manifestation of pronatalist pressure is the expectation that childless persons provide acceptable accounts of their behavior, in the form of excuses, explanations, or justification (Scott and Lyman, 1968). One of the problems confronted by childless couples is that even casual acquaintances show little reluctance in making very personal inquiries about their deviant status. Goffman (1963: 16) notes that ". . . the stigmatized individual is a person who can be approached by strangers at will, providing only that they are sympathetic to the plight of persons of his kind." In the same way that relative strangers will ask a single woman, "Why isn't a nice girl like you married?" friends and associates who would not dream of inquiring, "How's your sex life these days?" will feel quite free in asking "Hey, how come you don't have any kids?" Persons who opt for a childfree marriage are continually being asked to explain why they do not want children. Friends and relatives feel that they have a right to know; doctors and amateur psychiatrists hope to be able to help with the "problem," and casual acquaintances are frankly curious. Whether such queries are direct or indirect, they tend to make the childless resentful, defensive, uncomfortable and inarticulate.

The childless are not expected to be offended by the interest of outsiders in their behavior. In fact, however, childless persons typically resent being asked to explain their decision at all. It seems basically unfair that couples who opt to have children are never required to justify either their right to this alternative or their preference for it. The childless are put on the defensive when the request for information is seen as a thinly veiled criticism implying that one ought to want children, and that there is something wrong if one does not. The pervasiveness of the parenthood mystique is such that even those most committed to childlessness may occasionally have some doubts as to the wisdom and normalcy of their decision. The more such doubts are raised to the level of consciousness, the more defensive the childless become.

Defensive or not, the childless find themselves in an uncomfortable position when asked to defend the unpopular views of a small and deviant minority. Since most of the inquisitors are themselves parents, attempts to explain a disinclination to childbearing can be, and often are, interpreted as personal attacks on the others' child-centered lifestyle, leading to an unintentional but rapid escalation of hostilities. Typically, the childless feel that people will not understand their rejection of childbearing as a major life goal, and that attempts to explain and justify themselves will only lead to further estrangement.

When childless persons are required to explain their unusual behavior, they have two problems in formulating accounts: first, to offer an explanation which is credible as the "real" reason; and second, to find an explanation which is more or less socially acceptable. Thus, if a couple can explain that, although they do dearly love children, they are unable to have them because of the wife's heart condition, or because of an unfortunate genetic background, the couple can in varying degrees be defined as unfortunate, and therefore, a suitable object for pity or at least sympathy. However, if the reasons given concern career interests, freedom, lack of responsibility, or, worst of all, materialistic comfort, the character is blemished, and the couple are almost certain to be considered selfish.

Fear of childbirth *per se* is not generally considered a legitimate motive for avoiding it. Since medical advances have made death in childbirth very rare, and even serious complications very unlikely, fear tends to be discarded as a valid reason.[2] Similarly, although some persons may in fact avoid having children because of excessive concern with population pressures,[3] such accounts are not usually given much credibility. Devotees of the Zero Population Growth movement find it nearly impossible to convince anyone not committed to the same ideology that the "real" reason they do not intend to have children is that they are genuinely alarmed by the population explosion and the resulting deterioration of the environment. The public generally considers overpopulation to be a significant issue. In a recent Gallup Poll, in response to the question: "As you know, the population throughout the world is increasing at a fast rate. Do you think this is a serious problem or not?," sixty-nine per cent of Canadians answered in the affirmative. However, the perception that overpopulation is a serious problem does not usually imply that voluntary childlessness is a solution. The concern with population problems, however, although not an acceptable explanation for childlessness, does provide a supportive justification indicating that one is not necessarily socially irresponsible and neglectful of one's civic obligation if one does not reproduce.

Accounts which are credible to one audience may not be given equal weight by another. Childless couples, therefore, learn to adjust their "story" to the needs of the audience. For example, one successful woman who was taking a combined degree in medicine and biology found that her colleagues readily accepted her explanation that she was childless because she did not have time both to have a child and to

---

[2] Bernard's (1963: 91) discussion of couples who wish to adopt rather than to bear their own child is representative of this attitude.

> Others sometimes seek to bypass what may unduly frighten or repel them about the normal reproductive process. In general, *it is unwise to act upon unrealistic fears, even though they may be compelling*, especially when, as in adoption, the action involves several lives and permanently. In contrast, appropriate reassurance and in some cases psychological help may lead instead to the bearing of their own child [emphasis ours].

How does Bernard know that it is wise to disregard fears, especially when he admits they may be compelling? How does a counselor recognize an "unrealistic" fear as opposed, presumably, to a "realistic" one? The line between what constitutes a legitimate and valid motive, as opposed to a mere rationalization, is definitely drawn in spite of there being virtually no empirical criteria to distinguish one from the other.

[3] Among our respondents, no one indicated that population pressure was the major reason for their decision not to have children. In contrast to this finding, Gustavus and Henley (1971) report that in their study of seventy-two childless couples seeking sterilization, "population concern" was the most frequently mentioned reason for choosing to be childless.

maintain the high standards of professional excellence she had set for herself. This explanation, which made sense to other members of the scientific community, made no sense at all to her sister, who had only a high school education and who was excessively preoccupied with conventional feminine concerns. When talking with her sister, this woman expressed reservations about pregnancy in terms of what it would do to her figure. Concern with the possibility that one's husband might not find her attractive when pregnant was not an issue with which the sister happened to agree, but it was one she accepted as plausible. Consequently, for her it was a satisfactory account of the situation, and so forestalled further questioning. This same woman found that her women friends, who pooh-poohed the dangers and drawbacks of pregnancy and birth, were very sympathetic to the plight of the housebound wife-mother who, although supposedly in a "liberated" marriage, in fact did almost all of the child-care. To this group, the young scientist expressed reservations about having children in a society where a disproportionate amount of the work fell to the mother, with only token help from the father. This motivation easily satisfied them as a rational and valid reason for reluctance to have children. To some extent, all of these factors did contribute to the decision of this particular woman not to have children. However, she did fail to tell the whole truth, in that her most pressing reason related simply to her fundamental dislike of young children and of their childish concerns. When this finally came out in the interview, she said with a laugh:

> Well, I'm not under oath. I don't tell them lies, I just don't tell the whole truth. I learned long ago that I save myself a lot of trouble and nasty discussions that do no good if I come up with something they understand, and let it go at that. I could just tell them it was none of their business, but they would be offended. This way, they go away happy and leave me alone. I tell my mother it is because Sam would not be a good father—which he wouldn't—and that lets him be the bad guy instead of me.

Similarly, many couples, with varying degrees of awareness, structure a plurality of accounts to fit the predispositions of their various audiences.

After several years of marriage, most childless people become very skilled at accounting for their childless state. One of the important skills required is the ability to differentiate casual questions from serious demands for explicit accounts. An acquaintance who asks, "When are you going to start a family?" may be leading into an intense converstion about parenthood, culminating with an explicit "baby commercial." In many instances, however, such questions are offered in an offhand manner, and may reflect only a general expression of interest, or a simple attempt at conversation. At the early stages of trying to justify the decision not to have children, the childless are often oversensitive about pronatalism in society. They tend to be almost paranoid on the topic, and consequently over-react to perceived sanctions which are not in fact intended to comment on their childless state one way or the other. As a result, they tend to involve themselves in unnecessary conversations, and indeed may provoke the very kind of disapproval to which they object. Later on, when couples have become comfortable with being childless, they are less defensive, and are so able to pass over innocuous questions without notice or upset.

The childless also learn to protect their belief system by becoming very selective in the persons to whom they reveal their true feelings. Weinberg reports that nudists managed the problem of social disapproval by telling only those from whom they expected a favorable response. Thus, one nudist commented: "Everyone we talked to reacted favorably," but then went on to qualify his observations with the explanation: "If we didn't anticipate a favorable reaction, we wouldn't have talked with them" (Weinberg, 1970: 371). In the same way, voluntarily childless couples avoid expressing their views on children except to those people whom they expect to approve. If they are skillful in their judgments, they may experience almost no direct social disapproval. Demands that the childless account for their worldview are deftly turned aside with pat and stereotypic answers which do not inform, but serve to satisty curiousity, and protect the childless from elaborate and potentially disruptive coversations. The ability to maintain social relationships while avoiding explanations requires considerable skill and experience and is usually achieved only after several years of marriage.

Evasive Actions

One way of coping with pronatalistic pressure is to take evasive action and thereby to avoid confrontations. Some adopt the strategy of "resistance by relocation" (Prus, 1975: 11) and move from intolerant environments to more accepting ones. For example, couples may move from a rural area into a city, or deliberately move far way from in-laws who become too aggressively pronatalist. In many instances, however, such relocation is more figurative than literal and mainly involves increasing the "communicative and ideological distance" between oneself and persons whose opinions differ (Prus, 1975: 11). Some couples evade sanctions by resorting to concealment of their unusual decision; others achieve the same end by associating as much as possible only with those who share their worldview, or who are tolerant of it.

Camouflage

Some protection from pronatalism can be derived by assuming protective coloration, and pretending to be more "normal" than one actually is. Being voluntarily childless entails both a behavior (not having children) and an attitude (not wanting them). Although childless couples cannot hide the fact that they are not parents, they can exercise considerable subterfuge in camouflaging whether their childlessness is voluntary or involuntary, and whether their intentions are "honorable" or not.

One way of evading militant pronatalists is to convey the impression—implicitly or explicitly—that regardless of what one thinks about having children, the choice is beyond one's control because either the husband or the wife is sterile. Being sterile is considered an unfortunate state deserving of sympathy, whereas the deliberate avoidance of parenthood is considered selfish and immoral. The marked contrast between the stereotypes associated with involuntary and voluntary childlessness (Polit, 1978) suggests that this strategy is probably the most socially acceptable "out" for childless persons. As in the CBC television play *Dear Friends*, passing as sterile helps the childless to avoid the inevitable evaluative and sanctioning remarks of others. One husband reported simply:

> . . . it's not that I get a great deal of hassle from not having kids, it's just that the topic comes up often in casual conversations in my dealings with other men in my work. I've found that one way of getting off the subject of kids is to simply say that "we can't have any," and it works every time.

Implying sterility does not necessarily require an outright lie; subtle innuendo may suffice to make others, considering the subject a "delicate" one, drop the issue. A wife may simply counter: "How do you know we can have children?" which, without her saying anything further, conveys the suggestion of involuntary childlessness. One wife explains matter-of-factly that they do not have children because her husband cannot. While this is perfectly true, she neglects to mention that the cause of his sterility is a vasectomy which he had during the second year of their marriage with her full knowledge and consent.

Occasionally this technique may backfire. Unfortunately, sterility may be defined as even more stigmatic than deliberately avoiding parenthood, or the sanctioners may consider adoption an acceptable alternative. One wife who had received constant and blatant pressure from her father-in-law since the first year of her marriage had tried unsuccessfully to avoid the subject. In desperation, she decided simply to pretend they could not have children.

> He laughed and said "Ah, but you have forgotten, I too am a chosen son, you might choose one of your own." I had forgotten he was adopted. So I don't know if he really believed us or not, but he acted like he did. Like, if we could have them sometime, then we should keep trying. But if not, then there was no reason to wait and we should adopt right away. So the whole thing backfired and I wished I had just shut up and let him chatter on.

Another strategy for avoiding pronatalist pressure is to imply that one's present avoidance of childbearing is only a temporary one. In response to the query: "Surely you don't mean not ever?" a response of "Perhaps not" turns away the conversation, when a response of "Never, never" inevitably invites confrontation (Russell *et al.* 1978). The stalling tactic of "temporary" childlessness can be extended indefinitely if it is expanded to include the prospect of adoption. A couple who have in fact rejected the adoption alternative may find it socially useful to imply that such a possibility is still being considered.

Differential association

Many of the childless we spoke with reported that they gradually lost touch with their friends who have children, especially if those friends took their child-care responsibilities and privileges too seriously. Those friends who opted for parenthood were gradually replaced by persons who were likely to be tolerant of the decision to remain childless and/or who were likely to provide vicarious experiences congruent with the rejection of the parenthood mystique.

One strategy of differential association is to surround oneself with friends who could not reasonably be expected to have children, namely single people. For many persons, the break with friends of one's youth comes, not with marriages *per se*, but with marriage and parenthood. While this strategy works well for persons in their twenties, it is increasingly difficult for persons in their thirties or older when almost all persons are married.

A second strategy is to seek out the companionship of others who have made the same decision. In some unusual circumstances, such as on a progressive university campus, reference-group support may be forthcoming even for young unmarried persons (Houseknecht, 1976). In most instances, however, reference-group support from other married couples is rare.

A third strategy is to seek out persons who, although not childless, share similar attitudes towards children. Some parents openly acknowledge that they would have preferred to be childless had not fate intervened in the form of accidental pregnancies. Such parents may also make suitable companions if they have not allowed the mere fact of procreation to make a dramatic difference to their marriage and consider children to be only one minor facet of their complex lives. In the rhetoric of the childless, they are "sensible" about their children, meaning that their involvement with them is minimal and that almost all of their energies and interests are devoted to adult as opposed to childish concerns. Although such couples are rare, they are not as rare as other voluntarily childless couples and they do increase the pool of potential friends. Association with parents who opt to live as if they did not have children can provide some childless couples with consensual validation as to the appropriateness and the superiority of adult-centered living.

The observation that voluntarily childless couples tend to lose touch with their friends who have children should not be interpreted as necessarily involving a rejection of persons who are enthusiastic parents. Part of the differential association is a result of the parents' rejecting the childless. The refusal to interact, almost a kind of shunning, is in some circumstances an extreme social sanction. For example, one middle-aged realtor, remembering the early days of her marriage, recalled a typical incident:

> There was a couple we were good friends with—in fact, Sam was best man at their wedding. We were all about the same age and used to go around together all the time. A few months after they were married, we got talking one night over some wine about children, and we allowed as how we weren't keen on them. I guess we should have noticed their reaction right away, but we did not think it was so sensitive. They used to be Catholic, but they weren't religious and they had broken from the church long ago, we all had. Or so we thought. Well, they were outraged, and the more indignant they got, the more defensive we got. Finally, they as much as said, "What did you get married for then?" and we went home miffed. But we'd had arguments before, college kids spend half their time debating the fate of the cosmos. We didn't think much about it. But after that, they were sort of busy every time we phoned and we finally got the message and stopped calling. It seems a shame.

Special Pressures: Would-Be Grandparents

The maintenance of a deviant belief system through the strategy of physical and psychological isolation from nonbelievers is an effective strategy in dealing with many sanctioners. However, it is of only limited usefulness in the special case of dealing with one's own parents, who constitute a unique threat to the maintenance of a worldview supporting voluntary childlessness. Parents and in-laws often perceive an inconsistency between their own aspirations for grandchildren and the stubborn refusal of their children to produce the required babies on the required schedule. The voluntarily childless report that parents and in-laws are a major and persistent source of social pressure to procreate. Such pressure typically continues unabated until the couple have been married for five or six years, or until a sibling produces a child and so relieves some of the direct pressure. The most serious and unresolvable conflict occurs between the only child and his or her parents, where there are no alternative sources of grandchildren.

Several factors combine to make interaction with parents especially problematic. First, parents typically feel that their children's child-bearing aspirations, or lack of them, are a legitimate subject of interest and concern. Consequently, they may show relatively little hesitation in making extensive inquiries. Since they feel such decisions are within their province, they cannot be put off with appeals to privacy or with superficial answers. Second, in many if not most cases, parents feel that one of the rewards due to them for their years of child-care and support is the right to grandchildren. Their expectations and self-conceptions are oriented toward this future role, especially as their peers become grandparents. It is noteworthy that this motivation appears to be independent of their own satisfactions or dissatisfactions with the parenthood role. If their experiences with children were positive, they want to repeat them, this time with less of the responsibility and more of the joys. If their experiences with children were negative, they feel that, although they made many mistakes with their own sons or daughters, this time with their grandchildren they would do better. For them, grandparenthood would constitute a second chance to make up for their initial bad luck or ineptitude.

Another factor in the interaction between childless persons and would-be grandparents is that, to some extent, parents identify with their children and feel responsible for their upbringing as moral and right-minded citizens. An immoral decision, such as opting for voluntary childlessness, may suggest to the parents or to their peers that something was wrong with their child-bearing techniques, leading to the stereotypic "where-have-I-failed you?" response. Some childless persons are able to continue in their nonconforming behavior while simultaneously maintaining good relationships with their parents by managing to blame their spouse for the absence of children. For example, a young engineer reported:

> We made a deal a couple of years after we were married. You be the "heavy" with my parents, and I'll be the "heavy" with yours. So when Mom asks me, one more time, I look sad and pensive and talk about how maybe Marion will finally be ready to settle down in a few years. And Mom commiserates with me for having an over-liberated wife. It is a good thing our folks live so far apart. If they ever get together and compare notes, the jig will really be up. For now, it keeps everyone happy.

By blaming the spouse for the failure to have children, childless persons put their parents in a neat double-bind, in that the same persons who are *for* children are typically *against* divorce. The childless son or daughter can be viewed as an unfortunate "victim" rather than as willfully uncooperative. This strategy also gives the would-be grandparents hope, for by implication, if in the future their child were to be married to someone else, grandchildren might still be forthcoming from the second marriage.

Frustrated would-be grandparents could resolve their dilemma by choosing to abdicate from the grandparent role in favor of other statuses, but in most cases, they must be gradually resigned to the loss of this anticipated and valued status. If they are not going to continue to be unhappy, or to continue to make a fuss, they must be in some way reconciled to their fate. The first strategy for coping with parents who feel they are being "conned" out of the grandchildren who are rightfully theirs is simply stalling. A number of childless wives who are quite definite in their decision to avoid parenthood make a deliberate point of passing for potential parents when confronting their parents or in-laws. If, for example, they have opted for sterilization, they withhold this information from them, even though they may show little reticence in revealing it to other acquaintances. In many ways, the voluntarily childless strive to give their parents the maximum amount of time to become accustomed to the possibility of not having grandchildren and the maximum length of time during which they may continue to hope that such is not the case. The announcement of sterilization would precipitate a direct confrontation in that it would provide a specific point for vague feelings of being "had." Parents are literally the last to know when a final decision against childbearing has been made, and in many cases, they are never explicitly informed. One husband summarized the situation this way:

> We are both in our mid-thirties and have not mentioned having kids to our parents for ten years. And it's been about five years since they've even hinted about the subject with us. Yet, we aren't ready—and we're sure they aren't ready—to talk about our decision, not to mention justify it. This is why we didn't tell them about my vasectomy; what's the point? Maybe we'll talk it over with them someday . . . but probably never will.

Special Pressures: Pronatalistic Physicians

A number of voluntarily childless wives report receiving considerable pressure from their physicians to become mothers. The attitudes of physicians in advocating parenthood are of special significance for a variety of reasons. First, the prestige of the physician and his social role as a wise and learned person means that his opinion, biased or not, is given more weight than that of ordinary persons. He is assumed to know what is best for the patient, and his opinions pro or con therefore are taken more literally. Second, on the subject of fertility decision-making, physicians are consulted more often by more couples than are other professionals. Sometimes such consultations take the form of direct advice-seeking, but more often concern with social or psychological problems may be expressed under the guise of concern with physical problems. Third, and most important, the physician has direct control over his patient's fertility. Peers may exert pressures to parenthood, counselors may advocate childbearing as a strategy likely to increase adjustment and happiness, but only physicians can and do exert influence beyond verbal recommendations into the realm of the physical realities of conception and birth.

The amount of stress caused by physicians in their pronatalist advice-giving depends directly on the certainty of the childless wife that she does not want to conceive and on her tolerance for disapproval. For example, one wife, who had known since she was fifteen that she never wanted children, and who was not especially sensitive to the opinions of others, was not greatly distressed by her experience with an unsympathetic medical profession.

> When I was twenty-one, I went to the General Hospital for my annual checkup and I asked the intern who did it about having my tubes tied. He turned white and he went scurrying out, he came back in with a female gynecologist who had three children of her own and proceeded to tell me all about how it is possible to work and have children and how they fulfilled her life—and even if I went off the pill there were other methods of contraception. And I said: "Yes, but I don't want two children. I just don't want to have them." So they went away and got the head gynecologist who called me a silly, idiotic female and told me to shut up, I didn't know what I was talking about, and I didn't know what I would want. So they told me to come back in two years if I still felt the same.

Given the strength of her convictions about childbearing, she was not shaken or offended, but rather amused and indignant.

> You have the right to choose what you want. I guess I'm sort of rocking the boat a bit but—well, so it's irreversible, so what, big deal, having a kid is irreversible too, isn't it? You can't take it back if you change your mind. And they would think I was old enough to get knocked up if I wanted to, right?

However, another wife with a Roman Catholic background and a much more conformist self-image was affected more deeply. She went routinely to a Catholic physician. She reported that the first year he gave her a physical examination, prescribed the pill and told her to come back in a year; the second year he asked her why she was not having a baby, but seemed satisfied that she and her husband were still adjusting to one another; the third year he delivered a long lecture to the general effect that at twenty-seven she was getting old, and that if she knew what was good for them, she would have a baby now before it was too late. She relates that, "I went home from there feeling so damn guilty that I nearly cried. I thought it was something terrible in me."

Childless couples who are resolutely committed to not having children often manage to circumvent pronatalist pressure from physicians by the simple expedient of changing doctors until they find one sympathetic to their views. However, the idea of "shopping" for a physician is not widely accepted. In addition to being expensive, it implies flouting the authority and judgment of the first doctor, and so is particularily difficult for working-class couples who are not well educated. Couples who are not absolutely committed to remaining childless may well find that the "decision" has been made for them in the form of an accidental pregnancy.

The voluntarily childless have a major problem with fertility control in that, except for sterilization, none of the techniques of contraception can be safely used to prevent *all* births over a lifetime.[4] The voluntarily childless wife who marries young may have twenty to thirty years when she is at risk of becoming pregnant. If we ignore the more obviously unreliable contraceptive methods, such as rhythm and *coitus interruptus*, and consider only relatively safe methods such as a condom or a diaphragm, a woman might still expect to have one or two pregnancies before she reaches menopause. The intrauterine device (IUD) is a non-obtrusive and relatively effective method of birth control, with a failure rate of only five per cent. However, it is often not suitable for use with nulliparious women who experience higher rates of expulsion and more negative side effects than do mothers.

Oral contraceptives may be considered completely effective, if taken correctly. However, not all women can tolerate them without unpleasant side effects. More importantly, recent data suggest that concern with their dangerous side effects may be more justified than was first believed. Medical opinion on the risks associated with oral contraception has changed dramatically over the past several years. As recently as 1975, a review of clinical problems and choices associated with oral contraceptives concluded that:

> There seem to be relatively few side effects and no serious problems related to extended duration of pill use. There is no justification in the literature for the "rest period" after several months or years of pill usage, although many physician advocate one, for reasons of personal insecurity more than anything else. So many unwarrented conceptions have occured during these "rest periods" that the physician really provides the patient a disservice when less effective means of contraception are provided (Jones and Halbert, 1975: 123).

Since that time, however, other studies have suggested that such is not the case. The Royal College of General Practitioners (1977a) provides

---

4 The effectiveness of contraceptives is usually measured in terms of the rate of pregnancies per one hundred women years, using the Pearl Formula. Although the estimates of relative effectiveness vary from one source to the next, the general rank ordering of alternatives is quite consistent. When properly used, the failure rates of the condom, or of the diaphragm with spermicidal jelly, may be as low as four to seven pregnancies per one hundred women years. However, failure rates with these methods used with less precision can also reach as high as thirty or thirty-five, a rate which is nearly as high as the rhythm method (Southam, 1966: 386). Overall, a general estimate of the effectiveness of the condom or the diaphragm is approximately ten pregnancies per one hundred women years (Havemann, 1967; Wood, 1969). When considering the life chances of a particular woman, it is more meaningful to consider this statistic as a rate of one accidental pregnancy per ten years, or of several accidental pregnancies over several decades of exposure to pregnancy risk.

data from a prospective study of some 46,000 women of childbearing age. They report that women who have ever used the pill show an overall increase in mortality of 40 per cent, compared with non-users. The risk is especially great for women over the age of thirty-five, and for women who smoke. For example, Shapiro *et al.* (1979: 746) found that controlling for age, women who used contraceptives and who smoked heavily (more than 25 cigarettes a day) had 39 times the risk of heart attack than did women who neither smoked nor took contraceptives. The Royal College of General Practitioners (1977b) does not recommend changes in the current use of oral contraceptives for women under thirty. However, it does consider that women aged thirty to thirty-five ought to "reconsider" their use if they have been taking them continuously for five years or more or if they smoke, and suggests that all users over thirty-five "would be wise" to reconsider their method of contraception.

Whether or not a physician's unsolicited advice has an effect on a childless wife's attitude towards pregnancy, his refusal to grant credibility to her decision to avoid motherhood may jeopardize her chances of avoiding all conceptions. The physician who does not take seriously a woman's claim not to want children tends to be relatively unsympathetic to her insistence that birth control be not only relatively effective, but absolutely effective. For example, when concerned that a woman has been taking contraceptive pills for too long, a physician may recommend that she stop for a trial period and suggest that the couple use a diaphragm or a condom instead, meanwhile assuring her that these means are also "safe." Relatively well educated childless wives who are highly motivated to avoid motherhood may suspect this assertion to be untrue and, therefore, may resort to some combination of birth control techniques. However, it seems possible that less well informed or less committed women may be "tricked" into motherhood in this way by physicians who assume that they are acting in the woman's own best interests.

The attitudes of physicians concerning abortions for married, childless women may be critical in avoiding motherhood, in that abortion is often a necessary back-up technique for maintaining childlessness over a lifetime. Many members of the medical profession tend not to believe that the desire of a married woman to remain childless is, in and of itself, sufficient reason for terminating a pregnancy.[5] In assess-

[5] In Canada and many places in the United States, abortion is now presumably a lega right for every woman whose mental health would be endangered by having a child However, the so-called liberalization of abortion laws has not had the effect of providin even an approximation of abortion-on-demand. An unmarried woman, or a marrie woman with many children and extreme problems, has a good chance of obtaining a

ing the decisions of physician and patient concerning birth control, it is necessary to recognize that all effective and reliable procedures do entail some risk. However, it is also important to remember that pregnancy and childbirth also entail risks, especially for older women, quite apart from the psychological distress occasioned by an unwanted conception. After an evaluation of the risk associated with various alternatives, Rosenfield (1978) concludes that:

> With the exception of pill users who are heavy smokers in the age group 40 to 44, the use of no method is significantly more hazardous than any other alternative. The safest alternative is a combination of the use of traditional methods (diaphragm or condom), backed up by early first-trimester abortion (Rosenfield, 1978: 103).

Whether or not official policies permit abortions to be granted on demand to childless wives is of little significance if the involuntarily pregnant wives do not accept abortion as an alternative. The implications of pronatalist medical policies in prescribing contraception are especially serious for those wives who could in good conscience deliberately prevent a pregnancy, but who could not in good conscience deliberately terminate one once it had begun. The willingness to seek abortion as a means of fertility control may not depend upon one's commitment to the childfree lifestyle as much as upon one's attitude toward abortion *per se*.

The attitude of physicians toward voluntary childlessness is especially crucial in regard to the most effective of all means of birth control, namely sterilization. In terms of official policy, sterilization is ostensibly available to any adult.[6] In practice, however, many physi-

---

abortion if she is resourceful and determined. Before this can occur, however, she must have the written recommendation of a physician and must make a convincing case to an abortion board. Like the general public (Balakrishnan *et al.*, 1972), physicians tend not to believe that a first pregnancy can be a serious danger to a normal married woman's mental health.

[6] In the United States, voluntary sterilization is a legal operative procedure in all states for all persons qualified to give their consent, except in Utah where sterilization is allowed only for "medical indications." A similar restriction in Connecticut was repealed in 1971. In Canada there are no legal restrictions on sterilization, regardless of marital status, number of children or consent of spouse if married. The legal policies regarding sterilization are generally supported by the official policies of various professional groups in the health care field. For example, in 1970 the Canadian Medical Association took a liberal stand on sterilization, essentially favoring availability on demand. In 1971 the American College of Obstetricians and Gynecologists eliminated from their statement of policy on sterilization any reference to number of children. The National Medical Committee on Planned Parenthood-World Population has followed suit and has issued in its guidelines for vasectomy clinics operated by Planned Parenthood Affiliates the recommendation that "any adult should be accepted."

cians have been reluctant to perform sterilizations on unmarried persons or those without children. For example, one husband reported that when he broached the question of sterilization with their family physician, he was asked: "Why would you want to mutiliate yourself that way?" Such attitudes are changing as sterilization becomes more widespread among ordinary couples. For example, in the United States, among white couples married 5–9 years, in 1965 only 5 per cent had been sterilized, by 1970 this had increased to about 8 per cent; and by 1975 it had jumped to 22 per cent (Westoff and Jones, 1977: 154).

Antinatalism: An Emerging Counter-Culture

Many deviant constructions of reality, even those which are endorsed by only a small proportion of the population, still find a considerable amount of group support. The legitimacy of their behavior is defended by the emergence of a counter-culture. Under certain conditions, many people find that they have similar conflicts between the accepted institutional version of social reality and their own reality construction, and unite to form new institutional alternatives. "A final step in the career of a deviant is movement into an organized deviant group" (Becker, 1963: 17). Counter-cultures are extremely important in coping with negative social pressure, in that they provide a working philosophy for the deviant: ". . . explaining to him and to others why he is that way, that other people have also been that way, and why it is all right for him to be that way" (Becker, 1963: 38). In other words, they provide ready-made explanations and accounts.

Pronatalism and feminism

From one perspective, it might seem logical to assume that some counter-institutional support for voluntary childlessness might be forthcoming from the women's movement, in that some writers consider an inclination to avoid motherhood as a logical extension of the new feminism. Thus, Bernard (1972: 60) perceives a general "antimotherhood ambience" in the tenor of the times, and Lott (1973) notes a number of themes in the women's movement which appear to denigrate the functions of childbearing and child-rearing. It is difficult to generalize about a social movement as amorphous as the women's liberation movement, a rubric which incorporates many diverse and even contradictory attitudes. However, "a significant feature of the women's liberation movement is that, although its demands have been made on the basis of equality for women, it has not usually been anti-marriage or anti-children" (Commission on Population and the American Future, 1972: 68).

In many instances, the expression of feminist ideologies is actually pronatalistic. Considerable concern is expressed with the problems of successfully combining motherhood with other careers. However, motherhood is not perceived as an unfulfilling and unrewarding experience; rather, it is perceived as a positive experience which, although desirable, is not sufficient in and of itself for maximum self-actualization. Rather than advising women to abandon motherhood as a career, the new feminist literature advises them to consider other careers in addition to it, and advocates societal changes to make the motherhood role easier. Although devotees of the new feminism may provide some support for the idea that motherhood is neither necessary nor sufficient for fulfillment, they do still advocate that normally it will be an important part of that fulfillment. They do not tout childlessness as an especially desirable alternative, do not proselytize the childfree lifestyle, and in general, do not provide active encouragement for those women who reject motherhood.

Most of the childless wives interviewed were generally sympathetic with the women's liberation movement, especially regarding the more obvious and conservative goals such as equal pay for equal work. However, only a few were actively concerned with women's liberation, and all of these indicated that they did not become aware of the movement until after their decision not to have children had been made and their childfree lifestyle had been established.

Pronatalism and population problems

A second potential source of counter-cultural support for voluntary childlessness might be expected from political groups expressly concerned with the hazards of excess fertility, either at the individual level as reflected in groups such as Planned Parenthood, or at the societal level as reflected by groups such as Zero Population Growth (ZPG). Although devotees of these movements are notably less pronatalist than others, they still convey the assumption of universal parenthood. Thus, the expressed concern of the Planned Parenthood movement regarding the "right of every child to be wanted" also implies the expectation that "everyone wants a child." A local Planned Parenthood affiliate in the midwest dropped their slogan of "Have 'Em

When You Want 'Em" when they realized its implicit assumption that *when* was the only issue, not *if* you want children at all. Advocates of ZPG are careful to indicate that it is not procreation *per se* they are opposed to, but only excessive procreation. The slogan "Stop At Two" asserts that one should have no more than two children, but it also implies that perhaps one should have at least one or two.

Concern with population problems has helped to legitimize childlessness, in that it has tended to redefine the social meaning of parenthood as neither an obligation nor a right but a privilege. Questioning the motivations imputed to parents and nonparents can even make the "sacrifice" of some persons in not having children seem to permit others the "indulgence" of parenthood. Childlessness comes to be defined as in society's best interest, in that each couple who do not produce a child do not contribute to existing "people pollution." If there is an implicit endorsement of *The Case of Compulsory Birth Control* (Chasteen, 1972), then childlessness can seem like part of the solution, rather than part of the problem.

Some of the childless respondents interviewed were involved, at least superficially, with Planned Parenthood or with ZPG. However, in reviewing their commitment to childlessness, it was apparent that the ideological stance of these groups had not been of great importance in their decision-making. Identification with these social movements, like identification with the women's movement, tended to be not so much a cause of childlessness as a result of it, providing *ex post facto* justifications for remaining childless.

The National Organization For Nonparents

Although childless persons may gain some ideological support from social movements concerned with sexism or with the population explosion, these associations do not speak directly to the problems of being childless by choice in a world full of parents. The development of antinatalism as a counter-culture has been greatly facilitated by the emergence of an interest group of persons explicitly identified with this variant life style.[7] For the voluntarily childless, the explicit formulation

[7] In a unique book, *Old Man In*, Sagarin (1969) has described the growth and structure of a number of societies formed to provide group support for individuals who are defined as social deviants. The stigmata involved may range from physical deformities, as in the case of dwarfs, to character blemishes, as in the case of homosexuals. In many ways the emergence of NON parallels the development of other interest groups which offer consolation and advice to persons whose social identity has been flawed. The deliberately childless are stigmatized both physically, because they have not had children, and morally, because they have not desired them.

of an antinatalist counter-culture began with the organization of the National Organization for Nonparents (NON) in California in 1972.[8]

NON was originally incorporated as a tax-exempt non-profit educational organization founded: "to make the childfree lifestyle a realistic and socially accepted and respected option and to eliminate pronatalist social and economic discrimination." The initial step towards these goals involved raising the public consciousness concerning the nature and operation of pronatalism. Ellen Peck became the self-proclaimed spokesman of the voluntarily childless, and with her book *The Baby Trap* (1971), provided both a focus for media attention and a practical manual for articulating and defending antinatalist sentiments. Two years later, this approach was reinforced by Shirley Radl's proclamation that *Mother's Day Is Over* (1973). Membership in NON grew rapidly, and by 1974 it had branched out into thirty-four local chapters across the United States.

By the time of the second annual convention in 1975, however, NON showed the kinds of internal strain to be expected in a neophyte social movement. Initially, NON members tended to tout being childfree as a preferred life style. In many cases, passive resistance against pronatalism was supplemented by an active advocacy of antinatalism. As apologists for childlessness, the emotional tone was often aggressive and occassionally militant. After several years, NON began to attract members who were less extreme in their orientation, and who were concerned with a broader range of issues relating not so much to childlessness *per se* as to fertility decision making in general. The conflict concerning the direction NON should take was manifest in the issue of whether or not the name of the organization should be changed. By 1977, Ellen Peck was no longer affiliated with the group. After considerable internal disruption, NON was transformed in 1978 into the National Alliance for Optional Parenthood (NAOP).

NAOP presently involves some 1,600 members in 42 chapters across the United States. In spite of extensive publicity and able leadership and administration, NAOP has not grown as quickly as might have been expected. One of the problems of the organization is that for many childless persons, the primary appeal is in providing reassurance that not having children is in fact acceptable. Once that message has been

---

The original founders of NON were Norman Fleishman, Ellen Peck, William Peck, Shirley Radl, John R. Rague, and Sherwood Wallace. The first executive director, Shirley Radl, was succeeded in 1973 by an acting executive director, Audrey Bertolett, and in 1974 by the current executive director Ms. Carole Baker. NON moved from California to Baltimore in 1973, and from Baltimore to Washington in 1979. Its present mailing address is the National Alliance for Optional Parenthood, 2010 Massachusetts Avenue Northwest, Washington, D.C. 20036.

conveyed to everyone's satisfaction, there is only limited incentive to remain with the organization. Another problem relates directly to the shift in focus from the NON days. NAOP now offers a soft-sell message that disavows being childfree as deviance, and stresses the advantages of adult-centered living. It is most likely to appeal to persons who see themselves as postponing childbearing, and who are experiencing pressure as a result. However, the notion of postponement still conveys the clear impression that eventual reproduction is possible and perhaps desirable. Rather than conveying the message, implicitly or otherwise, that being childless is somehow the "best" way to be, NAOP now tends to convey the less controversial message that reproductive decision making should be thoughtful and rational. NAOP is now vaguely embarrassed by explicit antinatalists. While this shift in focus has increased the base of appeal of the group, making it relevant to a larger proportion of the population, it has rendered it less ideologically distinct from other groups, such as Planned Parenthood, who also advocate rational reproduction. In the shift, those persons who do actively reject parenthood and who wish to proselytize their views, have lost their advocate.

Chapter Eight: THE POLITICS OF PRONATALISM: IMPLICATIONS FOR SOCIAL RESEARCH AND SOCIAL POLICY

From its inception, our study of voluntary childlessness was modest in its scope. We began our research with an intense curiosity about what seemed a fascinating and neglected minority: childfree persons living in a child-centered world. In accepting from the start the limitations intrinsic in research based on a purposive sample, it was never our intention to offer firm conclusions which would be generalizable to all deliberately childless persons. Our 156 respondents were not selected as a representative sample of all childless couples; rather, they were selected because their probability of remaining permanently childless was very high, and because they were willing to speak openly and at length about their motivations and experiences. In talking with our respondents, we sought to learn how they had come to question the parenthood mystique, how they ultimately made the decision to reject it, and how their lives had been affected as a result of those atypical decisions. The information we collected was not easy to quantify, but it was qualitatively rich, and therefore ideal for stimulating more focused investigations. These new research initiatives will, we hope, consider our findings and tentative conclusions, and direct their attention to one or more questions related to the antecedents and consequences of being childless by choice.

The Increase in Voluntary Childlessness

Since the turn of the century, childlessness among Canadian and American women has shown wide fluctuations. From 1910 to 1940, rates of childlessness tended to increase. From the war years and postwar period until the mid-1960s, however, childlessness rates declined to the point where many experts declared that voluntary childlessness was virtually extinct (Whelpton, Campbell and Patterson, 1965: 163; Thomlinson, 1975: 148; Tomasson, 1966: 328; Westoff and Westoff, 1971: 35). Such conclusions appear to have been premature, in that the total incidence of childlessness still exceeded sterility estimates for most groups. Since the 1960's, studies of the incidence of childlessness confirm that childlessness has increased, especially among young wives.[1]

Predicting the incidence of childlessness in the future is hazardous, in that current expectations of births may or may not be realized in actuality. Although only a small minority of young childless wives expect never to have children, this minority is increasing. For example, in the United States in 1967, among white wives aged eighteen to thirty-nine, 3.0 per cent never expected to have children; by 1975, this had increased to 4.8 per cent (United States Bureau of the Census, 1976b: 5). Similarly, Blake (1974: 34) reports that from 1961 to 1971 the proportion of college women preferring childlessness increased from 1 per cent to 9 per cent. More important for predicting childlessness, however, are those women who say they intend to have a child eventually, but who are postponing starting a family. Some researchers predict a resurgence of fertility when presently childless young women near the end of their childbearing years (Blake, 1974: 43; Sklar and

[1] This finding is consistent in terms of period rates (Sell, 1974; DasGupta, 1975; DeJong and Sell, 1977) or of cohort analyses (Hastings and Robinson, 1974; Poston and Gotard, 1977). For example, in the United States, among white ever-married women aged twenty to twenty-four, the percentage remaining childless increased from 25.0 per cent in 1960 to 44.7 per cent in 1975. An equally dramatic increase occurred among slightly older wives aged twenty-five to twenty-nine, where rates jumped from 12.3 per cent in 1960 to 21.6 per cent in 1975 (United States Bureau of the Census, 1976a: 33).

Berkov, 1975). It seems likely, however, that a sizeable proportion of supposedly temporary postponements of childbearing will eventually become permanent postponements (Glick, 1975). Given the fundamental changes in fertility patterns which are occurring, it seems likely that low fertility is indeed here to stay (Bumpass, 1973). Present rates of childlessness are likely to be maintained and, given current trends towards contraceptive use, family norms, and sex roles, it seems likely that voluntary childlessness will continue to increase (DeJong and Sell, 1977; Poston and Gotard, 1977). Westoff (1978: 55) suggests that the developed countries of the world are witnessing an "ongoing retreat from parenthood." He concludes that:

> If current rates for first births were to persist, some 30 per cent of U.S. women now of childbearing age would never have children. The highest proportion on record was 22 per cent childless for U.S. women born in 1908. It seems likely that today's young women will break that record by a few percentage points (Westoff, 1978: 55).

Since there is no reason to expect an increase in sterility among young populations, the acceleration of rates of childlessness can be assumed to be almost entirely due to deliberate avoidance of parenthood. If Westoff's predictions hold, in the immediate future we would expect voluntary childlessness to characterize between 10 and 15 per cent of all couples— approximately three times as many as were found in the 1960's.

A Typology of Childlessness

Descriptions of childless couples have dichotomized them in terms of a number of variables: by whether they made their decision before ("early articulators") or after marriage ("Postponers"); by whether they achieved it independently or by negotiation; by whether they have high or low levels of commitment to it; and by whether they are primarily motivated by reactive or proactive factors. Our data seems to suggest that some useful hypotheses can be formulated regarding the relationships among these four dimensions. The cornerstone of this hypothesis is the notion that there are two quite different kinds of voluntarily childless persons: **rejectors** and **aficionados.**[2]

---

[2] Strong (1967: 2246) provides a similar distinction. In a study of over 300 childless Negro couples in Washington, two types were observed: the tradition-oriented who had had negative family experiences, and the upward-striving who had enjoyed positive family

Voluntarily childless persons whom we have designated as rejectors are those who disavow the parenthood mystique and who have actively and vehemently rejected the parenthood role. Rejectors are primarily motivated by *reaction* against the *dis*advantages of having children. Their decision is an immutable part of an idiosyncratic belief system in that they cannot imagine any circumstances under which they would want to have children. Rejectors often tend to dislike children, and to avoid being around them. A number of them flaunt their childlessness; others actively proselytize their antinatalist ideology and childfree lifestyle.

Aficionados are persons who are ardent devotees of voluntary childlessness because they appreciate the *advantages* of being childfree rather than the disadvantages of parenthood. They are not so much against children as they are intrigued and beguiled by some other interest which does not include children. Such enticements may range from hard science to pottery, from art to mountain-climbing, from literature to horse racing. Such persons are "buffs" who find, in the pursuit of their passion, that children would be an impediment. They made their decisions about parenthood primarily in terms of the positive attractions of other interests. They tend to negotiate their decision over the course of their marriage, in the context of the development of other interests, and to be less definite in their commitment to it. Generally, they like children, or at least have a neutral attitude towards them, and on the issue of natalism, they tend to be apolitical, endorsing neither the pronatalist nor the antinatalist perspective. In terms of comparisons with the general population, one might hazard a guess that aficionados are more similar to parents than are rejectors, who tend to have more varied and unconventional backgrounds and childhood experiences. Further specifications about the background and other characteristics of these two types would require considerably more in-depth interviews and study. Table 3, however, provides a useful method of comparing the expected patterns of response regarding the process by which each arrives at the decision to be childless.

All of the persons we interviewed were influenced both by some concern with the disadvantages of parenthood, and some concern with the advantages of being childfree. However, in most cases it was possible to differentiate those persons who were primarily characterized as re-

experiences. Strong suggests different central concerns of these two groups. "The tradition-centered group desired economic security and freedom from the impoverished and unstable background that many of them had known, while the upward-striving group emphasized maintaining the status quo which they had achieved."

Table 3. Ideal Type Model of Kinds of Voluntary Childlessness

Dimension	Rejectors	Aficionados
Timing of the decision	Early articulators: decision to remain childless made clearly before marriage	Postponers: decision to remain childless made gradually after marriage
Consensus on the decision	High consensus: both husband and wife independently opted for childlessness	Low consensus: husband and wife negotiated decision; one "converted" other to their view
Commitment to the decision	High level of commitment: parenthood rejected independently of present marriage and circumstances	Low level of commitment: parenthood might be accepted in different marriage or circumstances
Motive antecedents	Rejection of the negative aspects of a child-centered lifestyle	Attraction toward the positive aspects of an adult-centered lifestyle
Maintenance of variant worldview	Deviance avowal; acceptance-of-difference from parents; tend to dislike children	Deviance disavowal; rejection-of-difference from parents; tend to like children

jecting the parenthood mystique from those who were childless primarily because of their attraction to other pursuits. In future research on childlessness, it is important to maintain this distinction, and to recognize that in generalizations about childlessness, it is theoretically critical to differentiate the involuntary from the voluntary, and the rejectors from the aficionados.

The Consequences of Childlessness

The most important finding of our research is simply stated in one observation: from our vantage point, it seems clear that at least some voluntarily childless couples *do* achieve high levels of personal, marital, and social adjustment. Moreover, from our interviews, it seems clear to us that for many of the childless, the maintenance of sound mental health is not achieved in spite of being childless, but is predicated upon the continued avoidance of parenthood. This conclusion would perhaps seem "obvious" were it not for the fact that it contravenes a basic assumption of Canadian-American culture, namely that children are *necessary* for happiness and fulfillment. While it may well be that under many circumstances children do contribute to satisfactory life adjustment, the in-depth interviews we conducted do establish that, at least for some persons, alternative lifestyles may provide the same level of satisfaction.

The implications of this simple finding are manifold. The pronatalist premise that having children is a desirable goal for all persons must be modified to the more limited premise that is is not necessary for all and that for some persons under some circumstances childlessness may be a more desirable alternative. Presently, young couples are oriented towards a basic question: how many children do you want to have? More appropriately, we might rather orient them to the question: do you want to have any children?

It has always been known that some persons of eminence made noteworthy contributions in spite of, or perhaps because of, being childless. For such outstanding individuals, extra-ordinary achievements were often assumed to compensate for their lack of children. The fact that they could lead apparently fulfilled lives, however, is of little relevance for the everyday decision-making of ordinary people. A noteworthy feature of our respondents is that they were ordinary people. Although more advantaged than most of middle America, they could hardly be considered exceptional. Many of our respondents were successful by conventional standards, but none had as yet made outstanding contributions. Many were well off but none were rich. Many were well known in their local communities but none were celebrities From the point of view of ordinary people, it is of little consequence i the brilliant and the famous can be happy without children; it is however, of considerable consequence if ordinary people can.

Implications for Social Research

An ubiquitous cliché at the end of a research project is to note tha "more research is needed." In this instance, however, this really is th case, and a major purpose in our undertaking was to examine wha form such research might take. On the basis of our findings, we hav three specific recommendations: first, for research on voluntary chil lessness *per se*; second, for research comparing voluntary childless ness with parenthood; and third, for research on the development of "parent test" for predicting aptitude for child-rearing.

The nature of childlessness

Because childlessness involves only a small proportion of the population, and because deliberate childlessness is still a sensitive issue, the research initatives on childlessness have not been generalizable, sometimes constituting hardly more than case studies (Burnside, 1977; Goodbody, 1977). Respondents tend to be selective purposively from atypical groups, such as persons being sterilized (Gustavus and Henley, 1971; Magarick, 1975; Kaltreider and Margolis, 1977) or persons of exceptional achievements (Welds, 1976; Mommsen and Lund, 1977). Members of NAOP are convenient and cooperative respondents and so are frequently studied (Marcks, 1976; Lichtman, 1976; Barnett and MacDonald, 1976; Marciano, 1978). Given what is known about members of voluntary organizations, it is unlikely that NAOP membership encompasses the entire range of types of childless couples, although it may be as likely to do so as respondents such as ours, who reply to media appeals (Nason and Poloma, 1976; Cooper *et al.* 1978). A first step in the study of childlessness would be to broaden the basis of investigation to include a representative sample of the general public. Of special import would be the examination of voluntarily childless persons of all ages and all durations of marriage. In studies such as the present one, where one indicator of permanent commitment to childlessness is a duration of marriage of several years, the resulting survivors are atypical in that they are probably better adjusted and more happily married than childless couples in general.

Cross-sectional studies would provide a better basis of description of voluntary childlessness. However, even if comprehensive interviews could be done with respresentative samples, the dynamics of the decision-making process would remain obscure, in that persons would be recollecting how decisions had been made in the past. A more desirable approach would be a prospective cohort study, which would enable one to trace the decision process, and to ascertain the circumstances under which the intention to be childless is maintained or altered.

The consequences of parenthood

Our folklore assumes that parenthood has a benign effect on parents, and that it is a desirable goal to be sought, if not by everyone, then at least by all married persons. Moreover, it assumes that the absence of parenthood will have a deleterious effect on non-parents. Our evidence on the high levels of adjustment of some childless couples suggests that such is not necessarily the case, and that in some instances their lifestyle may be more satisfactory than the lifestyle of some parents. To assess fully the consequences of parenthood, we need systematic research not on childless couples, but on childless couples compared with parental couples.

Assuming that one could collect valid data from a representative group of persons who are truly voluntarily childless, it remains unclear with whom they would most appropriately be compared. The simplest and most obvious approach is to contrast them with parents in general. For example, Bernard (1972: 66) states flatly: "The general conclusion warranted from the research is that childless marriages tend to be happier than those with children. . . ." It is note worthy, however, that she then goes on to comment: ". . . and small families tend to be happier than large ones." Looking at childless versus parental persons may be confounding two very different groups: those who have a few children, most of whom were planned and wanted; and those who have many children, most of whom were unplanned and unwanted. In those few studies of voluntary childlessness which do involve a control group (Bram, 1978; Welds, 1976; Burnside, 1977), no attempt is made to distinguish between small, planned families and those exhibiting excess fertility. There is little doubt that the deleterious aspects of parenthood are directly associated with excess fertility (Terhune and Pilie, 1974). The voluntarily childless at least have the advantage of being successful in achieving their desired family size. The appropriate comparison group may therefore be, not all parents, but only those parents who have always been successful in planning the number and spacing of their pregnancies, a group who might be expected to have had relatively small families.

Development of a parent test

Systematic research is needed to assess the conditions under which parenthood is likely to have a benign effect on a couple and on their marriage, versus the conditions under which it is likely to affect them adversely. Since we do not yet know the consequences of parenthood, this step is of necessity more intuitive than rational. However, since decisions cannot await definitive research but are being made willy-nilly without guidance, it seems profitable for professionals to offer a "best guess" as to propitious circumstances. For example, twenty years ago in a cogent article which unfortunately has been largely ignored, Harper suggested a marriage counsellor's view of several criteria to be considered before advocating parenthood.

> The *only* time reproduction is truly desirable for the children, for the married couple, and for the general society is when (a) the husband and wife are considerably above average as phenotypes and (insofar as it can be determined) genotypes in such traits as mental and physical health, intelligence, emotional and social maturity, and creative and adaptive skills; (b) the marriage is a very happy one; and (c) *both* the husband and wife not only want children in a sentimental sense but are *eager to make parenthood their main enterprise* for the next quarter of a century and realize that this task means a lot of hard work, and the sacrifice of many other satisfactions (Harper, 1956: 9, emphasis in original).

Less radical, and hence less controversial, endorsements of the need for some kind of selective screening for parenthood, based on persuading individuals to assess themselves voluntarily, are recognized in two recent how-to-do-it books: Whelan's *A Baby? Maybe* (1975) and Peck and Granzig's *The Parent Test: How to Measure and Develop Your Talent for Parenthood* (1978). In addition, the National Alliance for Optional Parenthood provides a short brochure posing the question: "Am I Parent Material? Some thoughtful questions about one of the most important decisions you'll ever make." Their "test" is broken down into four sections on lifestyle changes,[3] motivations,[4] knowledge

---

[3] *Does having and raising a child fit the lifestyle I want?*

1. What do I want out of life for myself? What do I think is important?
2. Could I handle a child and a job at the same time? Would I have time and energy for both?
3. Would I be ready to give up the freedom to do what I want to do, when I want to do it?
4. Would I be willing to cut back my social life and spend more time at home? Would I miss my free time and privacy?
5. Can I afford to support a child? Do I know how much it takes to raise a child?
6. Do I want to raise a child in the neighborhood where I live now? Would I be willing and able to move?
7. How would a child interfere with *my* growth and development?
8. Would a child change my educational plans? Do I have the energy to go to school and raise a child at the same time?
9. Am I willing to give a great part of my life—AT LEAST EIGHTEEN YEARS—to being responsible for a child? And spend a large portion of my life being concerned about my child's well being?

[4] *What's in it for me?*

1. Do I like doing things with children? Do I enjoy activities that children can do?
2. Would I want a child to be "like me"?
3. Would I try to pass on to my child my ideas and values? What if my child's ideas and values turn out to be different from mine?
4. Would I want my child to achieve things that I wish I had, but didn't?
5. Would I expect my child to keep me from being lonely in my old age? Do I do that for my parents? Do my parents do that for my grandparents?
6. Do I want a boy or a girl child? What if I don't get what I want?
7. Would having a child show others how mature I am?
8. Will I prove I am a man or a woman by having a child?
9. Do I expect my child to make my life happy?

about child rearing[5] and finally the decision process itself.[6] They preface their "test" with a short introduction:

> If you decide to have a child, it'll be a decision that will affect you for the rest of your life. Think about it . . . Taking responsibility for a new life is awesome.
>
> These questions are designed to raise ideas that you may not have thought about. There are no "right" answers and no "grades"—your answers are "right" for you and may help you decide for yourself whether or not you want to be a parent. Because we all change, your answers to some of these questions may change two, five, even ten years from now.
>
> You *do* have a choice. Check out what you know and give it some thought. Then do what seems right for you.

Unfortunately, although these sources claim to provide a "parent test," neither the pamphlet nor the books provide a clear guide either for prospective parents themselves or for their counselors. What they do provide in the so-called "tests" is primarily a series of questions calling attention to the consequences of parenthood, with an implicit antinatalist bias towards an emphasis on its perils. Undoubtedly, the

---

5 *Raising a child? What's there to know?*

1. Do I like children? When I'm around children for a while, what do I think or feel about having one around all of the time?
2. Do I enjoy teaching others?
3. Is it easy for me to tell other people what I want, or need, or what I expect of them?
4. Do I want to give a child the love (s)he needs? Is loving easy for me?
5. Am I patient enough to deal with the noise and the confusion of the twenty-four-hour-a-day responsibility? What kind of time and space do I need for myself?
6. What do I do when I get angry or upset? Would I take things out on a child if I lost my temper?
7. What does discipline mean to me? What does freedom, or setting limits, or giving space mean? What is being too strict, or not strict enough? Would I want a perfect child?
8. How do I get along with my parents? What will I do to avoid the mistakes my parents made?
9. How would I take care of my child's health and safety? How do I take care of my own?
10. What if I have a child and find out I made a wrong decision.

6 *Have my partner and I really talked about becoming parents?*

1. Does my partner want to have a child? Have we talked about our reasons?
2. Could we give a child a good home? Is our relationship a happy and strong one?
3. Are we both ready to give our time and energy to raising a child?
4. Could we share our love with a child without jealousy?
5. What would happen if we separated after having a child, or if one of us should die?
6. Do my partner and I understand each other's feelings about religion, work, family, child raising, future goals? Do we feel pretty much the same way? Will children fit into these feelings, hopes and plans?
7. Suppose one of us wants a child and the other doesn't. Who decides?
8. Which of the questions in this pamphlet do we need to *really* discuss before making a decision?

nays have it, in that it is hard to imagine anyone who took their ominous questions to heart actually "passing" and therefore opting for parenthood. In developing a valid parent test, it is important that current pronatalist philosophies are not simply replaced by antinatalist ones, with the result that the parenthood prescription is simply replaced by an equally dubious parenthood proscription.

Implications for Social Policy

Presently available research has at least established the fact that all levels of adjustment asre possible for individuals with and without children, and that for some persons under some circumstances, remaining childless may be the most desirable alternative not only for them personally, but also for society in general. In the light of this contention, it seems to us that four goals in social policy would be desirable: first, increasing consciousness of parenthood as optional rather than compulsory; second, increasing rational debate of the pros and cons of parenthood; third, maintaining facilities whereby couples can effectively achieve their desire to have or not to have children; and fourth, providing support for those people who do opt for childlessness.

Consciousness-raising: to parent or not to parent

An insidious aspect of traditional pronatalism is the implicit assumption that parenthood is inevitable. Consequently, although there may be a choice of *how many* or *when*, the choice of *to parent* or *not to parent* is not raised to the level of awareness. It is not known how often pronatalism is in fact "coercive," in the sense of leading couples to have children they did not especially want for the sake of social approval, rather than for other reasons. There is reason to believe, however, that it does happen (Flapan, 1969: 409; Hardin, 1971: 265), and that such circumstances are not the most auspicious for either mother or child. Social policies which make implicit pronatalism explicit would go a long way towards lessening its undesirable effects, and towards making childlessness a viable option. Social scientists are not yet in a position to advocate with any certainty when a couple should or should not have a child. They are, however, in a position to make that process an increasingly conscious decision. By providing awareness that not *all* persons want to have children, and that those who do not are not necessarily unfortunate, they can raise the deliberation of parenthood to the level of awareness, and make "to parent or not to parent" a focus of conscious concern.

Debating the pros and cons: pronatalism versus antinatalism

Persons trying to debate the pros and cons of having children, and needing to come to a decision, cannot wait for social science to develop a "parent test" for guidance in their decision. In this instance, even the decision not to decide is eventually a *de facto* decision, as the biological and social reasons for having a child will pass and the couple will find that their option to have children has disappeared.

In assembling and weighing relevant evidence, a couple deliberating childbearing will find the pronatalist case excessively documented. In terms of social policy, there is no need to elaborate further the already elaborate mechanisms whereby young adults are bombarded with messages advocating parenthood. While pronatalism may provide essential psychological support for some persons facing the difficult task of child-rearing, it may also create unnecessary frustrations in others. The oversell of parenthood may lessen rather than enhance later adjustment to it, in that the actual experiences cannot live up to the romanticized expectations implicit in the advance billing. Some increase in the messages concerning the disadvantages of having children would help make expectations more realistic, and would make for a more balanced and informed decision.

Maintaining free choice: implications for physicians

Encouraging couples to debate the pros and cons of parenthood and, as much as possible, to make a "rational" decision, is of little utility unless they are then able to carry it out. Maintaining an atmosphere of free choice involves two components: first, avoiding permanent, irreversible decisions until the couple are indeed certain of their motivations; and second, providing the means whereby the final decision can be implemented. To achieve these ends, it is necessary to have unrestricted access to all of the means of birth control: contraception, abortion, and sterilization.

Availability of Contraception and Abortion. Barring the alternative of infanticide, the role of parenthood is an irrevocable one. Once a child is born, its parents are required to act as parents for some twenty years. The irreversible nature of the decision to have a child argues strongly for the position of the planned parenthood movement that it is a decision that should be made with deliberate foresight. Deciding to be childless is of little consequence if fate then intervenes in the form of an accidental pregnancy that a woman cannot or will not abort.

At the present time, attempts to control fertility have as their focal concern a target population of young married mothers. While this group certainly incurs the greatest number of pregnancies, wanted or otherwise, it is not the only segment of the population seeking freedom from the "tyranny of pregnancy." In terms of the law, fertility control is theoretically available to all adults; in actual practice, however, conscientious assistance with problems of fertility control is more likely to be forthcoming for mature married parents than for any other group.

Availability of Sterilization. Legally, all persons past the age of consent have a right to sterilization. In practice, however, many physicians are reluctant to sterilize persons who are unmarried or who are childless,[7] either because they are afraid of subsequent lawsuits, or because they personally disapprove. The film of childlessness entitled: *Surely You Don't Mean Not Ever?* focuses attention directly on an issue considered critical in responding to childlessness. Often, temporary childlessness may be more or less acceptable, whereas permanent childlessness is not. The important factor in such deliberations is the question of irreversibility. When couples postpone having children for a long period of time, there is always the possibility that when they do decide to have a child they will find they have become sterile, or at least sub-fecund. More dramatically, when a childless couple decide that one or the other or both should be sterilized, they assert that they *never* want to have children. The younger a couple are when they declare their intention to avoid parenthood, the more they are looked upon askance, and the less they are granted credibility. Often, it is assumed that young couples do not know their own minds and that when they "grow up,"

---

[7] In the past, the absence of legal restrictions regarding the rights of adults to be sterilized if they choose to do so was not reflected in common medical practice. For example, Landis (1966) studied the attitudes of 1,500 physicians toward vasectomy and found the simple reason of not wanting children was not considered acceptable for having the operation performed. Most (seventy per cent) indicated they would refuse a vasectomy to a single man and more than half (sixty per cent) said they would refuse a man with no children. Since children are commonly assumed to be more essential to women than to men, probably an even larger proportion of doctors would have refused to sterilize a childless women. Thus, after a review of a number of objections to vasectomy (such as religious conflicts, possible legal action for civil damages and problems of impotence), the American Medical Association (1968: 821) concluded, after no reference at all to the importance of number of children, that:

> . . . the following can serve as preliminary guidelines . . . if a man can reconcile the operation with his religion, *if he has several children*, if he lacks observable psychiatric sex-oriented stigma, and if his wife agrees to the operation . . . surely then he should be able to obtain a vasectomy for reasons of contraception alone [emphasis ours].

By implication, at that time in the editorial opinion of the AMA, a man who did not have children should not have been able to obtain a vasectomy simply as a means of birth control. Many doctors still refuse to perform sterilizations on unmarried people or on those without children.

they will change their views. The older couples who express a similar intention are taken more seriously because of their maturity, but they are also viewed with greater alarm. They are, after all, "old enough to know better," and they are cautioned not to wait too long, lest they find later they cannot have children and regret their lost opportunities. The possibility of regret is a relevant question, but unfortunately, is an unanswerable one. No one can be accountable for how he or she will feel in twenty years. Probably some childless couples do regret their lack of progeny. Certainly many parents lament, and loudly, their regret at having produced offspring. In 1975, a Gallup Poll of a representative sample of Americans found that in response to the question: "If you had it to do over again, would you have children?" one in ten parents said they would not (McLaughlin, 1975: 37). When considering childlessness, the question of irreversibility is a false issue in light of the fact that having a child is an irreversible decision, too. It is noteworthy that it would not be cause for comment or alarm if a person of twenty-one made the irreversible decision to have three children; however, it would be cause for considerable comment if she made the irreversible decision to have no children.

In our opinion, the control of fertility should be vested in the individual, rather than subject to unilateral decisions by a physician. To achieve this in practice as well as in theory, medical school curricula should include a discussion of moral and ethical issues with regard to pronatalism. Since pronatalism pressure from physicians may be covert as well as overt, it is important to sensitize physicians to the ways in which they may be implicitly imposing their own values upon their patients. Contraception and abortion should be equally available to all, regardless of marital or parental status. The sterilization of relatively young persons, assuming that they are past the legal age of consent should be seen as no more or less problematic than the decision of young persons to have one or more children.

Sustaining a variant choice: implications for counselors

Regardless of how much emphasis is placed on the free choice of bein or not being a parent, the vast majority of persons will continue to op for parenthood. It is likely, however, that those persons who are no well suited for parenthood and who have children anyway cause a greatly disproportionate number of problems for themselves and fo others. In terms of whatever formal or informal "parent test" i employed in such situations, counselors might consider advocating tha such persons either forego parenthood or at least postpone it.

Only a few years ago there was a rather extensive debate in the helping professions concerning whether or not responsible marriage counselors would ever be ethically justified in recommending divorce, rather than spending time, money and emotional energy in a futile attempt to reconcile irreconcilable differences. Although opinions still vary, many counselors have concluded that one of their functions in helping clients may be to help them overcome their fear of the stigma of divorce and other social pressures to stay married, thereby facilitating the dissolution of the marriage. Similarly, it may be time for a parallel debate concerning whether or not responsible marriage counselors would ever be ethically justified in recommending voluntary childlessness, rather than spending time, money and emotional energy in developing positive attitudes toward childbearing. There has been extensive professional concern with helping couples to adjust to the "crisis of parenthood," with adjustment usually being defined as modifying their behavior in ways which are felt to be in the best interests of the child or children. While there is certainly a place for such child-centered therapy, there may also be a place for adult-centered therapy, including concern with helping some couples to avoid the "crisis of parenthood" in the first place. The general social policy of professional therapists has been to advocate parenthood to almost all patients under almost all conditions. A more appropriate social policy would be for marriage counselors and other advisors to be sensitized to the possibility that for some clients, the parenthood experience may be permanently disruptive.

In at least some cases, the most appropriate role of the counselor or the therapist may be to help clients overcome their fear of the stigma of childlessness and other social pressures to have children, thereby facilitating deliberate childlessness as an acceptable option. The small minority of couples who do opt for childlessness, and /or who should be encouraged to do so, would benefit immensely from this rather special kind of support.[8] Rather than being uncritically pronatalistic, or being merely tolerant of some persons who wish to avoid parenthood, future counselors might be able to serve their clients better by articulating the childless option, and by taking an active part in mitigating the coercive effects of pronatalism.

---

8 For example, an ongoing project at the University of Minnesota offers a workshop specifically designed to serve childless couples (Russell, Hey, Thoen, and Walz, 1978). A relevant film, *Surely You Don't Mean Not Ever?* was written and directed by Martha Garrett Russell, and is available from the Media Resource Center of the University of Minnesota, Minneapolis, Minnesota. A recent issue of *The Family Planner* (1979) reports similar workshops being conducted in Los Angeles under the auspices of the Planned Parenthood Association.

Appendix: THE RECRUITMENT OF RESPONDENTS

The present research was based on data collected from a group of 156 childless persons. From 1972 to 1977, in-depth interviews were conducted with 120 childless wives and 36 childless husbands living in southern Ontario, primarily in the Toronto area. The methodological procedures used in the collection and presentation of the resulting data are admittedly unorthodox. In discussing the approach used, at least four main issues are involved: the rationale for the selection of a group of voluntarily childless persons; the procedures for locating suitable respondents; the processes involved in in-depth interviewing; and finally, the description of the characteristics of the respondents who were interviewed.

Stalking an Invisible Minority

Since unmarried persons are expected to remain childless, and since, with some exceptions, most of them deliberately do so, the social significance of voluntary childlessness focuses mainly upon married persons who choose not to have children in spite of being licensed and indeed expected to do so. The initial problem in the study of childlessness was simply to find appropriate married couples to interview. Unfortunately, the nature of the phenomenon of voluntary childlessness is such that conventional techniques for the selection of appropriate samples are not readily applicable. In the first place, individuals in this category are statistically only a very small minority, constituting about five per cent of the population. Second, the absence of children is not always a significant enough social characteristic to make childless couples readily visible in the population. Third, even when childless couples are identified, without actual interviews one cannot distinguish persons who happen not to have become parents from those who have deliberately and permanently opted out of parenthood. Finally, intentional childlessness is still a sensitive issue, in that it is perceived by many to be abnormal and immoral. Even if persons could be contacted on a random basis, and could be correctly categorized, it is unlikely that most deliberately childless persons would be willing to talk freely about a status which is considered deviant and which carries a significant social stigma.

The fact that individuals in a particular social category constitute only a small fraction of the total population, and are not readily identifiable, does not mean that they cannot and should not be studied by social scientists. It does mean that conventional techniques are often inappropriate. Worthwhile studies have been done with a number of kinds of deviant individuals, such as transvestites, married virgins, prostitutes, drug addicts, homosexuals, members of minority religious cults, and various kinds of criminals (Buckner, 1971). Although nonrandom sampling has many limitations, it is often the only alternative to abandoning the inquiry. Availability samples provide a legitimate alternative, especially in instances such as the present work which are exploratory in nature.

The search for deliberately childless persons included several stages of publicity. Initially, word-of-mouth requests among acquaintances yielded some suitable subjects. These few were supplemented by persons responding to direct advertisements in local newspapers. Later, several journalists became interested in the research and offered newspaper accounts of the project. These efforts, which predictably appeared in the so-called "women's section" of the paper were quite successful, especially when the article was supplemented by photographs. The subject of childlessness was also discussed on several radio and television talk shows in which a tag-line to the lecture was an appeal to interested respondents.

Screening Volunteers: Four Criteria

The public response to media appeals was considerable. A total of 206 persons called or wrote to ask for information and to volunteer themselves, and sometimes their mates, as participants in the study. All of these persons were themselves childless. However, since our research interest was not in childlessness in general but only in deliberately childless couples who were unlikely ever to have children, only 156 of the 206 volunteers were considered to be appropriate persons to be interviewed. Because the selection of respondents was nonrandom, making it impossible to generalize results to all childless couples, it was doubly important to insure at least that every one of the respondents was definitely and unambiguously voluntarily childless and almost certain to remain so.

Marital status

Of all couples who live together as man and wife, about two per cent are not legally married (Westoff, 1978: 54). Because illegitimacy is still somewhat stigmatic, couples who live together without marriage have an important, socially acceptable reason not to have children. It is of course possible that some deliberately childless persons reject marriage for much the same kinds of reasons that they reject parenthood. For our purposes, however, only respondents who were legally married, and who were living with their mates, were interviewed. Future research might also be concerned with the interface between unconventional, unconforming attitudes towards fertility norms, and unconventional, unconforming attitudes towards marriage norms.

Duration of marriage

Childlessness is known to be inversely correlated with duration of marriage.[1] For the first few months of marriage childlessness is the preferred rather than the deviant state.[2] For the first few years of marriage, childlessness does not occasion comment, in that couples are assumed either to be waiting for conception to occur, or to be temporarily postponing having their first child. However, the delay in beginning a family is related to both physiological and psychological factors: persons

---

[1] For the first years of marriage, the correlation of childlessness and marital duration seems primarily related to the increased risk of conception (Rhee, 1973); after ten years, the correlation is usually not substantial (Titmuss and Grundy, 1946; Grabill and Glick, 1959: 74; Veever, 1971d).

[2] Although ideally, married couples do not become parents until they have been married for some time, in reality many have children quite precipitately. In the United States, approximately 8 per cent of women have a child before their first marriage, and another 16 per cent do so before they have been married seven months. The median interval from marriage to the birth of the first child is less than 20 months (United States Bureau of the Census, 1976b: 13).

who postpone having children always increase the risk of never having them, in that later they may be less fecund,[3] or may change their minds on the desirability of becoming parents. Whatever the ultimate reason, the key question becomes: how long after marriage can a couple postpone having a child before it becomes very likely that they will permanently remain childess? Of all first births, 90 per cent occur within the first five years of marriage (United States Bureau of the Census, 1976b: 13). Althought exceptions undoubtedly occur in particular instances, in general couples who are still childless after five years of marriage seem likely to remain so. This is especially true of wives who marry for the first time in their late twenties, and so are already over thirty when that interval had passed. Among persons who volunteered, interviews were done only with those who had been legally married for at least five years.

Since the purpose of the five-year criterion was to eliminate persons who were presently childless but who were likely later to become parents, several exceptions were made. In one instance, a couple married only three years was accepted because the wife had already been sterilized, indicating an irrevocable commitment to permanent childlessness. In several other cases, although the couple had been married for less than five years, the wife was already over forty years of age, making it virtually impossible for her still to become a mother.
become a mother.

Fecundity

A man's ability to sire a child, or a woman's ability to conceive and to bear one, can never be absolutely established until a child has actually been born. However, in the absence of known fecundity impairments, it

---

3 Until the age of menopause, it is reasonable to assume that most women remain fecun and could therefore conceive and bear a child. In reality, however, fecundity is known t decline with advancing age (Rindfuss and Bumpass, 1976). Some women who coul readily have conceived and born a child when they were in their twenties will becom subfecund or even sterile in their thirties. In addition, male fertility also declines wit age, and for older couples the problem is further compounded by the effects of less fre quent intercourse (Fabe and Wikler, 1979: 280-282). Although mothers over thirty ma continue to have more children, if a woman has not become a mother by the age of thirty it is very unlikely that she will ever do so. For example, it is estimated that amon childless wives aged thirty to thirty-four, it is 93.3 per cent certain that they will nc have a child (Poston, 1976: 203). Since women who tend to postpone having children als tend to postpone getting married, it is likely that some couples will find that they hav waited too long, and that by the time they desire conception it is no longer possible. A this point, their classification as voluntarily or involuntarily childless is open to cor siderable debate.

can be assumed that a sexually active couple could produce a child if they so desired. To be included in the study, respondents had to report either that they believed themselves fecund and were therefore using birth control to prevent conception or that they had deliberately been sterilized. In the absence of conclusive tests for fecundity, there is always the ironic possibility that couples who assiduously practice birth control to prevent conception may be subfecund or sterile, so that conception would not occur in any case.[4] In our terms, the important factor was the perception of oneself as fecund, and the taking of appropriate measures to prevent conception.

Parental roles

Parenthood is a social as well as a biological phenomenon. Since part of our concern was with the impact of children upon adults, respondents were screened in terms of their **parenting experience**. No one was accepted who had ever assumed the role of a parent, either by adopting a child or by caring for a step-child. This eliminated a number of second marriages, in which one spouse had a child by a previous marriage, and the other, although biologically childless, was at least peripherally involved in its care. Although such quasi-parental roles are themselves worthy of study, for present purposes it was unclear whether such a person "really" was or was not a "parent." Unfortunately, childlessness, including voluntary childlessness, is known to be associated with complex marital histories.[5] Imposing these criteria inadvertently eliminated from potential respondents some persons who

---

[4] Conversely, some infertile couples are in a sense deliberately childless, in that they prefer to live without children, have no inclination to adopt, and regard their sterility not as a problem to be cured, but as an incidental convenience. From the sociological point of view, the essential component in defining persons as voluntarily childless is not their biological status as fecund or sterile, but their psychic preference not to procreate and their subsequent avoidance of the parenthood role. However, in order to be certain that our respondents were unambiguously deliberately childless, we omitted from consideration one wife who claimed to be voluntarily childless, but who had serious fecundity problems and was probably sterile, and one husband who reported that he had not gotten a vasectomy because the doctor told him his sperm count was already very low.

[5] Demographic studies suggest that among ever-married women, rates of childlessness are lowest for those who are married only once and who are currently living with their husbands. Among other ever-married women, rates are lower for widows than for separated women, and lower for the separated than for divorcées (Grabill and Glick, 1959; Rhee, 1973). Among women who marry more than once, rates of childlessness are substantially higher, especially among remarried divorcées (Bogue, 1969: 727). For some, involuntary childlessness may have been a precipitating factor in divorce and remarriage. More likely, however, the association between childlessness and multiple marriage is due to deliberate avoidance or postponement of parenthood.

were themselves voluntarily childless but who were involved in reconstituted families in their second or third marriages.

Finally, respondents were asked about their **parenting aspirations.** Volunteers were only accepted as respondents if they had no plans to have a child in the forseeable future. This criterion excluded those who planned definitely to have a child by a specific date, no matter how far that point was in the future, but included those who conceded some possibility of eventually having a child, or of adopting one. It is, of course, possible that some persons who do not intend to have children will accidentally have them, or will later change their minds. Conversely, it is possible for some persons who want children some time in the future to find that, in the end, they do not have them. In trying to find couples who will permanently remain childless, it is very likely that persons married more than five years who have avoided having a child, and who have no specific plans to have one, will never actually become parents.

Eventually, over the course of six years, interviews were conducted with 156 persons who had been married for at least five years, who were living with their mates, who had no known fecundity impairments or who had been deliberately sterilized, who had never been in the role of parent, and who did not aspire to parenthood. Of the childless persons interviewed, 120 were women, and 36 were men. For 29 couples, it was possible to interview both husband and wife. However, in most instances wives (N = 91) provided data on both themselves and their husbands. In a few cases (N = 7), husbands alone provided information on the family. In total, therefore, data were collected concerning a total of 127 deliberately childless marriages, with an average duration of marriage of 9.6 years.

In-Depth Interviews: Collecting Life Histories

The initial approach to the study of voluntary childlessness followed the conventional approach of survey interviewers. A number of studies pertaining to fertility and to family interaction were examined, and a detailed questionnaire was constructed using a self-report format similar to the kind offered by Blood and Wolfe (1960). This questionnaire was then administered to a number of childless men and women. Examination of the data soon made it apparent that the instruments, as conventionally constructed, were not subtle enough to pick up the intricacies and fine points which really differentiated the orientations and attitudes of childless persons from their more traditional counterparts. Unless one is researching an area which is already quite familiar to social science, one cannot have a great deal of confidence that one is, in fact, asking "appropriate" questions (Denzin, 1970). The factual data collected by such approaches are of little relevance in attempting to explain the subjective aspects of the phenomenon of childlessness and the career paths whereby some men and women come to reject parenthood.

In addition to the limitations of questionnaires in assessing subjective factors and situational contingencies, it became apparent that questionnaire items which initially seemed appropriate and innocuous were in fact "leading the witness" in ways which did not necessarily correspond with the respondent's worldview. For example, in one of the early studies of attitudes towards parenthood, the suggestion that: "Childlessness may some day be cause for regret" was checked by 33 per cent of the husbands. When it was not included in the questionnaire, however, no one volunteered supplemental information indicating this motive (Dennison, 1940: 69). Similarily, it seemed to be obvious that the population explosion would be a significant factor in individuals' decisions not to have children. When questions about population were asked directly, many respondents agreed that such issues were indeed important. However, left to their own devices, very few spontaneously volunteered anything at all about population or ecology, suggesting that in fact these issues were at best tangential to their own concerns. Structured questionnaire items about these issues would have suggested a preoccupation with aging, or a concern with over-population, which did not actually characterize the respondents.

All volunteers were contacted initially by telephone and an appointment for an interview was arranged, usually at least a week in advance. Although very little was said about the nature of the interview or the study, it was made clear that the interview would take several hours and that it was undesirable for persons other than the couple to be present. Interviews were conducted during the evenings and weekends, favorite times being Saturday and Sunday mornings. In most instances, the interviews were taped using a small, unobtrusive audio tape recorder without a detached microphone. Permission was always requested to tape the interviews, with the explanation that it was easier than taking notes, and no one refused permission or appeared bothered by the tape or even especially aware of it. One upper-class woman of some prominence was very concerned with the question of privacy, and although confident her name would not be used, felt that a description of her case would be readily recognizable to many people in her community. She was persuaded to continue with the interview only after it was promised that no case history involving her, however disguised, would be released to the public without her knowledge and consent. Following this experience, similar assurances were given to other respondents.

The unstructured in-depth method is described and discussed in some detail by Denzin (1970: 219-259). Following his orientation, our interviews took the form of orienting questions in which the childless were encouraged to tell their own life story, in their own time and in their own words, with the focus of attention directed toward those aspects of their life relevant to their sexual and marital adjustment and to their feelings about parenthood. Since there existed few reliable materials concerning the nature of voluntary childlessness, and few theoretical frameworks adequately accounting for it, there were few reliable guidelines suggesting which factors were of sociological significance. In this context, the themes and issues subjects chose not to discuss, or to discuss only cursorily, were at least as significant as the themes and issues they chose to elaborate on at length. This open-ended procedure allowed closer approximation of the version of reality constructed by the subjects themselves. No assumptions were made about what was or was not important in the reality-construction process; no order on the presentation was imposed to suit the thinking of the interviewer; and no specific instances of kinds of behavior were necessarily assumed to have uniform meanings for the individuals interviewed.

One of the advantages of working with a self-selected sample of volunteers is that all respondents are more or less willing informants who come to the interview predisposed to cooperate. To start the conversation, respondents were first invited to describe some aspects of their daily round. Routine and emotionally-neutral questions were posed concerning such things as the nature of their work, their satisfaction with their place of residence, or their basic domestic arrangements. After a brief period, respondents were then asked: "How do people respond to you when they find out that you do not have children?" This query proved to be especially useful in establishing rapport, in that it provided an introduction to the topic of childlessness which was not at all threatening. All respondents reported a wide range of negative responses from others. In relating vignettes of what had been said about them or done to them, attention was directed not towards themselves and their own possible inadequacies, but towards the foibles of others. After a few minutes of ventilation about what they perceived to be unfair stereotypes and unwarrented pronatalist pressures, they had become deeply immersed in the topic and were almost eager to expound their views.

Interviews averaged a length of approximately four hours, ranging from a minimum of two and a half to a maximum marathon session of nearly eight. The interviews touched on many aspects of life which would ordinarily fall within the private sphere. Most respondents seemed to have anticipated that such would be the case, and implicitly agreed to such intimate discussions when they agreed to be interviewed. Once involved in the discussion, most respondents were willing to go beyond the confines of the usual interview situation, and to discuss almost all aspects of their lives in which interest was expressed. In most cases, interaction with respondents did not end with the end of the formal interview, and in a number of cases, the discussions after the interview were almost as informative as the interview itself. Morgan (1963) reports that in interviewing the families of schizophrenics, he obtained a great deal of his most valuable information during the "second day seminar" in which the families really began to "level" with him about what was going on in the family. Although in the present study the home visits were never as extensive as Morgan's, who sometimes spent several days with the family, several techniques did provide something of a "second day" effect. In many cases an interview lasting several hours was followed by a host-guest relationship lasting for another several hours, during which time the spouse was often present, and was included in a general conversation. Such discussions were not deliberately focused on parenthood, but inevitably returned to some variation on this theme. Respondents often extended invitations for lunch or dinner, and in some instances it was possible to accept. Some respondents further illustrated their interviews by showing objects or environments which they felt crucial in the expression of their lifestyle.[6] Without exception,

For example, a doctoral student in zoology invited me to see her basement laboratory set up for the study of bird behaviors, and explained in some detail the nature of the problem and the progress of her research. An amateur musician and her husband displayed with some pride the harpsicord they were building in the spare bedroom, explaining with enthusiasm the details of its construction. Two sculptors provided a tour of their studio, explaining many facets of their work and discussing the responses of their critics. Couples to whom a secluded country lifestyle was important suggested a walk over their grounds. Couples who were conspicuously "house-proud" inevitably offered a tour of their home, pointing out at length the special features of their interior decor. A couple whose soical life centered mainly around a country club extended an invitation for an informal picnic with friends.

all respondents expressed a willingness to be interviewed again, either in the near future or in several years.

Childlessness, whether deliberate or not, is a sensitive issue, and interviews concerning it therefore meet with the same kinds of pitfalls and obstacles as do discussions of sensitive family topics (Gelles, 1976). Although persons who volunteer to be interviewed are by definition willing to talk about themselves and their problems, all couples showed reluctance to discuss at least some aspects of their lives. It is interesting to note, however, that the definitions of what was or was not "too personal" to discuss varied widely from one person to the next. For example, one respondent felt quite comfortable discussing her self-induced abortion, including details to the mechanical techniques selected and how each step was performed. However, this woman would not reveal what her bank balance was and, when finally persuaded that financial concerns were relevant, would only give a range "to the nearest $5000." One middle-aged man was willing to discuss in detail several extramarital affairs but would not comment in any way on anything he considered "politically compromising." A young accountant was enthusiastic about reporting financial concerns, to the point of bringing out the family books and budget and explaining in detail how all of the money was saved or spent. However, he would not discuss his religious preferences beyond; "It's between me and God and God's not listening." Every person had some area, other than childlessness *per se*, which was for them emotionally charged and very sensitive; however, there was no discernible pattern and no way to predict whether this "taboo" area would be sexual, political, financial, religious, or economic.

With volunteer subjects, it is always relevant to question, at least obliquely, why they have come forward. One motivation for volunteering for the study seems to have been to learn more about childlessness. However, to prevent biasing subjects' answers, no information was given during the interview except in response to direct questions, and to these the minimum amount of information was given, such as: "Some couples feel that way." The norm of reciprocity was also apparent in the subjects' interest in my own background and feelings and in the way in which the study came to be done. Questions on these areas were answered with a promise to tell them everything they wanted to know but only *after* the interview was over. Most expressed interest in the outcome of the study and wanted access to the report when it was completed.

In-depth interviews on sensitive issues provide an opportunity for an emotional catharsis for respondents, which for some persons was ob viously rewarding (Gelles, 1976). Once rapport was established, it was often difficult to get respondents to *stop* talking. This was especially true of older respondents who, compared with younger couples, felt a sense of pluralistic ignorance. The sense of being very much alone in their antinatalist feelings meant that, when they finally encountered what they perceived to be a sympathetic audience, there was a long outpouring of salient but generally unexpressed feelings.

The processing of in-depth interviews, once they have been collected, is difficult and of necessity subjective. In the early stages of the research, some of the interviews were transcribed in their entirety. However, this process proved very time-consuming and yielded unmanageable results, with a single interview running to nearly one hundred pages of typescript. For most of the interviews, the tapes were played several times. Many direct quotations were transcribed verbatim and were organized both by individual respondent and by general topic. A précis was made of the interview, which was later abbreviated still further into biographies for each respondent. Although the biographies themselves were later abandoned, being too objective and structured to be immediately relevant to the problem at hand, writing them was a very instructive exercise and provided a necessary basis for contemplating masses of detailed but unsystematized data. Factual data, such as age, age at marriage, education, and religion, which would ordinarily constitute face sheet data on a standard questionnaire, were coded on summary sheets, enabling concise summary statements to be made concerning some selected objective characteristics of respondents.

Characteristics of Respondents

Because respondents were volunteers who were then selected in a purposive manner, and because the major focus of concern was upon the construction of reality by voluntarily childless persons rather than upon their objective charcteristics, there was little utility in a statistical analysis of our interviews. Nevetheless, it is useful to know something about the kinds of persons who were interviewed, and to be able to make at least tentative comparisons between their demographic characteristics, and those of the general population.

Every year at the University of Chicago, the National Opinion Research Center (NORC) conducts a survey of opinions and attitudes held by a representative sample of all persons in the United States over

Table 4. Selected Characteristics of Childless Respondents, Compared with Married Parents: United States, 1977[1]

Characteristic	% Childless Respondents (N = 254)	% Reference Population of Parents (N = 419)
Self-Perception of Own Social Class		
Lower class	—	2
Working class	15	50
Middle class	74	45
Upper class	11	3
Religious Preference		
Protestant	23	61
Catholic	3	29
Jewish	—	2
None	74	7
Other	—	1
Religion Raised In		
Protestant	82	63
Catholic	11	29
Jewish	1	3
None	6	4
Other	—	1
Family Background		
Lives with both parents at age 16	93	80
Other arrangement at age 16	7	20
Mother's Employment		
Mother did work after marriage	17	55
Mother never worked after marriage	83	45
Number of Siblings		
None	21	7
One	16	15
Two	23	21
Three	14	15
Four	8	13
Five or six	6	13
Seven or more	12	17
Mean size, family of origin	3.7	4.8
Marital History		
Primary marriage	98	81
Previously divorced or separated	2	19

[1] NORC data on a representative cross-section (N = 1,530) of total population in continental United States: sub-sample of white persons aged twenty-five to forty-nine who are currently married, are living with their spouse, and who have had at least one child. Due to rounding, percentages do not always total exactly 100 per cent.

the age of eighteen.[7] Data from this survey provide a suitable reference population for comparison with our group of childless respondents. To maximize comparability, the total NORC sample in 1977 (N = 1,530) was restricted to only those persons most like our respondents, namely those who were white, aged twenty-five to forty-nine, presently married, living with their spouse, with at least one child. The result was a randomly selected reference population (N = 419) for the purposes of comparison with our group of childless respondents (N = 254) as shown in Table 4. With regard to some specific characteristics, such as age at marriage and education, typical patterns were known to be different for men than for women. In these instances, the reference group was divided into fathers (N = 185) and mothers (N = 234) for the purposes of comparison with childless husbands and childless wives (N = 127) as shown in Table 5.

Respondents who came forward to be interviewed were typically in their mid-thirties: the **mean age** for wives was 34.1 years, compared with 37.4 years for husbands. Although criteria for inclusion in the study entailed a minimum length of marriage of only five years, the **mean duration of marriage** was 9.6 years. Consistent with other studies, the **age at first marriage** for childless persons tended to be later than for other married couples.[8] Among our respondents, the mean age at first marriage was 24.9 years for wives and 26.8 years for husbands, nearly five years later than the age of first marriage in the

---

The NORC survey is conducted under the auspices of the Inter-University Consortium for Political and Social Research at the University of Chicago. Details of the sampling technique and of the specific instruments used are provided annually (National Opinion Research Center, 1978). Computer access to this data has proved to be an invaluable resource in this and other research endeavors and is greatly appreciated.

A number of researchers have observed that high rates of childlessness tend to be associated with relatively late age at first marriage (Titmuss and Grundy, 1946; Grabill and Glick, 1959; Rice, 1964; Rele, 1965; Ritchey and Stokes, 1974). In attempting to account for the phenomenon of late marriages among the voluntarily childless, one would assume that a selection factor would be operative. Very fecund young women who become pregnant quite readily may be more likely than others to incur a premarital pregnancy and consequently to be "forced" into an early marriage (deJong and Sell, 1977: 133). Moreover, part of the correlation is no doubt due simply to the fact that late marriage reduces the number of years before menopause when the woman is at risk of becoming pregnant, and since fecundity is known to decline with advancing years, this effect is further exaggerated. A year of unprotected intercourse at age twenty incurs more risk of pregnangy than does one at age thirty. Although part of the correlation between childlessness and late age of marriage may, therefore, be due to subfecundity, it seems more likely that the same social and psychological factors which predispose men and women to delay marriage may also predispose them to delay, and ultimately forego, parenthood. Fluctuations in the age of first marriage contribute to, but do not account for, fluctuations in the incidence of childlessness.

Table 5. Selected Characteristics of Childless Husbands and Wives Compared with Fathers and Mothers: United States, 1977[1]

Characteristic	% Males: Childless Husbands (N = 127)	% Males: Reference Population of Fathers (N = 185)	% Females: Childless Wives (N = 127)	% Females: Reference Population of Mothers (N = 234)
Age				
Under 25	—	—	2	—
25-29	12	15	14	18
30-34	25	21	39	22
35-39	33	19	25	22
40-44	16	24	8	20
45-49	4	22	6	18
Over 50	10	—	6	—
Mean age	**37.4**	**38.0**	**34.1**	**36.7**
Age range	**26–78**	**25–49**	**23–71**	**25–49**
Age at First Marriage				
Under 20	2	19	8	48
20–21	8	30	12	24
22–23	14	21	14	13
24–25	25	12	24	7
26–29	37	15	33	6
over 30	14	3	9	2
Average age	**26.8**	**22.4**	**24.9**	**20.3**
Education				
Less than high school	4	27	—	23
High school graduate	16	39	19	47
Some college	20	13	23	12
Undergraduate degree	28	12	21	12
Some postgraduate training	8	3	11	1
Postgraduate degree	24	7	26	5
Employment status				
Working full time	85	89	83	37
Working part time	—	2	3	12
Retired	4	—	3	—
In school	8	2	11	—
Keeping house	—	—	—	51
Other	3	7	—	—

[1] NORC data on a representative cross-section (N = 1,530) of total population of the continental United States: sub-sample of white persons, aged twenty-five to forty-nine who are currently married, are living with their spouse, and have at least one child. Due to rounding, percentages do not always total exactly 100 per cent.

reference population. The **age range** of respondents varied considerably, from a young school teacher of twenty-three to a retired carpenter of seventy-eight. The **range of marriage duration** varied comparably. The shortest marriage involved the young woman of twenty-three who, although married for only three years, was included in the study because she had already been sterilized; the longest marriage observed was a retired couple in their late sixties who had recently celebrated their thirty-fifth wedding anniversary.

The **social class position** of the childless persons we talked with was mainly upper middle class, and they tended to define themselves in these terms. None of them defined themselves as lower class, and only fifteen per cent felt that they were working class, compared with half of the reference population. Voluntary childlessness seems to be predominantly a middle-class phenomenon, associated with higher-than-average income and occupational prestige.[9] The respondents interviewed may also constitute an atypical selection, in that middle-class persons are the most likely to be aware of media appeals, and to respond to them. The middle-class bias is most clearly reflected in the high **level of education** of our respondents, especially of the women. Most of the persons interviewed had some university education, and one-quarter had at least one postgraduate degree. This discrepancy compared with the general public was true for both men and women, but was especially marked when comparing childless wives with mothers, and is consistent with the findings of previous research.[10]

---

[9] Contrary to the well-documented observation that *The Poor Get Children* (Rainwater, 1960), early studies reported an inverse relationship between childlessness and income (Kunz, Brinkerhoff, and Hundley, 1973). Later data suggest that such is not always the case, and that in many instances the relationship is in fact curvilinear (Poston, 1974). A more precise hypothesis is that although the relationship between income and involuntary childlessness may be inverse, the relationship between income and voluntary childlessness may be direct. Wolowyna's (1977) comparative analysis of data on British Protestants versus French Catholics lends additional support to the validity of this hypothesis. Generally, the voluntarily childless can be expected to be higher than average in terms of income and occupational prestige (Polonko, 1978).

[10] Although in certain instances the rates of childlessness are higher for women with only elementary school training than for those with high school training (Grabill and Glick, 1959: 80), generally the more years of schooling a woman has, the more likely she is to remain childless (Rhee, 1973). This relationship appears to hold for expected as well as actual childlessness and to hold for husbands as well (Ritchey and Stokes, 1974: 352). The association between childlessness and advanced education is especially pronounced among women who have had four or more years of college (Bogue, 1969: 726). The interaction between childlessness and education is convoluted. Some subfecund or sterile persons may seek advanced education to compensate for failure to fulfill maternal or paternal roles. Some parents—especially mothers—may be denied advanced education because an early pregnancy precluded staying in school, regardless of inclination. However, among groups known to be voluntarily childless, both men and

Among the childless persons interviewed, the **employment status** o wives was unusual, in that *all* of the childless women under the age o sixty-five were actively engaged in some occupation. The literatur suggests a clear association between childlessness and paid employ ment.[11] Although most young married women without children are nov gainfully employed,[12] our respondents would seem to be atypical o childless persons in general, in that there are some wives who neithe work nor take care of children. Our data do not provide any materia relevant to such cases. Hopefully, future research might consider ye another kind of childless couple which, unlike our respondents, doe not automatically involve a dual-income, dual-career family. Most o the childless wives who worked were salaried employees, but some ex ceptional women were self-employed in the arts, or as artisans or en trepreneurs. Although childless working wives did earn less than thei husbands, they usually provided nearly half of the family income.

In terms of **religion**, the childless respondents were clearly unlik the reference population, in that three-quarters reported they had "n religion," a pattern consistent with that reported in previou research.[13] Among the non-believers, the husbands appeared mor

---

women have high educational attainments (Gustavus and Henley, 1971: 281; Magaric 1975; Nason and Paloma, 1976). Part of this may be due to incidental factors, in tha women with advanced education tend also to be urban, to delay their first marriag and to be relatively effective contraceptors both before and after marriage. More lik ly, however, the same factors relating to wanting an education may be related to nc wanting children. Especially for women, parenthood may be postponed until a satisfa tory level of education is reached, by which time childbearing goals no longer see compelling. Although it is, of course, possible for mothers to achieve high levels c education, it is clear that motherhood leads to attrition at every stage of the educatio process.

11 Wives who are employed are known to have substantially higher rates of childlessne than do wives who are not employed (Grabill and Glick, 1959; deJong and Sell, 1977 This relationship holds for all ages, for both white and non-white women (Rhee,1973 and for present and expected fertility (Ritchey and Stokes, 1974: 353). It is unclea whether career involvement is a cause or a consequence of childlessness. Low rates c childlessness among housewives, however, have suggested to some that childlessne and unemployment are "incompatible" (Ritchey and Stokes, 1974).

12 In Canada in 1971, of childless wives ages twenty-five to thirty-four, 75 per cent we employed (Veevers, 1977: 22). In the United States in 1975, of childless wives unde thirty-five, 77 per cent were in the labor force (Glick and Norton, 1977: 11). In a gener survey in Chicago, Gove and Geerken (1977) found an approximately equal incidence employed and unemployed childless wives. Renne (1976: 195) found not only that on third of childless wives did not work, but that the happiest marriages appeared to b those in which the wife was neither a mother nor gainfully employed.

13 Similar over-representation of non-religious persons among the childless has bee reported by Rice (1964), Gustavus and Henley (1971), Rhee (1973), Bram (1978 Magarick (1975), Marcks (1976), Barnett and MacDonald (1976), Ory (1978), Kaltreid and Margolis (1977), Toomey (1977), Goodbody (1977) and Theon (1977).

eady to declare themselves to be atheists, whereas the wives were nore likely to temporize and call themselves agnostics. In either case, heir religious commitment was virtually nil. Even among those persons vho claimed a nominal affiliation, the level of religiosity was ex- eedingly low, as measured by ritual involvement, by private belief, or imply by level of interest. In terms of religious background, although nly a few non-religious persons came from non-religious homes, such ersons were more likely to have Protestant than Catholic ackgrounds. Although most persons who profess "no religion" do narry and become parents, their fertility rate is consistently lower han for those who profess to be associated with a religious denomina- on (Scott, 1976: 38). The strong and generally consistent association etween religious apostacy and voluntary childlessness suggests the ypothesis that the questioning of traditional religious beliefs is a elevant—perhaps even a necessary—predisposing factor leading to a orresponding questioning of beliefs concerning pronatalism.[14]

The **family background** of respondents was remarkably un- emarkable, in that most came from homes unbroken by either ivorce or death, in which the mother had never worked after she was narried. One atypical point of note is that a disproportionate number, bout one in five (or three times what would be expected) were only hildren. Generally, childless persons came from smaller families than id parents, and were more likely to be the first born than later born.

The **marital histories** of respondents was also remarkably uniform, n that with four exceptions, all respondents were in primary mar- ages. Persons who have complex histories are known to be more isposed than others to childlessness, both voluntary and involuntary. he absence of divorced persons is due primarily to the selection riterion eliminating those who had had experience in the parenting ole, even in the capacity of step-parent. Hopefully, future research ill address itself to the question of what happens in childless mar- ages which are also remarriages.

In summary, the 156 men and women interviewed seem not nrepresentative of voluntarily childless couples in general, in that ney are disproportionately drawn from the urban, well-educated, pper-middle class, and exhibit remarkably low religiosity. They are ertainly atypical in that all persons were white and were in marriages hich had survived for at least five years, and almost all were in rimary marriages in which both partners were employed.

In contradiction to this hypothesis, Poston (1976: 206) reports the one exception to this generalization, in that although data from the 1965 National Fertility Survey do in- dicate an excess of childless persons with no religious preference, their incidence in his study was only "slightly disproportionate."

Bibliography

Albee, Edward

1963 *Who's Afraid of Virginia Woolf?* New York: Antheneum.

Albert, E. M.

1966 "The unmothered woman," pp. 34–40 in S. M. Farber and R. H. L. Wilson (eds.), *The Challenge to Women.* New York: Basic Books.

Allport, Gordon

1937 "The functional autonomy of motives," *American Journal of Psychology*, 50: 141–156.

American Medical Association

1968 "Editorial: voluntary male sterilization," *Journal of the American Medical Association*, 204 (May): 163–164.

Andrews, Frank J., and Stephen B. Withey

1976 *Social Indicators of Well-Being: Americans' Perceptions of Life Quality.* New York: Plenum.

Arasteh, Josephine D.

1971 "Parenthood: some antecedents and consequences: a preliminary survey of the mental health literature," *The Journal of Genetic Psychology*, 118 (June): 179–202.

Bacon, Francis

1854 *Essays and Historical Works.* London: Henry G. Bohn.

Balakrishnan, T. R., J. F. Kantner, and J. D. Allingham

1975 *Fertility and Family Planning in a Canadian Metropolis.* Montreal and London: McGill–Queen's University Press.

Balchin, N.

1965 "Children are a waste of time," *The Saturday Evening Post* (October 19): 10–11.

Bardwick, Judith M.

1974 "Evolution and parenting," *The Journal of Social Issues*, 30(4): 39–62.

Barnett, Larry D.
1978 "Population growth, population organization participants, and the right of privacy," *Family Law Quarterly* 12 (Spring): 37–60.

Barnett, Larry D., and Richard H. MacDonald
1975 "The values of social movement participants: a study of the National Organization for Non-Parents," unpublished manuscript, available from Dr. Barnett at Nova University Law Center, Ft. Lauderdale, Florida 33314.

Barnett, Larry D., and Richard H. MacDonald
1976 "A study of the membership of the National Organization for Non-parents," *Social Biology*, 23 (Winter): 297–310.

Becker, Howard S.
1963 *Outsiders: Studies in the Sociology of Deviance.* New York: Free Press.

Berelson, Bernard, and Gary A. Steiner
1964 *Human Behavior: An Inventory of Scientific Findings.* New York: Harcourt, Brace and World.

Bell, Norman W.
1971 "Dimensions of the family: a critical view," paper presented at the Annual Meetings of the Canadian Sociology and Anthropology Association, St. John's, Newfoundland.

Bem, S. L.
1974 "The measurement of psychological androgyny," *Journal of Consulting and Clinical Psychology*, 42 (April): 155–162.
1975 "Sex-role adaptability: one consequence of psychological androgyny," *Journal of Personality and Social Psychology*, 31 (April): 634–543.

Benedek, Therese
1970 "The psychobiologic approach to parenthood," p. 109–208 in E. James Anthony and Therese Benedek (eds.), *Parenthood: Its Psychology and Psychopathology.* Boston: Little, Brown and Company.

Berger, Peter, and Hansfried Kellner
1970 "Marriage and the construction of reality," pp. 50–73 in H. Q Drietzel (ed.), *Recent Sociology No. 2.* London: Macmillan.

Berger, Peter L., and Thomas Luckman
1966 *The Social Construction of Reality: A Treatise in the Sociology of Knowledge.* New York: Doubleday.

Berkow, S.
1937 *Childlessness: A Study of Sterility, Its Causes and Treatment* New York: Lee Furman.

Bernard, Jessie
1972 *The Future of Marriage.* New York: Bantam.
1974 *The Future of Motherhood.* New York: Penguin.

Bernard, V.
1963 "Adoption," pp. 70–108 in A. Deutsch and H. Fishman (eds.), *The Encyclopedia of the Social Sciences.* New York: Franklin Watts.

Bierkens, B. P.
1975 "Childlessness from a psychological point of view," *Bulletin of the Menniger Clinic,* 39(2): 177–182.

Blake, Judith
1973 "Coercive pronatalism and American population policy," pp. 85–109 in Robert Parke, Jr. and Charles F. Westoff (eds.), *Aspects of Population Growth Policy.* Washington, D.C.: Commission on Population Growth and the American Future.
1974 "Can we believe recent data on birth expectations in the United States?" *Demography,* 11 (February): 25–44.
1978 "Is zero preferred? American attitudes towards childlessness in the 1970's," paper presented to the Population Association of America at their Annual Meeting in Atlanta, Georgia, April 13–15.

Blazer, John A.
1964 "Married virgins—a study of uncomsummated marriages," *Journal of Marriage and the Family,* 26 (May): 213–214.

Blood, Robert O., and Donald M. Wolfe
1960 *Husbands and Wives.* New York: Free Press.

Bogue, Donald J.
1969 *Principles of Demography.* New York: John Wiley.

Bram, Susan
1978 "Through the looking glass: voluntary childlessness as a mirror of contemporary changes in the meaning of parenthood," pp. 368–391 in Warren B. Miller and Lucile F. Newman (eds.), *The First Child and Family Formation.* Chapel Hill, North Carolina: Caroline Population Center.

Brown, Judith K.
1970 "A note on the division of labor by sex," *American Anthropologist,* 72 (October): 1073–1078.

Buckner, H. Taylor
1971 *Deviance, Reality and Change.* New York: Random House.

Bumpass, Larry
1973 "Is low fertility here to stay?," *Family Planning Perspectives,* 5 (Spring): 67–69.

Burgess, E. W., and Paul Wallin
1953 *Engagement and Marriage*. Philadelphia: J. B. Lippincott.

Burnside, Beverly
1977 *Gender Roles and Lifestyles: A Sociolcultural Study of Voluntary Childlessness*. Ph.D. dissertation, University of Washington, Seattle, Washington.

Byrne, Susan
1977 "To breed or not to breed? That is the question," *Playgirl* (September): 35–38.

Calhoun, A.
1919 *A Social History of the American Family from Colonial to Present Times*. Cleveland: The Arthur H. Clark Co.

Cameron, Paul, Cynthia Carr, and Kathy Scott
1976 "The effects of progeny upon lethality," paper presented to the Eastern Psychological Association at their Annual Meeting, New York, New York, April.

Campbell, Argus
1975 "The American way of mating: marriage si, children only maybe," *Psychology Today* (May): 37–43.

Campbell, Argus, Philip E. Converse, and Willard L. Rodgers
1976 *The Quality of American Life: Perceptions, Evaluations, and Satisfactions*. New York: Russell Sage.

Carr, Genevieve Delta
1963 *A Psychosociological Study of Fertile and Infertile Marriages*. Ph.D. dissertation, The University of Southern California, Los Angeles, California. *Dissertation Abstracts*, 1963–64, 24: 5598–5599.

Cavan, Ruth
1959 *American Marriage: A Way of Life*. New York: Thomas Y. Crowell.

Centers, R., and G. H. Blumberg
1954 "Social and psychological factors in human procreation," *Journal of Social Psychology*, 40(2): 245–257.

Chapman, Judi Anne
1978 *The Social Role of Household Pets*. Unpublished Master's thesis, Department of Sociology, The University of Western Ontario, London, Ontario.

Chasteen, Edgar
1972 *The Case for Compulsory Birth Control*. Englewood Cliffs, New Jersey: Prentice-Hall.

Chester, Robert
1972 "Is there a relationship between childlessness and marriage breakdown?" *Journal of Biosocial Science*, 4(4): 443–454.

1976 "Official statistics and family sociology," *Journal of Marriage and the Family*, 38 (February): 117–126.

Chester, Robert, and Jane Streather

1972 "Cruelty in English divorce: some empirical findings," *Journal of Marriage and the Family*, 34 (November): 706–712.

Christensen, Harold T.

1968 "Children in the family: relationship of number and spacing to marital success," *Journal of Marriage and the Family*, 30 (May): 283–289.

Christensen, Harold T., and Robert E. Philbrick

1952 "Family size as a factor in the marital adjustment of college students," *American Sociological Review*, 17 (June): 306–312.

Clarkson, Adrienne

1971 *True to You in My Fashion*. Toronto: New Press.

Clarkson, Frank E., Susan R. Vogel, Inge K. Broverman, Donald M. Broverman, and Paul S. Rosenkrantz

1970 "Family size and sex role stereotypes," *Science*, 167 (January): 390–392.

Cohen, J. M., and M. J. Cohen (eds.)

1971 *A Dictionary of Modern Quotations*. New York: Penguin.

Cohen, Sarah Betsy and James A. Sweet

1974 "The impact of marital disruption and remarriage on, fertility," *Journal of Marriage and the Family*, 36.

Commission on Population Growth and the American Future

1972 *Report*. Washington, D.C.: Commission on Population Growth and the American Future.

Cooper, Pamela E., Barbara Cumber, and Robin Hartner

1978 "Decision-making patterns and postdecision adjustment of childfree husbands and wives," *Alternative Lifestyles*, 1 (February): 71–94.

Cope, P.

1928 "The woman of *Who's Who*: a statistical study," *Journal of Social Forces*, 7 (December): 212–224.

Cowan, Carolyn Pape, Philip A. Cowan, Lynne Coie, and John D. Coie

1978 "Becoming a family: the impact of the first child's birth on the couple's relationship," pp. 296–324 in Warren B. Miller and Lucile F. Newman (eds.), *The First Child and Family Formation*. Chapel Hill, North Carolina: Carolina Population Center, University of North Carolina.

Cox, Nancy

1974 "Pronatal influences in home economics texts in a junior high school," pp. 99–113 in Ellen Peck and Judith Senderowitz (eds.), *Pronatalism: The Myth of Mom and Apple Pie*. New York: Thomas Y. Crowell.

Crum, Frederick S.
1914 "The decadence of the native American stock," *American Statistical Association Journal*, 14 (September): 215–222.

Cuber, John P., and Peggy B. Haroff
1966 *Sex and the Significant Americans: A Study of Sexual Behavior Among the Affluent*. Baltimore, Maryland: Penguin Books.

Cumber, Barbara F.
1977 *To Have or Not to Have: Married Couples' Decision to be Childfree*. M.A. dissertation, The University of Connecticut, Storrs, Connecticut.

Cutright, Phillip and Karen Polonto
1977 "Areal structure and rates of childlessness among American wives in 1970," *Social Biology*, 24 (Summer): 52–61.

Das Gupta, Prithwis
1975 "A method of computing period rates of spinsterhood and childlessness from census data applied to the United States," *Social Biology*, 22 (Summer): 134–142.

DeJong, Gordon F., and Ralph R. Sell
1977 "Changes in childlessness in the United States: a demographic path analysis, *Population Studies*, 31 (March): 129–141.

Dennison, Charles
1940 "Parenthood attitudes of college men," *Eugenic News*, 25: 65–69.

Denzin, Norman K.
1970 *The Research Act*. Chicago: Aldine Publishing Co.

Dexter, Lewis Anthony
1958 "A note of selective inattention in social sciences," *Social Problems*, 6 (Fall): 176–184.

Eickhoff, Andrew R.
1966 *A Christian View of Sex and Marriage*. New York: Free Press.

Epenshade, Thomas J.
1977 "The value and cost of children," *Population Bulletin*, 32 (April): 1–47.

Erikson, Erik K.
1963 *Childhood and Society*. New York: W. W. Norton.

Fabe, Marilyn, and Norma Wikler
1979 *Up Against the Clock*. New York: Random House.

Falk, Z. W.
1966 *Jewish Matrimonial Law in the Middle Ages*. London: Oxford University Press.

Family Planner, The
1979 "Investigating the cost: has raising a child become a luxury?" *The Family Planner*, 10 (Winter): 2–3.

Farber, B., and L. S. Blackman
1956 "Marital role tensions and number and sex of children," *American Sociological Review*, 21 (October): 596–601.

Fawcett, James T.
1973 "The value of children: theory and method," *Representative Research in Social Psychology*, 4 (January): 23–36.

Feiffer, Jules
1960 *The Explainers*. Toronto: The New American Library of Canada.

Feldman, Harold
1971 "The effects of children on the family," pp. 197–125 in Andrée Michel (ed.), *Family Issues of Employed Women in Europe and America*. Leiden, The Netherlands: E. J. Brill.

Figge, Margaret
1932 "Some factors in the etiology of maternal rejection," *Smith College Studies in Social Work*, 2: 237-260.

Figley, Charles R.
1973 "Child density and the marital relationship," *Journal of Marriage and the Family*, 35 (May): 272-282.

Flapan, Mark
1969 "A paradigm for the analysis of childbearing motivations of married women prior to the birth of their first child," *American Journal of Orthopsychiatry*, 39 (April): 402–417.

Fletcher, Ronald.
1968 *Instinct in Man*. London: Unwin University Books.

Foote, Nelson M.
1956 "A neglected member of the family," *Marriage and Family Living*, 18 (August): 213–218.

Ford, Clellan Stearns
1945 *A Comparative Study of Human Reproduction*. New Haven: Yale University Publications in Anthropology.

Frank, M., and C. Kiser
1965 "Changes in the social and demographic attributes of women in *Who's Who*," *The Milbank Memorial Fund Quarterly*, 43 (January): 55–75.

Franzwa, Helen H.
1974 "Pronatalism in women's magazine fiction," pp. 68–77 in Ellen Peck and Judith Senderowitz (eds.), *Pronatalism: The Myth of Mom and Apple Pie*. New York: Thomas Y. Crowell.

Friedan, Betty
1963 *The Feminine Mystique*. New York: Dell Publishing.

Friedman, L. J.
1962 *Virgin Wives: A Study of Unconsummated Marriages*. Springfield, Illinois: C. C. Thomas.

Gelles, Richard J.
1976 "Methods for studying sensitive family topics," paper presented to The National Council on Family Relations at their Annual Meeting in New York, New York, October.

Glick, Paul C.
1975 "A demographer looks at American families," *Journal of Marriage and the Family*, 37 (February): 15–27.

Glick, Paul C., and Arthur J. Norton
1977 "Marrying, divorcing, and living together in the U.S. today," *Population Bulletin*, 32 (October): 1–41.

Goffman, Erving
1952 "On cooling the mark out: some aspects of adaptation to failure," *Psychiatry*, 15 (November): 451–463.
1963 *Stigma: Notes on the Management of Spoiled Identity*. Englewood Cliffs, N.J.: Prentice-Hall.

Goldstein, Joseph, and Jay Katz (eds.)
1965 *The Family and the Law*. New York: The Free Press.

Goodbody, Sandra Toll
1977 "The psychological implications of voluntary childlessness," *Social Casework*, 58 (July): 426–434.

Goode, William J.
1963 *World Revolution and Family Patterns*. New York: The Free Press.
1964 *The Family*. Englewood Cliffs, New Jersey: Prentice-Hall.
1968 "Pressures to remarry: institutionalized patterns affecting the divorced," pp. 331–341 in Norman W. Bell and Erza F. Vogel (eds.), *A Modern Introduction to the Family*. New York: The Free Press.

Gove, Walter R., and Michael R. Geerken
1977 "The effect of children and employment on the mental health of married men and women," *Social Forces*, 56 (September): 66–76.

Grabill, W. C., and P. C. Glick
1959 "Demographic and social aspects of childlessness: census data," *Milbank Memorial Fund Quarterly*, 37 (January): 60–86.

Greenbaum, Henry
1973 "Marriage, family, and parenthood," *American Journal of Psychiatry*, 130 (November 11): 1262–1265.

Greenburg, Dan
1965 *How to Be A Jewish Mother*. New York: Price, Stern, Sloan.
Greene, Gaile
1963 "A vote against motherhood," *The Saturday Evening Post* (January 26): 10–12.
Griffith, Janet
1973 "Social pressure on family size intentions," *Family Planning Perspectives*, 5 (Fall): 237–242.
Grindstaff, Carl F.
1975 "The baby bust: changes in fertility patterns in Canada," *Canadian Studies in Population*, 2:15–22.
1976 "Trends and incidence of childlessness by race: indicators of black progress over three decades," *Sociological Focus*, 9 (August): 265–284.
Gustavus, Susan O., and James R. Henley, Jr.
1971 "Correlates of voluntary childlessness in a select population," *Social Biology*, 18 (September): 277–284.
Hagan, John
1977 *The Disreputable Pleasures: Crime and Deviance in Canada*. Toronto: McGraw-Hill Ryerson.
Hardin, Garrett
1971 "Multiple paths to population control," pp. 259–266 in Daniel Callahan (ed.), *The American Population Debate*. New York: Doubleday.
Harper, Robert A.
1959 "The responsibilities of parenthood: a marriage counsellor's view," *Eugenics Quarterly*, 6 (March): 8–13.
Hartner, Robin L.
1977 *Childfree Couples' Perception of Pronatalist Pressures from Others*. M.A. dissertation, The University of Connecticut, Storrs, Connecticut.
Hass, Paula H.
1974 "Wanted and unwanted pregnancies; a fertility decision decision-making model," *Journal of Social Issues*, 30 (4): 125–164.
Hastings, D. W., and J. G. Robinson
1974 "Incidence of childlessness for United States women, cohorts born 1891–1945," *Social Biology*, 21 (Summer): 178–184.
Havemann, Ernest
1967 *Birth Control*. New York: Time Incorporated.
Hawke, Sharryl, and David Knox
1977 *One Child By Choice*. Englewood Cliffs, N.Y.: Prentice-Hall.

Heath, L. L., B. S. Roper, and C. D. King
1974 "A research note on children viewed as contributors to marital stability: the relationship to birth control use, ideals, and expected family size," *Journal of Marriage and the Family*, 36 (May): 304–306.

Hobbs, Daniel F., Jr.
1968 "Transition to parenthood: a replication and an extension," *Marriage and the Family*, 30 (August): 413–417.

Hollingworth, Leta S.
1916–1917 "Social devices for impelling women to bear and rear children," *American Journal of Sociology*, 22 (July): 19–29.

Houseknecht, Sharon K.
1976 "A social-psychological model of voluntary childlessness," paper presented to the American Psychological Association at their Annual Meeting, Washington, D.C., September.
1977 "Reference group support for voluntary childlessness: evidence for conformity," *Journal of Marriage and the Family*, 39 (May): 285–294.
1978 "Voluntary childlessness: a social psychological model," *Alternative Lifestyles*, 1 (August): 379–402.

Humphrey, Michael
1969 *The Hostage Seekers: A Study of Childless and Adopting Couples*. London: Longmans.
1975 "The effect of children on the marital relationship," *British Journal of Medical Psychology*, 48 (September): 273–279.
1977 "Sex differences in attitude to parenthood," *Human Relations*, 30 (August): 737–750.

Jakobovits, Immanuel
1959 *Jewish Medical Ethics*. New York: Block Publishing Company.

Jacobson, Paul H.
1950 "Differentials in divorce by duration of marriage and family size," *American Sociological Review*, 15 (April): 235–244.

Jacoby, Arthur P.
1969 "Transition to parenthood: a reassessment," *Journal of Marriage and the Family*, 31 (November): 720–727.

Jones, D. E. Darnell, and David R. Halbert
1975 "Oral contraceptives: clinical problems and choices," *American Family Physician*, 13 (October): 115–123.

Kaij, L., and A. Malmquist
1971 "Motherhood and childlessness in monozygous twins. Part 1: Early relationships," *British Journal of Psychiatry*, 118 (February): 11–21.

Kaltreider, Nancy B., and Alan B. Margolis
1977 "Childless by choice: a clinical study," *American Journal of Psychiatry*, 134 (February): 179–182.

Karwoski, Rev. Francis A.
1955 *A Comparison of the Matrimonial Impediments of the State of Ohio and the Code of Canon Law*. Rome: Catholic Book Agency.

Kenkel, W.
1966 *The Family in Perspective*. New York: Appleton, Century, Crofts.

Kiesler, Sara B.
1977 "Post hoc justifications of family size," *Sociometry*, 40 (March): 59-67.

Kirk, D.
1957 "The fertility of a gifted group: a study of the number of children of men in *Who's Who*," pp. 78–98 in *The Nature and Transmission of the Genetic and Cultural Characteristics of Human Population*. New York: Milbank Memorial Fund.
1964 *Shared Fate*. New York: Free Press.

Kiser, Clyde V.
1939 "Voluntary and involuntary aspects of childlessness," *The Milbank Memorial Fund Quarterly*, 17 (January): 50–68.
1959 "Psychological factors in infertility: a demographic appraisal," paper presented to the Society for the Scientific Study of Sex at their Annual Meeting, New York, New York, November 7.

Kiser, Clyde V., and N. Schacter
1949 "Demographic characteristics of women in *Who's Who*," *The Milbank Memorial Fund Quarterly*, 27 (October): 392–433.

Kuczynski, R. R.
1938 "Childless marriages," *Sociological Review*, 30 (April): 120–144; (July): 213–235; (October): 346–364.

Kunz, Philip R., and Merlin B. Brinkerhoff
1969 "Differential childlessness by color: the destruction of a cultural belief," *Journal of Marriage and the Family*, 31 (November): 713–719.

Kunz, Phillip R., Merlin B. Brinkerhoff, and Vickie Hundley
1973 "Relationship of income and childlessness," *Social Biology*, 20 (June): 139–142.

Landers, Ann
1976 "If you had it to do over again, would you have children?," *Good Housekeeping*, 182 (June): 100–101, 215–216, 223–224.

Landis, Judson T.
1966 "Attitudes of individual California physicians and policies of

state medical societies on vasectomy for birth control," *Journal of Marriage and the Family*, 28 (May): 227–283.

LeMasters, E. E.
1957a "Parenthood as crisis," *Marriage and Family Living*, 19 (August): 352–355.
1957b *Modern Courtship and Marriage*. New York: Macmillian.
1959 "Holy deadlock: a study of unsuccessful marriages," *Midwest Sociologist*, 21 (July): 86–91.
1970 *Parents in Modern America*. Homewood, Illinois: The Dorsey Press.

Lemert, E. M.
1951 *Social Pathology*. New York: McGraw-Hill.

Levinson, Boris M.
1972 *Pets and Human Development*. Springfield, Illinois: Charles C. Thomas.

Lichtman, Carl H.
1976 *"Voluntary" Childlessness: A Thematic Analysis of the Person and the Process*. Ph.D. dissertation, Columbia University Teacher's College, New York. *Dissertation Abstracts*, 1976, 37: 1484–1485.

Lindenmayer, Jean-Pierre, Maurice D. Steinberg, Darla A. Bjork, and Herbert Pardes
1977 "Psychiatric aspects of voluntary sterilization in young, childless women," *Journal of Reproductive Medicine*, 19 (August): 87–91.

Loesch, John G., and Nahman H. Greenberg
1962 "Some specific areas of conflicts observed during pregnancy: a comparative study of married and unmarried pregnant women," *American Journal of Orthopsychiatry* 32 (July): 622–636.

Lorimer, F., *et al.*
1954 *Culture and Human Fertility. A Study of the Relation of Cultural Conditions to Fertility in Non-industrial and Transitional Societies*. Paris, Zurich: UNESCO.

Lott, Bernice E.
1973 "Who wants the children? Some relationships among attitudes toward children, parents, and the liberation of women," *American Psychologist*, 28 (July): 573–582.

Luckey, Eleanore B. and J. K. Bain
1970 "Children: a factor in marital satisfaction," *Journal of Marriage and the Family*, 32 (February): 43–44.

MacIntyre, Sally
1974 "Who wants the babies? The social construction of 'instincts'," pp. 150–173 in Diana Barker and Sheila Allen (eds.), *Sexual Divisions and Society: Process and Change.* London: Tavistock.

Magarick, Ronald Herbert
1975 *Social and Emotional Aspects of Voluntary Childlessness in Vasectomized Childless Men.* Ph.D. dissertation, The University of Maryland, College Park, Maryland. *Dissertation Abstracts*, 1976, 37: 1256.

Magarick, Ronald H., and Robert A. Brown
1976 "Social and emotional aspects of voluntary childlessness in vasectomized childless men," paper presented to the American Public Health Association at their Annual Meeting, Miami Beach, Florida, October 21.

Mai, François
1978 "The diagnosis and treatment of psychogenic infertility," *Infertility*, 1 (1): 109–125.

Malmquist, A., and L. Kaij
1971 "Motherhood and childlessness in monozygous twins. Part 2: The influence of motherhood on health," *British Journal of Psychiatry*, 118 (February): 22–28.

Marciano, Teresa Donati
1978 "Male pressure in the decision to remain childfree," *Alternative Lifestyles*, 1 (February): 95–112.

Marcks, Beatrice R.
1976 *Voluntarily Childless Couples: An Exploratory Study.* M.Sc. dissertation, Syracuse University, Syracuse, New York.

McFadden, Chas. J.
1961 *Medical Ethics (Fifth edition).* Philadelphia: F. A. Davis.

McLaughlin, Mary
1975 "Parents who wouldn't do it again," *McCall's*, 103 (November): 37–38.

Mead, Margaret
1949 *Male and Female.* New York: William Morrow.

Michel, Andrée, and Françoise L. Feyrabend
1969 "Real number of children and conjugal interaction in French urban families: a comparison with American families," *Journal of Marriage and the Family*, 31 (May): 359–363.

Michels, Lynnell
1970 "Why we don't want children," *Redbook Magazine* (January): 10–14.

Miller, Brian

1978 "Rocking the cradle and ruling the world: an exploratory study of gender role convergence and family patterns in *Who's Who*," paper presented to the Pacific Sociological Association at their Annual Meeting, Spokane, Washington, April.

Mills, C. Wright

1959 *The Sociological Imagination.* New York: Oxford.

Mommsen, Kent G.

1973 "Differentials in fertility among black doctorates," *Social Biology*, 20 (February): 20–29.

Mommsen, Kent B., and Dale A. Lund

1977 "Zero parity in the black population of the United States," paper presented to the Population Association of America at their Annual Meeting, St. Louis, Missouri, April.

Monahan, Thomas P.

1955 "Is childlessness related to family stability?," *American Sociological Review*, 20 (August): 446–456.

1962 "When married couples part: statistical trends and relationships in American divorce," *American Sociological Review*, 27 (October): 625–633.

Morgan, Ralph W.

1963 "The extended home visit in psychiatric research and treatment," *Psychiatry*, 26 (May): 168–175.

Morrow, Lance

1979 "Wondering if children are necessary," *Time*, 113 (March 5): 60–61.

Movius, M.

1976 "Voluntary childlessness: the ultimate liberation," *The Family Coordinator*, 25 (January): 57–63.

Nason, Ellen M., and Margaret M. Poloma

1976 *Voluntarily Childless Couples: The Emergence of a Variant Lifestyle*. Beverly Hills: California: Sage Publication.

National Opinion Research Center

1978 *National Data Program for the Social Sciences Spring 1977 General Social Survey* (ICPSR Study Number 7573). Ann Arbor, Michigan: Inter-University Consortium for Political and Social Research.

Nortman, Dorothy

1974 "Parental age as a factor in pregnancy outcome and child development," *Reports on Population/Family Planning*, 16 (August): 1–51.

Nye, F. Ivan, and Felix M. Berardo
1973 *The Family: Its Structure and Function.* New York: Macmillan.

Ory, Marcia G.
1978 "The decision to parent or not: normative and structural components," *Journal of Marriage and the Family,* 40 (August): 531–539.

Parsons, Talcott, and Robert T. Bales
1955 *Family, Socialization and Interaction Processes.* Glencoe, Illinois: The Free Press.

Payne, Judy
1978 "Talking about children: an examination of accounts about reproduction and family life," *Journal of Biosocial Science,* 10 (October): 367–374.

Peck, Ellen
1971 *The Baby Trap.* New York: Bernard Geis.
1974 "Television's romance with reproduction," pp. 79–97 in Ellen Peck and Judith Senderowitz (eds.), *Pronatalism: The Myth of Mom and Apple Pie.* New York: Thomas Y. Crowell.

Peck, Ellen, and Judith Senderowitz (eds.)
1974 *Pronatalism: The Myth of Mom and Apple Pie.* New York: Thomas Y. Crowell.

Peck, Ellen, and William Granzig
1978 *The Parent Test: How to Measure and Develop Your Talent for Parenthood.* New York: G. P. Putnam.

Peel, J., and G. Carr
1975 *Contraception and Family Design.* Edinburgh: Churchill Livingstone.

Perrucci, Carolyn Cummings
1970 "Minority status and the pursuit of professional careers: women in science and engineering," *Social Forces,* 49 (December): 245–259.

Pohlman, Edward
1965 "Wanted and 'unwanted': toward a less ambigious definition," *Eugenics Quarterly,* 12 (March): 19–27.
1968 "Burgess and Cottrell data on 'Desire for Children': an example of distortion in marriage and family textbooks," *Journal of Marriage and the Family,* 30 (August): 433–437.
1969 *The Psychology of Birth Planning.* Cambridge, Massachuestetts: Schenkman.
1970 Childlessness: intentional and unintentional," *The Journal of Nervous and Mental Disease,* 151 (1): 2–12.

Polit, Denise F.

1978 "Stereotypes relating to family-size status," *Journal of Marriage and the Family*, 40 (February): 105–114.

Polonko, Karen

1978 "A comparison of the patterns associated with voluntary childlessness and low birth intentions," paper presented to the American Sociological Association at their Annual Meeting, San Francisco, California, September.

Popenoe, Paul

1936 "Motivation of childless marriages," *Journal of Heredity*, 27 (December): 469–472.

Poston, Dudley L., Jr.

1974 "Income and childlessness in the United States: is the relationship always inverse?," *Social Biology*, 21 (Fall): 296–307.

1976 "Characteristics of voluntarily and involuntarily childless wives," *Social Biology*, 23 (September).

Poston, Dudley L., Jr., and Erin Gotard

1977 Trends in childlessness in the United States, 1910 to 1975," *Social Biology*, 24 (Fall): 212–224.

Pratt, Lois, and P. K. Whelpton

1955 "Interest in and liking for children in relation to family planning and size of planned family," *The Milbank Memorial Fund Quarterly*, 33 (October): 430–463.

Prus, R.

1975 "Resisting designations: an extension of attribution theory into a negotiated context," *Social Inquiry*, 45 (1): 3–14.

Radl, Shirley L.

1973 *Mother's Day is Over*. New York: Charterhouse.

Rainwater, Lee

1960 *And the Poor Get Children: Sex, Contraception and Family Planning in the Working Class*. Chicago: Quadrangle.

1965 *Family Design: Marital Sexuality, Family Size and Contraception*. Chicago: Aldine Publishing Company.

Ranulf, Svend

1964 *Moral Indignation and Middle Class Psychology: A Sociological Study*. New York: Schocken.

Rao, S. L. N.

1974 " A comparative study of childlessness and never pregnant status," *Journal of Marriage and the Family*, 36 (February): 149–157.

Reader's Digest

1975 *The Reader's Digest Treasury of Modern Quotations*. New York: Reader's Digest Press.

Reed, R. B.
1947 "The interrelationship of marital adjustment, fertility control, and size of family," *The Milbank Memorial Fund Quarterly*, 25 (October): 383–425.

Reed, Richie H., and Susan McIntosh
1972 "Costs of children," *Research Reports*, Volume 2, Commission of Population Growth and the American Future. Washington, D.C.: Government Printing Office.

Reiss, Ira L.
1967 *The Social Context of Premarital Sexual Permissiveness*. New York: Holt, Rinehart and Winston.

Rele, J. R.
1965 "Some correlates of the age at marriage in the United States," *Eugenics Quarterly*, 12 (March): 1–6.

Renne, Karen S.
1970 "Correlates of dissatisfaction in marriage," *Journal of Marriage and the Family*, 32 (February): 54–60.
1976 "Childlessness, health and marital satisfaction," *Social Biology*, 23 (Fall): 183–197.

Rhee, Jung-Mo
1973 *Trends and Variations in Childlessness in the United States*, Ph.D. dissertation, University of Georgia, Athens, Georgia. Dissertation Abstracts, 1974, 34: 5351.

Rice, Ann Smith
1964 *An Economic Life Cycle of Childless Families*. Ph.D. dissertation, The Florida State University, Tallahassee, Florida. *Dissertation Abstracts*, 1966, 26: 7292.

Rice, Berkeley
1968 *The Other End of the Leash*. Boston: Little Brown.

Rindfuss, Ronald R., and Larry L. Bumpass
1976 "How old is too old? Age and the sociology of fertility," *Family Planning Perspectives*, 8 (September/October): 226–230.

Ritchey, P. Neal, and C. Shannon Stokes
1974 "Correlates of childlessness and expectations to remain childless," *Social Forces*, 52 (March): 349–356.

Rogers, Joseph W., and M. D. Buffalo
1974 "Fighting back: nine modes of adaptation to a deviant label," *Social Problems*, 22 (October): 101–118.

Rollin, Betty
1970 "Motherhood: who needs it?," *Look*, 34 (September): 11–17.

Rollins, B. C., and H. Feldman
1970 "Marital satisfaction over the family life cycle," *Journal of Marriage and Family*, 32 (February): 20–28.

Rollins, Boyd C., and Kenneth L. Cannon

1974 "Marital satisfaction over the family life cycle: a reevaluation," *Journal of Marriage and Family*, 36 (May): 271–282.

Rosenblatt, Paul C.

1974 "Behavior in public places: comparison of couples accompanied and unaccompanied by children," *Journal of Marriage and the Family*, 36 (November): 750–755.

Rosenblatt, Paul C., and Walter J. Hillabrant

1972 "Divorce for childlessness and the regulation of adultery," *Journal of Sex Research*, 8 (May): 117–127.

Ronsenblatt, Paul C., P. Peterson, J. Portner, M. Cleveland, A. Mykkanen, R. Foster, G. Holm, B. Joel, H. Keisch, C. Kreuscher, and R. Phillips

1973 "A cross-cultural study of responses to childlessness," *Behavioral Science Notes*, 8 (3): 221–231.

Rosenfield, Allan

1978 "Oral and intrauterine contraception: a 1978 risk assessment," *American Journal of Obstetrics and Gynecology*, 132 (September): 92–106.

Rosengren, William R.

1961 "Social sources of pregnancy as illness or normality," *Social Forces* 39 (March): 260–267.

1962 "Social instability and attitudes toward pregnancy as a social role," *Social Problems*, 9 (Winter): 371–378.

Rossi, Alice S.

1977 "A biosocial perspective on parenting," *Dedaelus*, 106 (Spring): 1–31.

Royal College of General Practitioners

1977a "Mortality among oral-contraceptive users," *The Lancet*, 8041 (October 8): 727–731.

1977b "Recommendations arising out of the findings by the RCGP oral contraception study on the mortality risks of oral contraceptive users," *Journal of the Royal College of General Practitioners*, 27 (November): 700.

Russell, Candyce Smith

1974 "Transition to parenthood: problems and gratifications," *Journal of Marriage and the Family*, 36 (May): 294–302.

Russell, Martha Garrett, Richard N. Hey, Gail A. Thoen, and Tom Walz

1978 "The choice of childlessness: a workshop model," *The Family Coordinator*, 27 (April): 179–183.

Russo, Nancy Felipe
1976 "The motherhood mandate," *Journal of Social Issues*, 32 (Summer): 143–153.

Ryder, Robert G.
1973 "Longitudinal data relating marriage satisfaction and having a child," *Journal of Marriage and the Family*, 35 (November): 604–607.

Safran, Clair
1975 "Motherhood is not my game," *Today's Health* (May): 39–41.

Sagarin, Edward
1969 *Odd Man In: Societies of Deviants in America*. Chicago: Quadrangle Books.

Scanzoni, John and Letta Scanzoni
1976 *Men, Women, and Change: A Sociology of Marriage and Family*. New York: McGraw-Hill.

Scott, Jack
1976 *Canada's Religious Composition*. 1971 Census Profile Series. Catalogue 99-710, Volume V, Part 1 (Bulletin 5.1-10). Ottawa: Information Canada.

Scott, Marvin B., and Stanford M. Lyman
1968 "Accounts," *American Sociological Review*, 33 (February): 46–62.

Sells, Lucy W.
1975 *Sex, Ethnic, and Field Differences in Doctoral Outcomes*. Ph.D. Dissertation, The University of California, Berkeley. *Dissertation Abstracts*, 1976, 37: 637.

Sell, Ralph
1974 *Childlessness: A Demographic Path Analysis of Changes Among Married Women 18–40 Years Old, 1960–1970*. M.A. dissertation, Pennsylvania State University, University Park, Pa.

Shapiro, Samuel, Dennis Slone, Lynn Rosenberg, David W. Kaufman, Paul D. Stolley, and Olli S. Miettinen
1979 "Oral-contraceptive use in relation to myocardial infarction," *The Lancet*, 8119 (April 7): 743–746.

Silka, Linda, and Sara Kiesler
1977 "Couples who choose to be childless," *Family Planning Perspectives*, 9 (January-February): 16–25.

Silverman, Anna and Arnold Silverman
1971 *The Case Against Having Children*. New York: David McKay.

Simmel, George
1950 *The Sociology of George Simmel.* (Translated by Kurt H. Wolff). New York: The Free Press.

Simmons, J. L.
1964 "On maintaining a belief system: a case study," Social Problems 11 (Winter): 251–256.

Simpson, George
1966 *People in Families: Sociology, Psychoanalysis and the American Family.* New York: Meridan.

Sklar, June, and Beth Berkow
1975 "The American birth rate: evidences of the coming rise," *Science,* 189 (August 29): 693–700.

Slater, E., and M. Woodside
1951 *Patterns of Marriage.* London: Cassell.

Slater, Philip E.
1963 "On social regression," *American Sociological Review,* 28 (June): 339–364.

Sly, D., and S. Richards
1972 "The fertility of a sample of American elites," *Social Biology* 19 (December): 393–400.

Sohn, Sara A.
1971 "The cost of raising a child," unpublished monograph. New York: The Institute of Life Insurance.

Southam, Anna L.
1966 "Contraceptive methods: use, safety, and effectiveness," pp. 375–396 in Bernard Berelson (ed.), *Family Planning and Population Programs.* Chicago: University of Chicago Press.

Stannard, Una
1971 "The mask of beauty," pp. 118–130 in Vivian Gornick and Barbara K. Moran (eds.), *Women in Sexist Society: Studies in Power and Powerlessness.* New York: Basic Books.

Stein, Jess, and Laurence Urdang (eds.)
1971 The Random House Dictionary of the English Language. New York: Random House.

Stokes, C. S., and P. N. Ritchey
1974 "Some futher observations on childlessness and color," *Journal of Black Studies,* 5 (2): 203–209.

Strong, Ethelyn Ratcliff
1967 *The Meaning of Childlessness to Childless Negro Couples.* Ph.D. dissertation, The Catholic University of America, Washington, D.C. *Dissertation Abstracts,* 1967, 28: 2346.

'troup, Atlee, L.
1966 *Marriage and the Family: A Developmental Approach*. New York: Appleton-Century-Crofts.
'zasz, Kathleen
1968 *Petishism: Pets and Their People in the Western World*. New York: Holt, Rinehart and Winston.
'aylor, Shelley E., and Ellen J. Langer
1977 "Pregnancy: a social stigma?" *Sex Roles*, 3 (February): 27–35.
'erhune, Kenneth W., and Roland J. Pilie
1974 *A Review of the Actual and Expected Consequences of Family Size*. Washington, D.C.: U.S. Department of Health, Education and Welfare.
'erman, Lewis M.
1938 *Psychological Factors in Marital Happiness*. New York: McGraw-Hill.
'hoen, Gail Ann
1977 *Commitment Among Voluntary Childfree Couples to a Variant Lifestyle*. Ph.D. dissertation, University of Minnesota, Minneapolis, Minnesota. *Dissertation Abstracts*, 1977, 38: 3760.
'homlinson, Ralph
1965 *Population Dynamics*. New York: Random House.
'hompson, Vaida D.
1974 "Family size: implicit policies and assumed psychological outcomes," *Journal of Social Issues*, 30 (4): 93–124.
'hornton, Arland
1977 "Children and marital stability," *Journal of Marriage and the Family*, 39 (August): 531–540.
'ietze, Christopher
1977 "New estimates of mortality associated with fertility control," *Family Planning Perspectives*, 9 (March/April): 74–76.
'ietze, Christopher, John Bongaarts, and Bruce Schaerer
1976 "Mortality associated with control of fertility," *Family Planning Perspectives*, 8 (January/February): 6–14.
'itmuss, Richard M., and Fred Grundy
1946 "Childlessness and the small family: a fertility survey in Luton," *The Lancet* 251 (November): 687–690.
oman, Walter
1970 "Birth order rules all," *Psychology Today*, 4 (December): 45–49.
omasson, Ralph
1966 "Why has American fertility been so high?," pp. 327–338 in

Bernard Farber (ed.), *Kinship and Family Organization.* New York: John Wiley.

Toomey, Beverly Guella

1977 *College Women and Voluntary Childlessness: A Comparative Study of Women Indicating They Want to Have Children and Those Indicating They Do No Want to Have Children.* Ph.D. dissertation, Ohio State University, Columbus, Ohio. *Dissertation Abstracts*, 1978, 38: 6944–6945.

Turner, Ralph H.

1972 "Deviance avowal as neutralization of commitment," *Social Problems*, 19 (Winter): 307–321.

Udry, J. Richard

1966 *The Social Context of Marriage.* New York: J. B. Lippincott.

1971 *The Social Context of Marriage (Revised edition).* New York: J. B. Lippincott.

United States Bureau of the Census

1971 "Previous and Prospective Fertility: 1967," *Current Population Reports*, Series P-20, No. 211. Washington, D.C.: U.S. Government Printing Office.

1976a "Fertility of American Women: June 1975," *Current Population Reports*, Series P-20, No. 301. Washington, D.C.: U.S. Government Printing Office.

1976b Fertility History and Prospects of American Women: June 1975," *Current Population Reports*, Series P-20, No. 288. Washington, D.C.: U.S. Government Printing Office.

1977 "Fertility of American Women: June 1976," *Current Population Reports*, Series P-20, No. 308. Washington, D.C.: U.S. Government Printing Office.

United States National Center for Health Statistics

1971 "Parental ratings of behavioral patterns of children," *Vital and Health Statistics*, Series 11, Number 108.

1978 *Facts of Life and Death.* DHEW Publication No. (PHS) 79–1222. Washington, D.C.: U.S. Government Printing Office.

Van Keep, P. A.

1971 "Ideal family size in five European countries," *Journal of Biosocial Science*, 3 (July): 259.

Van Keep, P. A., and H. Schmidt-Elmendorff

1975 "Involuntary childlessness," *Journal of Biosocial Science*, 7 (January): 37–48.

Vaughan, Barbara, James Trussell, Jane Menken, and Elise F. Jones

1977 "Contraceptive failure among married women in the United States," *Family Planning Perspectives*, 9 (November - December): 251–258.

Veenhoven, Ruud

1974 "Is there an innate need for children?," *European Journal of Social Psychology*, 4 (4): 495–501.

Veevers, J. E.

1971a "The liberalization of Canadian abortion laws," pp. 33–39 in Craig Boydell, Carl Grindstaff and Paul Whitehead (eds.), *Critical Issues in Canadian Society*. Toronto: Holt, Rinehart and Winston.

1971b "Differential childlessness by colour: a further examination," *Social Biology*, 18 (September): 289–291.

1971c "Sample size and interpretation of census data," *Social Biology*, 18 (December): 431–433.

1971d "Rural-urban variation in the incidence of childlessness," *Rural Sociology*, 36 (December): 547–553.

1971e "Childlessness and age at first marriage," *Social Biology*, 18 (September): 292–295.

1972a "The violation of fertility mores: voluntary childlessness as deviant behavior," pp. 571–592 in Craig Boydell, Carl Grindstaff and Paul Whitehead (eds.), *Deviant Behavior and Societal Reaction*. Toronto: Holt, Rinehart and Winston.

1972b "Declining childlessness and age at marriage: a test of a hypothesis," *Social Biology*, 19 (September): 285–288.

1972c "Factors in the incidence of childlessness in Canada: an analysis of census data," *Social Biology*, 19 (September): 266–274.

1973a "Voluntary childlessness: a neglected area of family study," *The Family Coordinator*, 22 (April): 199–205.

1973b "Voluntarily childless wives: an exploratory study," *Sociology and Social Research*, 57 (April): 356–366.

1973c "Parenthood and suicide: an examination of a neglected area," *Social Science and Medicine*, 7 (February): 135–144.

1973d "The child-free alternative: rejection of the motherhood mystique," pp. 183–199 in Marylee Stephenson (ed.), *Women in Canada*. Toronto: New Press.

1973e "The social meanings of parenthood," *Psychiatry: Journal for the Study of Interpersonal Processes*, 36 (August): 291–310.

1973f "Estimating the incidence and prevalence of birth orders: a technique using census data," *Demography*, 10 (August): 447–458.

1974a "Voluntary childlessness and social policy," *The Family Coordinator*, 23 (October): 397–406.

1974b "The parenthood prescription," *Alternatives: Perspectives on Society and Environment*, 3 (Spring): 32–37.

1975a "The life style of voluntarily childless couples," pp. 395–411 i Lyle Larson (ed.), *The Canadian Family in Comparativ Perspectives*. Toronto: Prentice-Hall.

1975b "The moral career of voluntarily childless wives: notes on th defense of a variant world view," *The Family Coordinator*, 2 (October): 473–487.

1977 *The Family in Canada*. 1971 Census Profile Series. Catalogu 99–725, Volume V, Part 3 (Bulletine 5.3–3). Ottawa: Informa tion Canada.

1979 "Voluntary childlessness: a review of issues and evidence, *Marriage and Family Review* (forthcoming).

Veevers, J. E., and D. F. Cousineau

1980 "The heathen Canadians: atheists, agnostics, apostates, *Pacific Sociological Review*, (forthcoming).

Veevers, J. E., and Charles R. Figley

1978 "Perspectives on pronatalism: assumptions and issues," pape presented to the Groves Conference on the Family at their An nual Meeting, Washington, D.C., April 27–30.

Veroff, Joseph, and Sheila Feld

1970 *Marriage and Work in America*. New York: Van Nostranc Reinhold.

Waller, Willard, and Reuben Hill

1951 *The Family: A Dynamic Interpretation*. New York: Hol Rinehart and Winston.

Waller, J. H., B. Raja Rao, and C. C. Li

1973 "Heterogeneity of childless families," *Social Biology*, 20 (June 133–138.

Ward, Charles D.

1964 "A further examination of birth order as a selective facto among volunteer subjects," *Journal of Abnormal and Socic Psychology*, 69 (3): 311–313.

Weinberg, Martin S.

1970 "The nudist management of respectability: strategy for an consequences of the construction of a situated morality," pp 375–403 in Jack D. Douglas (ed.), *Deviance and Respectability The Social Construction of Moral Meaning*. New York: Basi Books.

Welds, Kathryn

1976 *Voluntary Childlessness in Professional Women*. Ph.D. disser tation, Harvard University, Cambridge, Mass.

Westoff, Charles F.

1978 "Marriage and fertility in the developed countries," *Scientifi American*, 239 (December): 51–57.

Westoff, Charles F., and Elise F. Jones
1977 "Contraception and sterilization in the United States, 1965–1975," *Family Planning Perspectives*, 9 (July–August): 153–157.
Westoff, Charles F., and Raymond H. Ptovin
1967 *College Women and Fertility Values*. Princeton, New Jersey: Princeton University Press.
Westoff, Leslie A., and Charles F. Westoff
1971 *From Now to Zero: Fertility, Contraception and Abortion in America*. Boston: Little Brown and Company.
Whelan, Elizabeth
1975 *A Baby? Maybe*. New York: Bobbs-Merrill.
Whelpton, Pascal K., A. Campbell and J. Patterson
1966 *Fertilty and Family Planning in the United States*. Princeton, New Jersey: Princeton University Press.
Williams, S. N.
1973 "The argument against the physiological determination of female roles; a reply to Pierre L. van den Berghe's rejoinder to William's extension of Brown's articles," *American Anthropologist*, 75 (October): 1725–1728.
Williamson, Nancy E.
1978 "Boys or girls? Parents' preferences and sex control," *Population Bulletin*, 33 (January): 1–35.
Windsor Star
1971 "A little bundle of joy," November 25, 1971.
Wolowyna, Jean E.
1977 "Income and childlessness in Canada: a further examination," *Social Biology*, 24 (Winter): 326–331.
Wood, Clive
1969 Sex and Fertility. London: Thames and Hudson.
Wortman, J., and P. T. Piotrow
1973a "Laparoscopic sterilization: a new technique," *Population Reports Series C* (January), Number 1.
1973b "Sterilization: laparoscopic sterilization II. What are the problems?," *Population Reports Series C* (March), Number 2.
1973c "Sterilization: Culpotomy—the vaginal approach," *Population Reports Series C* (June), Number 3.
Wrong, Dennis
1961 "The oversocialized conception of man in sociology," *American Sociological Review*, 26 (April): 183–193.
Wyatt, Frederick
1967 "Clincial notes on the motives of reproduction," *Journal of Social Issues*, 23 (4): 29–56.

Index

P

R